CHANNELING THE STATE

COMMUNITY MEDIA AND

POPULAR POLITICS IN VENEZUELA

Naomi Schiller

DUKE UNIVERSITY PRESS

Durham and London

2018

© 2018 DUKE UNIVERSITY PRESS
All rights reserved
Printed and bound by CPI Group (UK) Ltd, Croydon, CR0 4YY
Designed by Courtney Baker
Typeset in Minion Pro and Trade Gothic by Westchester Publishing Services

Library of Congress Cataloging-in-Publication Data
Names: Schiller, Naomi, [date–] author.
Title: Channeling the state : community media
and popular politics in Venezuela / Naomi Schiller.
Description: Durham : Duke University Press, 2018. | Series: Radical Amêricas
Identifiers: LCCN 2018008251 (print) | LCCN 2018010314 (ebook)
ISBN 9781478002529 (ebook)
ISBN 9781478001119 (hardcover : alk. paper)
ISBN 9781478001447 (pbk. : alk. paper)
Subjects: LCSH: CatiaTVe (Television station :
Caracas, Venezuela) | Television in politics—Venezuela. |
Television and state—Venezuela. | Political participation—Venezuela. |
Local mass media—Venezuela.
Classification: LCC HE8700.76.V4 (ebook) |
LCC HE8700.76.V4 S35 2018 (print) | DDC 384.550987—dc23
LC record available at https://lccn.loc.gov/2018008251

Cover art: Catia TVe's television studio, 2004. Courtesy of the author.

CHANNELING THE STATE

RADICAL AMÉRICAS

A series edited by Bruno Bosteels
and George Ciccariello-Maher

To my mom,

NINA GLICK SCHILLER

Contents

Preface

I started examining some of the issues explored in this book in 2000, when I spent eight months conducting research in a rural community outside of Cumaná, a small city in eastern Venezuela. I wanted to understand how campesino men and women engaged with commercial television's flashy depictions of elite urban experience and melodrama. Sitting for hours with women from the mountain valley, and occasionally local men, I watched endless hours of telenovelas, Latin American soap operas. Together with Anahi, one of the women with whom I had grown particularly close, I watched the concluding chapter of *Maria Rosa Búscame una Esposa* (Maria Rosa Find Me a Wife), a Peruvian telenovela about a secretary who—surprise!—falls in love with her wealthy boss. During the final episode, the boss recognizes his feelings for his secretary and the two live happily ever after. Anahi and I cried.

At this point, Hugo Chávez had been president for less than two years. Along with my interlocutors, I had paid limited attention to Chávez or the central government. The social welfare programs that would become the hallmark of Chávez's presidency did not yet exist. The campesinos with whom I was living had yet to feel any change in their everyday lives under Chávez, beyond being annoyed when he interrupted their telenovelas with long-winded speeches. For the most part they remained loyal to Democratic Action, the political party in Venezuela that had done most to solidify identification with rural Venezuelans through efforts at land reform and limited wealth redistribution.

I conducted this initial field research project at a time of increased anthropological attention to the role of media in people's everyday lives. I was drawn to analyses that recognized that audiences were not dupes of bourgeois values and aesthetics, although they did not always have access to tools that would allow them to negotiate all of television's messages (Abu-Lughod 1995). At the same time, I came away from this period of research knowing that commercial television encouraged very poor women to aspire to middle-class lifestyles, relating and comparing the ups and downs of their daily lives to the characters on the telenovelas.

I was eager to learn more about the Venezuelan "media world," the process of production, circulation, and engagement of media, and the social relations that create both mass and small media (Ginsburg, Abu-Lughod, and Larkin 2002). I began to learn about Venezuelan community television. I first heard about the community television station Catia TVe, the subject of this book, at a conference on neoliberalism organized by *Left Turn* magazine at New York University in 2002. Conference organizers invited Blanca Eekhout, a young middle-class Venezuelan woman, to speak about Catia TVe, the station she founded together with activists from a poor neighborhood. I returned to Venezuela in 2003 to learn more about Catia TVe, based in Caracas, and what Hugo Chávez and his allies' called the Bolivarian Revolution, named after the early nineteenth-century liberator of Latin America, Simón Bolívar. My experience watching telenovelas with very poor women in a marginal area of the country fueled questions about the urban poor's experience of media production in the nation's capital. I set out to do ethnographic research on how people teach, learn, and advocate for community media production as a means to construct a more just society.

When I arrived in Caracas in 2006 to do long-term fieldwork, and after spending three summers getting to know Catia TVe's founders, I decided to accept the invitation of the director of Catia TVe to live with him, his wife (who also worked at Catia TVe), and their two children in Manicomio, the neighborhood where Catia TVe was founded. I paid them rent. Living in Manicomio, I experienced the rhythms of daily life in a barrio: the occasional electrical blackouts, the long waits to pay 900 *bolivares* (about forty cents) to ride a minibus down the hill to where one could catch the metro, and the sounds of motorcycles buzzing up and down the narrow *callejon* (passageway) between the cement block houses. While I did not conduct research in or about life in Manicomio, this experience informed my understanding of people's lives at Catia TVe and the context from which their political project emerged.

I became part of the daily life at the station as well as I could. I accompanied staff and volunteers into the field, where they filmed meetings, marches, press conferences, and dance performances. I observed and participated in Catia TVe's weekly studio shows, the editing and transmission of programming, and the station's classes for new volunteers. I also attended workshops, conferences, and meetings in poor neighborhoods and state institutions alongside Catia TVe producers. I was excluded from most internal meetings of Catia TVe's directors, as well as many meetings with state officials. I conducted over fifty interviews with Catia TVe's staff and volunteers, staff at an official state television station called ViVe TV, and government officials.

When I became more involved, co-producing programs with Catia TVe producers and filming on my own, the video camera served me, as it did Catia TVe producers, as an entry vehicle into official state institutions and barrio meetings. Given my appearance (dark hair with "white but not bright white" skin, as one Catia TVe producer described me), people often assumed that I was a Catia TVe staff member. I had to make a conscious effort to alert people to my status as an American researcher—that is, until I opened my mouth and let loose my gringa Spanish. Given the inundation of foreigners who arrived to document and study aspects of life in Caracas at the time, most people found my being there unremarkable. People embraced me as an additional avenue for publicity, alongside Catia TVe producers. This presented its own challenges, as I attempted to make clear the long-term time frame of my research and writing.

Like so many others who visited Venezuela in the first decade of the 2000s, I had set out hoping to find a successful social movement. I witnessed many scholars, observers, and tourists turned off by the complexity of the political process they found in Venezuela. For my part, I had to come to terms with the gaps between the political ideals of Catia TVe producers and some of their practices. I saw how everyday interactions at times reproduced hierarchies, particularly of gender and class. The anthropological methodology of long-term engagement with our research subjects was vital in allowing me time to process messy realities and understand the history and perspectives of my interlocutors.

The challenge of writing this book has been one that Catia TVe producers have also faced. Creating representations of the world is part and parcel of constructing the world. Just as the production of all knowledge is a practice of mediation, so I struggled with striking the right balance, unearthing the complexity of Catia TVe producers' experiences, choosing which moments to highlight to show the deep problems as well as the possibilities. I hope that this book honors as much as possible the challenges that Catia TVe producers embraced.

As this book focuses on research I conducted in the early 2000s, I use the past tense to describe Catia TVe's struggle to tip the balance of forces in the direction of poor people's leadership. What I observed during this time period does not represent the position or outlook of my interlocutors for all time. My use of the past tense is not meant to indicate that Venezuelans have stopped struggling for a better world. The people I describe in this book continue to change and to develop new strategies in the face of shifting and increasingly difficult circumstances.

Acknowledgments

My deepest thanks go to the men and women at Catia TVe who welcomed me into their lives and shared their insights and experiences. Without their patience and willingness to allow me to observe and participate in their work, this book would not have been possible. My hope is that this project honors the complex challenges these media producers faced. I am grateful to have had the opportunity to learn from them, debate with them, and share passions for a better world.

This project began at New York University, where I had the opportunity to work closely with Faye Ginsburg, Thomas Abercrombie, Bruce Grant, Greg Grandin, and Rafael Sánchez. The media production skills and knowledge I gained from Cheryl Furjanic, Meg McLagan, and Peggy Vail, through NYU's Program in Culture and Media in the Department of Anthropology, proved enormously important in allowing me to participate in the work of television production in Caracas. I am indebted to Faye Ginsburg for inspiring my interest in understanding the social practice of media production and for her ongoing intellectual engagement. Bruce Grant's continued generosity as a mentor and interlocutor has been vital. I am thankful for support for this project from the National Science Foundation Graduate Research Fellowship, the McCracken Graduate Fellowship of New York University, a Dissertation Research Fellowship from the Wenner-Gren Foundation for Anthropological Research, Temple University's Center for the Humanities Faculty Fellowship, a CUNY Graduate Center's Gittell Junior Faculty Award, and a fellowship from CUNY's Center for Place, Culture, and Politics. Support for this project was also provided by a PSC-CUNY Award, jointly funded by The Professional Staff Congress and The City University of New York.

My sincere thanks goes to Lila Abu-Lughod, my undergraduate advisor, who first helped me craft a project to study media in Venezuela, and to Robert Albert, Julio Alvarez, Steven Bloomstein, and Susan Reyna for welcoming me to intern at the Turimiquire Foundation in Cumaná.

Great joy came from working with and learning from a wonderful group of friends and colleagues at the different institutions where I have made my life. At NYU, I benefited from the support and intellectual energy of Haytham Bahoora, Amahl Bishara, Maggie Clinton, Priya Lal, Deborah Matzner, John Patrick Leary, Shane Minkin, Tsolin Nalbantian, and Sherene Seikaly. In Caracas, I received vital feedback on the central ideas of this book from Chelina Sepúlveda and Andrés Antillano. Over the years, I have received helpful input from Anthony Alessandrini, Cristina Beltran, Dominic Boyer, George Ciccariello-Maher, Luis Duno Gottberg, Steve Ellner, Sujatha Fernandes, Judith Goode, Joseph Keith, Antonio Lauria, William Mazzarella, Natalia Roudakova, Robert Samet, Krupa Shandilya, Julie Skurski, Sam Stark, Constance Sutton, Miguel Tinker Salas, Alejandro Velasco, and K. Eva Weiss. Maggie Clinton, Crystal Parikh, and Jini Kim Watson were a continuous source of constructive criticism, intellectual guidance, and support. I am fortunate to have terrific colleagues at Brooklyn College, including Patricia Antoniello, Jillian Cavanaugh, and Katie Rose Hejtmanek. In addition, I am indebted to two anonymous readers for Duke University Press, who provided invaluable feedback and posed challenging questions that helped me improve the manuscript.

My family has been a source of unending encouragement. Thank you to my parents, Nina Glick Schiller, Steve Reyna, David Schiller, and Jessie Sullivan. I am grateful to my mother, Nina, who generously provided feedback on every chapter of this book. I draw strength from her support, wisdom, and passion for anthropology and social justice. I am proud to follow her example. Thanks to my father, David, for his faith in me and the pursuit of knowledge. His commitment to learning and his love for me have been a constant source of sustenance. Thank you, my closest friend and sister, Rachel Schiller, and to Devan and Isobel Aptekar. Finally, my love and appreciation go to Noah Biklen for his patience, kindness, humor, and delicious meals. Noah's constant encouragement to trust the process made completing this book much less onerous. Our daughters, Anika and Sari, have brightened my life and made me understand in new ways the urgent necessity of fighting for a better world.

Introduction

Passing through multiple security checkpoints staffed by heavily armed guards, Nestor, Jesica, and I made our way inside Miraflores, Venezuela's presidential palace.[1] Nestor and Jesica proudly presented their press credentials: small homemade squares of laminated cardboard emblazoned with the name of their community television station, Catia TVe. Once inside, we crowded beside nine professional camera crews in the back of a rectangular room with stadium seating. Nestor squeezed his skinny frame through the tangle of camera operators to place Catia TVe's microphone alongside those of major commercial television networks, a community radio station, and a state-run network.

A heavyset cameraman who worked for a state-run station eyed Catia TVe's palm-size video camera. Smiling, Jesica adjusted the height of Catia TVe's lightweight tripod and quipped, "¿Más criollo, no?" (It's more native, no?). The cameraman laughed at her suggestion that Catia TVe's low-priced video equipment made in Japan was somehow more Venezuelan, more of "the people," than his professional gear.

Jesica and Nestor's low-cost camera gear was not the only detail that marked them as different from most of the other media producers in the room. Jesica, twenty-four years old, and Nestor, eighteen years old, were younger, had darker complexions, and were more casually dressed than most of the journalists, photographers, and camera people. Jesica was the only female camera operator. She and Nestor had grown up in the same poor neighborhood of west Caracas, where they both dropped out of high school. After enrolling in a free video production class together at Catia TVe, they spent several months as volunteer producers at the station, making short programs about a local dance troop and the problems plaguing trash collection in their neighborhood. Jesica and Nestor had joined Catia TVe's staff, which was mostly from the poor neighborhoods of Caracas, just six months before. Their attendance at this February 2007 press conference challenged long-established boundaries of class, race, and gender.

Jesica and Nestor's presence in the midst of a packed room of national and international journalists was one sign of the tumultuous changes occurring in Venezuela. By the turn of the twenty-first century, President Hugo Chávez had made Venezuela a steady source of front-page international news. Venezuela was long viewed in the United States as a politically stable and friendly supplier of oil. Chávez's effort to challenge U.S. influence in Latin America and launch what he called the Bolivarian Revolution attracted extensive scrutiny from the international and Venezuelan press. Although the Chávez government embraced some of the formal mechanisms of liberal democracy—such as a strong emphasis on the constitution and regular elections—it challenged the basic liberal norm of the necessary autonomy of media and social movements from the state. In the wake of Chávez's 2005 declaration that Venezuela was building "twenty-first-century socialism," pundits, human rights organizations, and politicians in the United States and elsewhere almost uniformly argued that Chávez was an aspiring dictator who sought to use the state to trample freedom.

Much of this analysis overlooked the perspectives of young people like Jesica and Nestor, whose experiences of state power began to change when Chávez was elected president in 1998. Although Miraflores was located less than a mile from the barrio where Jesica and Nestor grew up, poor people had few opportunities to enter the presidential palace, let alone participate in the media coverage of their own neighborhoods or of official state affairs before Chávez's election. After being marginalized for decades by poverty and violence under the rule of liberal democratic governments, by the early 2000s community media activists found themselves involved in an unpredictable turnabout. By the time of my long-term fieldwork in 2007, almost thirty community television stations and hundreds of community radio stations had begun operating across the country.

Nearly two hours after we arrived, President Chávez entered the press conference room, flanked by several ministers. The sound of camera shutters reached a frenzied pitch. Half the reporters in the room extended him a warm applause. The other half remained unmoved. Nestor clapped loudly, while Jesica jumped up and down to get a better view. The floor shook as her

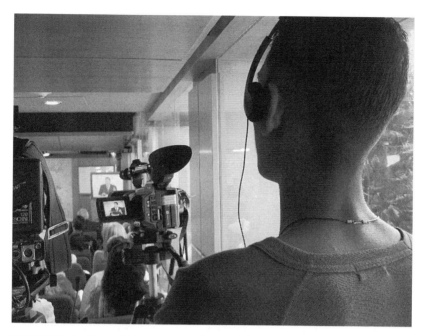

FIGURE I.1. Nestor films a Chávez press conference, February 1, 2007. Photo by the author.

feet hit the floor, eliciting angry glances from neighboring camera operators whose tripods and cameras registered every movement. Jesica and Nestor, like their Catia TVe colleagues, were ardent Chávez supporters, whom many in Venezuela and beyond have called *chavistas*. They identified with the president's humble roots; his mestizo, black, and indigenous features; and his call for social and economic justice.

Once considered the "voice of the voiceless" against the elite-controlled commercial media and the state, Catia TVe and many other community media producers became close collaborators with officials seeking to transform the state. By the time of my research in 2007, Catia TVe was not only politically aligned with the Chávez government and the Bolivarian Revolution, but was also financially dependent on state institutions to pay their staff and maintain their equipment and facilities.[2] This shift from dissident activists to government allies raised a lot of questions. Given their political and financial alignment with the Chávez-led Bolivarian movement, could Catia TVe generate what activists and scholars often refer to as "voices from below" when they were aligned with the state and supported financially "from above"? For many observers, the most pressing question is, Can state-supported media criticize the state?

Revising the Question, Rethinking the State

This question seems straightforward enough. Yet when I first began my fieldwork with Catia TVe, I found myself tongue-tied when people asked me if community media producers could criticize the state. My research suggested not only that the people I was studying had different expectations about the state than many of my friends, family, and colleagues, but also that their understandings of the state were shifting. Nestor and Jesica's experience at the palace that morning was one of many instances I observed over fourteen months of fieldwork that encouraged Catia TVe producers to view the state as an unfolding and messy collection of ideas, practices, individuals, and institutions that had the potential to improve the lives of the poor and expand their access to political participation.

Over time I came to realize that embedded in the question about whether Catia TVe producers could criticize the state were several major assumptions that made it difficult to understand Catia TVe's media practice. To begin with, the question takes for granted that we already know what the state means. Most crucially, the question assumes that the central aim of media producers should be to monitor and criticize the state from an independent position, as liberal democratic definitions of press freedom assert. Widely accepted understandings of the state led only to the conclusion that Catia TVe was a client-mouthpiece for the Chávez government. From this starting point, Catia TVe's close alignment with Venezuela's central state institutions seemed like a problem for freedom and democracy.

What we have been missing is greater attention to what the state means in various sites of media production. Instead of beginning with ready-made understandings of the media and the state to evaluate Venezuela in the Chávez era, this book is about how barrio-based community media producers and their allies experienced, understood, and created the state through the process of making media. In order to answer the question about Catia TVe's relationship with the state, we must understand what the state meant to these media makers and how they were engaged in producing it. One of the many strengths of ethnography is that it allows scholars to approach the state as an open question rather than as a known object of inquiry.

Exploring Catia TVe producers' perspectives and analyzing their day-to-day work allowed me to view Nestor and Jesica's presence at the Chávez press conference as a practice of everyday statecraft. While the work of statecraft is often associated with trained elite professionals in formal governing positions, I build on the work of anthropologists and historians who have focused attention on the participation of the poor and historically disenfranchised in the production of the state (Joseph and Nugent 1994).[3] From this perspective, statecraft (also referred to as state formation) is an ever-unfolding result of daily power-laden interactions between poor and elite social actors who jointly create the state through practices that are local, regional, and global. I argue that Catia TVe's work of media production was a form of statecraft. Catia TVe producers' efforts to make media in their own barrios, in the television studio, and inside central state institutions provided them a way to shape the emerging state project in the interest of the poor.

Official government press conferences in Venezuela, like the one I have been describing, are examples of the performance of state power. As a "made for media" ritual or play, press conferences are not simply created by the state but are constitutive of the state itself (Pedelty 1995). Even before Chávez walked into the room—before a single camera shutter clicked or a journalist asked a question—Nestor, Jesica, and their community media colleagues were already an essential part of a process of creating ideas and representations of the state. Together, the official actors—most prominently, President Chávez—and the press corps not only produced media content and coverage, but also granted the state meaning and power.[4] Jesica and Nestor, as barrio-based media producers, were a new piece of this performance. Their presence asserted that poor men and women of color had the right and the ability to participate in politics. For the government and for its supporters, their attendance was an important display of the government's redistribution of wealth and its commitment to the empowerment of the poor. Catia TVe's budget camera equipment and cheerful community logo helped proponents of the Bolivarian Revolution authenticate claims that the revolution was the product of grassroots participation. In the chapters that follow, I trace how Catia TVe producers worked to make these displays of popular power not simply window dressing, but meaningful opportunities for the poor to participate in revolutionary statecraft.

Taking seriously Catia TVe producers' perspectives on state institutions means having to allow for uncertainty about what the state means. In this book, I ask readers to join me in assuming a critical distance from what have become commonsense definitions of the state, especially in the United States. To be sure, given the history of authoritarianism and state violence, it is impossible to dismiss suspicions of state power. Many people around the world experience the state primarily as an antagonistic, coercive, or mystifying force. This book examines another possibility, one that challenges a uniform narrative of the state. Catia TVe producers and many of their allies rejected notions that the state was either a coherent thing to be seized or a collection of institutions always already predisposed to enacting a particular kind of politics.[5]

In their struggle to participate in the construction of a democratic socialist state, the pressing question for Catia TVe producers was not how to assert autonomy from the state so that they could criticize it. Instead, these media makers continually asked whose state they were constructing, which social class this state represented, and how to expand social justice and equality as they developed relationships with members of the middle class who had long monopolized influence over official state institutions. Catia TVe producers attempted to make Venezuelan state institutions sites of class struggle over how to use and dismantle the existing unjust economic and political system. I show how and why Catia TVe producers saw the state as a process rather than as a coherent object to be captured once and for all. Throughout this book I uncover how Catia TVe's work in poor neighborhoods and inside central state institutions created unique openings for the urban poor and their allies to embrace statecraft as a collective endeavor with the potential for creating positive social change.

In contrast to theorists and observers who argue that states are inherently oppressive, I draw attention to the contingency, unpredictability, and negotiation between popular movements and official state actors. I argue that state institutions are continuously made and remade rather than inevitable and unchangeable forms for the exercise of elite power. In emphasizing how the state is an uneven, variable process, I suggest that the state is a condition of possibility for popular mobilization at certain junctures. At the same time, the uncertainty about the meaning, boundaries, and possibility of the state left Catia TVe producers vulnerable. As I write this in 2017, Venezuelans face grave political and economic turmoil. Although Catia TVe producers anticipated many of the risks that their embrace of a revolutionary state project posed, some of which have come to fruition, they nevertheless wagered that this vulnerability was necessary and important. This book explains why. It offers insights into the state, class conflict, populist politics, gendered power, liberal notions of press freedom, and the challenges that revolutionary movements face in Venezuela and beyond.

Don't Watch Television, Make It!

Poor and working-class activists planted the seeds for Catia TVe in the late 1980s, a time when sectors of the Venezuelan military were unleashing murderous violence against poor people who had risen up to reject the government's decision to embrace neoliberal reforms. The founders of the station were drawn to community media as a form of social activism for two central reasons: first, they saw the enormous potential of video production to generate interest and inspire participation in their barrio; and second, they wanted to counter the power of the privately owned commercial media who, they believed, stood in the way of any meaningful political change.

The experience of community media producers who grew up in poor neighborhoods in the 1970s, 1980s, and 1990s differed markedly from the celebrations of Venezuela's democracy that I read about in many scholarly accounts. Beginning in the late 1950s, Venezuelans had regularly gone to the polls to elect leaders from two major political parties, the social-democratic party, Democratic Action (AD), and the social-Christian party, the Independent Political Electoral Organizing Committee (COPEI). To many observers, Venezuela seemed stable and relatively prosperous, especially in contrast to the conditions of state violence, civil war, and dictatorships that plagued other Latin American nations, including Chile, Argentina, and Uruguay. These celebrations, however, overlooked the fact that substantive political participation, social equality, and access to resources remained elusive for the vast majority of Venezuelans. Indeed, despite prominent claims that Venezuela had a "racial democracy" that avoided the virulent, race-based discrimination of the United States, the unequal distribution of resources and political power largely fell along racial lines (Wright 1990).[6] While women of all racial backgrounds have encountered deep structural inequalities, women of color in Venezuela have faced enormous levels of discrimination and have been impoverished at higher rates than light-skinned women (Friedman 2000; Rakowski and Espina 2011).

Despite their skepticism about the ability of the kind of democracy they grew up in—one that was liberal and capitalist—to create a free and fair society, Venezuelans I worked with had not given up on the state as an apparatus that ideally works to secure socioeconomic security as well as political rights. This view stems in part from the ideas proposed by the elite political leaders who founded Venezuela's liberal democracy in the late 1950s. The system they created was democratic, insofar as its founders established universal suffrage and a representative political system, and liberal, in the sense that leaders made commitments to the central values of political liberalism, including individual rights, private property, and a constitutional rule of law. To legitimize their rule, the architects of Venezuelan democracy argued that all Venezuelans were entitled to a share of the profits from selling Venezuela's oil (Coronil 1997).[7] They framed natural resources as communal property to be managed by the state in the interest of the people. This discourse has had an enduring impact. From my first research in rural Venezuela in 2000 through the fieldwork on which this book is based, I regularly heard Venezuelans express the idea that the population should have an equal share of the nation's oil wealth. My informants at Catia TVe assumed that it was common sense that Venezuelans have rights not only to vote or to express their opinions—what we generally think of as political rights—but also socioeconomic rights including access to shelter, food, health care, and education.

In practice, the ruling parties engineered a formal liberal democracy that allowed elites to maintain control of Venezuela's oil wealth and largely limited political participation to elections. During oil booms, leaders used oil-derived wealth to create spectacular development projects that made the state seem magical and out of reach (Coronil 1997). After the price of oil plummeted in the mid-1980s, Venezuela's government adopted neoliberal economic principles to reduce state support for public welfare, which proved disastrous, especially for the poor. If, by the early 1990s, the state appeared to much of the Venezuelan population as impenetrable, corrupt, violent, or even otherworldly, it did not strike popular activists as beyond recovery.

With the election of Chávez in the late 1990s, social activists demanded that the Venezuelan government invest resources from the sale of petroleum not only in social programs involving health and education, but also in community media initiatives. Rather than seeking to create autonomy apart from state institutions, Catia TVe producers demanded that they be able to participate in the remaking of these institutions so that they could fulfill their commitments to popular well-being. Catia TVe's central motto, "Don't watch television, make it!" provides an important starting point to understand how the station's producers saw media and the state during what would turn out to be a high tide of the Bolivarian Revolution.

When I returned to Caracas to do long-term fieldwork in 2006 after spending three previous summers getting to know Catia TVe's founders, the station's motto had already become a rallying cry for media producers across the country. Boldly proclaimed on a massive billboard that was perched atop the station's headquarters in Caracas, the motto demands production in place of reception. As I learned over the course of my research, the maxim referred to more than just television. It insisted that people from low-income barrios could shape the world around them. Catia TVe producers aimed to encourage people in low-income barrios to recognize their capacity not only to make television, but also to remake the broader social web of institutions

FIGURE I.2. Catia TVe headquarters with billboard that reads "Don't Watch Television, Make It!" January 25, 2006. Photo by the author.

and social relations they called the state. For my interlocutors at Catia TVe, the state was not a fixed and uniform thing, but rather a potentially revolutionary set of institutions and a process in gestation.

Despite the clarity of Catia TVe's slogan, it took me many months of fieldwork to understand that my interlocutors were quite serious about their motto. Like many grassroots video producers throughout Latin America, rather than seeing media as a product and imagining the effect that their programming might have on audiences, Catia TVe's thirty staff and nearly a hundred regular volunteers approached media as a process (Rodríguez 1994; Valdeavellano 1989). They worked to shape the immediate political terrain around them as they organized film shoots, conducted interviews, and documented their neighbors' problems. They did not aim to generate passive media audiences; they advocated for direct, engaged participation. Catia TVe's founders identified media production, not reception, as a practice that encouraged the discussion and debate necessary to create a truly participatory and democratic state. They attempted to bring this new state into being through their day-to-day participation in activities in poor neighborhoods and official state institutions where they asserted the right of the poor to participate and lead.

Media production provided Catia TVe producers an entry into statecraft in ways that I did not anticipate when I began my fieldwork. It is commonplace to understand that media outlets are important brokers of power in society. But this is often understood as a result of the influence of media coverage on audiences. An unexpected finding of my research was that the practice of media production—generating interviews, filming community meetings, asserting their right to attend official press conferences—was much more vital to their political activism than the influence of their finished media product on viewers. This approach had its contradictions. Audience numbers are the evidence that we use to judge the reach of media; my own effort to measure audiences and official polling revealed that community media audiences remained proportionately very small.

Regardless of their audience numbers, seizing the tools of media production and demanding institutional legal recognition allowed Catia TVe's founders to gain a foothold in an arena—"the press"—that many people across social sectors see as highly influential. This access—and the accompanying "media ideologies" (Gershon 2008) concerning the importance of television's impact on audiences—granted them a degree of political authority. In their effort to work with their allies who had greater class power and access to official state institutions, Catia TVe producers leveraged widespread beliefs about the power of television programming to sway the political opinion of audiences and influence political outcomes. In practice, Catia TVe's leaders demonstrated that their central goal was getting people to make television, not to watch it. And by the end of my fieldwork, I understood their motto, "Don't watch television, make it!" as another way of saying, "Don't sit by and watch the state, make it!"

The Historical Conjuncture

Much of what I document and analyze in the chapters that follow took place between 2006 and 2007, a time of ad hoc invention and change in Venezuela. This was a high point for the Bolivarian Revolution. Chávez was first elected in 1998 with the claim that his government would remake the relationship between state and society by granting the population direct control over governance and decision-making. To advance this vision, the government joined forces with active social movements to create a complex web of new programs in health care, education, housing, and media, some of which granted leadership to grassroots groups while others replicated previous patterns of paternalism. At the same time, Chávez concentrated power in the executive branch and centralized leadership in his own hands. In the wake of Chávez's 2005 declaration that Venezuela was on the road to building twenty-first-century socialism, the government formed a mass socialist party; nationalized key industries, expropriating them with compensation; and promoted local self-governing organizations called communal councils. The president and his supporters asserted that their aim was to create a kind of socialism that was neither derived from Soviet or Cuban socialism, nor limited to the formal channels of representative liberal democracy.

Chávez was reelected in December 2006 by a wide margin, granting him a firm mandate, even in the face of a wealthy and globally influential political opposition. Chávez's reelection followed three years of economic expansion. Oil prices were high and state funding for social programs was plentiful. Socioeconomic indicators for the period between 2003, when the government gained control over the state oil industry, and Chávez's reelection in 2006 reveal improved life conditions for the population (López Maya and Lander 2011b). Chávez emerged as a key leader in Latin America. He voiced the perspective of a growing number of progressive governments that challenged U.S. political and economic hegemony in the region.

Catia TVe producers were hopeful that through the Bolivarian Revolution they could advance social justice and equality in Venezuela and beyond. Intermingled with my informants' optimism, however, was a sense of uncertainty. The Bolivarian Revolution unfolded through sharp and pervasive contradictions. Over lunch one afternoon in 2007, Hector, an assistant director at Catia TVe, referenced aspects of these inconsistencies, noting, "This revolution is too easy." We had spent almost ten minutes searching for seats in the crowded food court of a mall in a working-class neighborhood of west Caracas. Tables were packed with families and young people enjoying pizza, fried chicken, and falafel sandwiches at prices that were more than double the cost of lunch from the informal vendors that lined the streets just outside the mall. The Bolivarian Revolution's redistribution of resources allowed many poor and lower middle-class people newfound access to commodities. The incongruous mix of capitalist and socialist ideals that shaped daily life in west Caracas was particularly notable in the mall, a space that serves as a kind of laboratory for aspirational class identities (Dávila 2015).

Hector worried about the fact that redistribution relied on high oil prices. The material gains we saw in poor communities around Catia TVe were not the result of a hard-fought struggle to upend the capitalist world system and re-order production and distribution through collective worker control. Instead, the poor and middle-class advocates of the Bolivarian Revolution attempted

FIGURE I.3. Caracas street mural, November 24, 2006. Photo by the author.

to build a new state on the foundation of an existing mono-crop export economy, which continued to keep Venezuela reliant on and deeply interconnected
to what Hector saw as an unjust and destructive international capitalist system.
In addition to being concerned about Venezuela's dependence on oil, most of
my interlocutors at Catia TVe were also anxious about the hostility of the
previous ruling elites, the opportunism they encountered within the ranks of
chavistas, and the overreliance of the Bolivarian movement on Chávez's leadership. Nevertheless, they believed that revolutionary change was possible.

At the time of my research, my interlocutors at Catia TVe had already
participated in advancing profound challenges to the status quo. They were
part of a mass popular rebellion that helped reverse a 2002 coup attempt
against Chávez, which Venezuela's commercial media owners and business
leaders orchestrated and the U.S. government endorsed. This was no small
achievement, given the violent history of U.S.-backed coups in the region
(Grandin 2006). Moreover, Catia TVe producers were active in building and
benefiting from programs in health, education, community media, and food
distribution. They were optimistic about their efforts to expand political
participation in state formation and develop meaningful popular control
through the Bolivarian Revolution.

To understand their sense of possibility, it is vital to comprehend how the particular historical conjuncture of the first decade of the 2000s created openings for political change. The multiple interconnected forces that informed daily life in Caracas and globe-spanning politics during this period included a shifting political landscape created by the collapse of Venezuela's two-party political system in the 1990s; the growing popular rejection in Latin America of neoliberal policies imposed by the United States; the charismatic contradictory leadership of Hugo Chávez; widespread denunciation of U.S. intervention in the aftermath of the American invasion of Afghanistan and Iraq; and, of course, the rise in the price of oil, which was itself a complex outcome of the interplay of the Chávez government's policies and global politics. These conditions produced uncertainty and opportunity; Catia TVe producers and their allies were hopeful they could exploit this situation to build state institutions by and for the poor majority.

Ten years later, the easiness that concerned Hector is a distant memory. Much of my informants' optimism has turned to despair. With Chávez's death in 2013, the precipitous drop in the price of oil, a reconsolidated political opposition, and the calamitous leadership of Chávez's successor, Nicolás Maduro, Hector and his allies face a remarkably different conjuncture. As I finish this book, my informants from Catia TVe fear the violence and political paralysis that shapes everyday life in Caracas. The poorest have been hit the hardest by the current economic collapse. Catia TVe is struggling to stay in operation in the face of budget cuts and the new challenges of everyday survival. The crisis Venezuela now faces is a consequence of at least three factors: first, the difficulty of altering the structure of dependency created by a mono-crop export economy; second, the pressure imposed by national and international interests who seek to curb anticapitalist politics that would upend the class structure; and third, the challenge of countering corruption in the midst of a chaotic and ad hoc process of transformation.

Given the formidable challenges Catia TVe producers and their allies faced in asserting popular leadership of state institutions, they were less attuned to analyzing and trying to intervene in the problems of Venezuela's dependence on the global oil market and its interconnections with global geopolitics. In the midst of high oil prices, some of the inconsistencies and tensions of the effort to build socialism on the foundation of a capitalist extraction-based economy could be temporarily sidestepped. Their horizon and practice of statecraft were focused on the local, national, and short term.

In focusing on the specific day-to-day work of statecraft in 2006 and 2007, I emphasize the opportunities that Catia TVe producers missed, especially in addressing inequalities internal to the Bolivarian movement. I make clear that the direction the revolution has taken and the problems that have emerged were not inevitable, as some observers contend. I emphasize how the lack of internal critique of power relations among supporters of the Bolivarian movement created a weak basis on which to navigate the contradictions of the movement and the hostility of the local and global forces aligned against popular leadership. Careful assessment of the gains and missteps of the many projects, like Catia TVe, that emerged with the Bolivarian process will enable us not only to understand the Bolivarian movement but also to grasp the limits and challenges of the conceptual categories we use to understand revolutionary politics.

By now, many scholars and observers have worked to untangle the knots of co-optation and empowerment that held together the Bolivarian Revolution and the process of state formation in Venezuela under Chávez.[8] I take up and extend a valuable thread in this scholarship that highlights how the state is produced on an everyday basis outside as well as inside formal state institutions. With many of the institutions of the Bolivarian Revolution under extreme duress, if not already dismantled, it becomes even more pressing to understand how and why social activists engaged with the state as a condition of possibility during the period that I analyze.

Anthropological Approaches to States

What became clear to Catia TVe activists and to me, as a scholar who is sympathetic with their efforts to construct a more just world, is that "one's theory of 'the state' does greatly matter in formulating strategies for political action" (Gupta 1995, 394). We must address the perennial questions of what the state is and why our theories matter. While states play important roles in people's everyday lives, states are not easy to define or delineate. One might imagine a state in institutional terms—organizations of appointed, elected, or hired people who run the police, the military, and the official bureaucracies that order our lives through both violent and banal coercion. But on close inspection, it becomes difficult to draw boundaries between state and non-state. In a now classic article, Philip Abrams (1988) calls the state a "triumph of concealment"; the very idea of the state hides the way power works in the world by making it seem as if there were a unified, self-operating force of legitimate power separate from the workings of the economy and society. Forgetting that people make the state—like a god or an idol—the state appears to have a life force all its own (Taussig 1993). The common spatial metaphor of the state as "above" and "outside" society inhibits an analysis of how power hierarchies are reproduced and challenged in daily interactions that are at once local and global (Coronil 1997; Ferguson and Gupta 2002).

Informed by thinkers such as Gramsci and Poulantzas, anthropologists, historians, and political theorists have challenged, on the one hand, orthodox Marxist notions that states are straightforward instruments of the dominant capitalist class and, on the other hand, liberal approaches to the state as an entity ideally autonomous from civil society and the economy (Fernandes 2006; Joseph and Nugent 1994; Mitchell 1999). The processual approach to the state that I take up throughout this book sees the state, as Michel-Rolph Trouillot contends, as "a set of practices and processes and their effects" (2001, 131), which are thoroughly embedded in our everyday actions, concrete experiences, and relationships. My research resonates with that of scholars who have argued that the state is not a fixed form or a "thing" at all, but rather a social web that extends not only through individual societies but also across the globe (Abrams 1988; Coronil 1997; Mitchell 1991). Thus, the state not only includes formal institutions like prisons and schools, but also, as Aradhana Sharma and Akhil Gupta note, "is within other institutional forms through which social relations are lived—family, civil society, and the economy" (2006, 9). A processual notion of the state takes into account how the unfolding social relationships that shape daily life are part of a network of unequal and global power relations.

Debates about the state are a steady fixture of everyday life for most Venezuelans. These discussions have generated extensive anthropological attention. Whether approached as "magical" (Coronil 1997; Taussig 1997), "festive" (Guss 2001), "hybrid" (Fernandes 2010b), or as a "process of everyday formation" (Schiller 2013; Valencia 2015), the state plays an outsized role in scholarly understandings and imaginations of Venezuela. My vantage point from Catia TVe allowed me to see that poor activists were using statecraft—the everyday process of creating ideas and representations about what the state is and can be—to try to create a more just world. This finding was distinct from most of what I had read about states and social movements.

Statecraft as a Weapon of the Weak

In the late twentieth and early twenty-first centuries, many anthropologists turned their attention away from organized revolutionary movements to focus instead on "unlikely" and "everyday forms of resistance" (Abu-Lughod 1990; Scott 1990). James Scott encouraged anthropologists to consider both the importance of unorganized acts of resistance and the great danger of large-scale state projects to "improve the human condition" (1998). Ethnographers traced how subjugated populations resisted relations of subordination by employing "weapons of the weak" (Scott 1985), including not only foot-dragging and dissimulation but also the "subtle, unorganized, diffuse and spontaneous" forms of oppositional culture, such as laughter and humor (Goldstein 2003, 98). As Lila Abu-Lughod (1990) notes, these studies uncovered the complexity of processes of domination, directed attention to everyday struggle, and deepened our understandings of power both as an exercise of hegemony and as brute violence. However, a weakness of the focus on unlikely and commonplace forms of resistance is that it downplayed the importance of overt organized forms of opposition and misrepresented resistance and local knowledge as separate from or outside of state power (Gutmann 1993; Li 2005).

At the same time that many anthropologists were devoting attention to small-scale everyday acts of resistance, social scientists studying Latin America increasingly directed their analyses to the "new social movements" that arose in the 1980s and 1990s. These scholars argued that conventional theories envisioned political practice in narrow terms that included only electoral, party, and other formal political institutions, overlooking the role of social movements in constructing and configuring democracy (Alvarez, Dagnino, and Escobar 1998). In the struggle against the bloody dictatorships in Latin America's southern cone and in their aftermath, social movements engaged in political activism in unconventional spheres outside the formal state apparatus. These activists were suspicious of or rejected outright the possibility that the state was a site of collective reference in the pursuit of justice (Dagnino 1998, 45).

My research on Catia TVe and the Bolivarian Revolution differs markedly from studies of social activists who determined that the state was a lost cause. In contrast, I analyze why in the first decade of the twenty-first century many activists in Venezuela approached statecraft as a weapon of the weak. These efforts were always, in every moment, shaped by power inequalities of class, gender, race, and the kinds of access to decision-making these hierarchies afforded, as I demonstrate. Rather than waiting to engage the state once more equitable relations were established, they used the process of statecraft as a way to try to bring into being a more equitable world. Catia TVe producers wrestled with their relationships with official state institutions and agents, which, as I will show, were simultaneously constraining and enabling. However, establishing autonomy from the state along the lines that liberal approaches to press freedom mandated was neither desirable nor possible for Catia TVe producers, given their political commitments to the Bolivarian Revolution and their view that the state resources on which they depended rightly belonged to them. They sought to create the necessary space for criticism in order to deepen the revolutionary process according to their agenda of popular empowerment.

Catia TVe producers' everyday forms of resistance included their efforts to develop radical interdependencies with, rather than absolute autonomy from, state institutions.[9] My informants at Catia TVe openly collaborated with officials, institutions, and a broad and diverse network of social movement actors who claimed affinity with a process of progressive social change. Catia TVe producers interchanged knowledge, material resources, and symbolic and material power with people working within state institutions. They aimed for these interdependent relations to be radical in the sense that they were in the interest of sweeping changes in the structures of liberal capitalist society. Catia TVe producers' efforts to create mutual reliance with official institutions involved maintaining long-standing ties and creating new relationships with allies who often exercised greater class power. In many moments, rather than radical interdependency, Catia TVe producers and their interlocutors created a kind of mutual instrumentality. In other moments, they created tenuous and fleeting forms of radical interdependence with official actors who worked within tumultuous state institutions, some of which were much more aligned than others with Catia TVe's goals of radical transformation and popular leadership. To engage in revolutionary statecraft in and through Venezuela's already existing liberal capitalist state institutions required Catia TVe producers to embrace the reality of an uneven playing field. They chose not to wait until they enjoyed conditions of equality with their allies to act. This process was conflict-ridden, frustrating, and sometimes tedious.

Making the Media and the State Ordinary

Let us return to the palace.

Considerable tension buzzed just below the staid collegiality of the press conference I began describing in the opening of this introduction. Just a few months before, Chávez had announced that his government would not renew the broadcast license for a commercial television station harshly critical of the Bolivarian Revolution. This announcement sparked the widespread conclusion that Chávez threatened press freedom. Tackling criticism

FIGURE I.4. Chávez speaks at press conference, February 1, 2007. Photo by the author.

of his government head on, Chávez opened his address to the national and international press that morning by pledging that he loved what he called "the battle of ideas." Taking a sip of espresso from a tiny porcelain cup, Chávez instructed his audience, "One should say what one wants, as long as they are responsible about what they say. The public should freely watch, listen, analyze, and come to their own conclusions. This is part of the Bolivarian Revolution. So that everyone knows, people here say what they want."

Chávez's declaration of commitment to freedom of expression, a right central to the framework of liberal democracy, ran counter to most pronouncements. But the president's qualification that press freedom entailed a "responsibility" on the part of speakers to manage their own expression pointed to exactly the kind of ambiguity that critics argued would allow the government to unilaterally censor any material it deemed reckless.[10]

Chávez moved on to other topics. Many other topics. About two hours into the president's four-hour monologue, Nestor and Jesica's excitement at being inside the palace for the first time, alongside the international and national professional press crews, slowly dissipated. Chávez regularly spoke for hours on end. As usual, he interspersed his formal discussion of policy with off-the-cuff commentary peppered with songs, jokes, and accessible lessons in political ideology. But even the most passionate supporters of the president grew bored as the tedium of being tightly packed against other film crews set in. Being in the same room as Chávez began to feel remarkably ordinary.

Nestor, Jesica, and I distracted ourselves by gazing through the windows of the control room behind us, where heavyset men in suits and ties operated dials and keyboards. Based on their experience in Catia TVe's studio, Jesica and Nestor explained to me—in short whispers—that these men were rotating between three different camera feeds to stitch together a seamless recording of the press conference, which they broadcast live over the airwaves of the principal state television channel. After a while, though, even this elaborate display of media production grew boring. Jesica and Nestor busied themselves exchanging text messages with friends. Like Chávez's presence, the behind-the-scenes action of this important site of official media production and state power had become altogether too familiar.

Nestor and Jesica's boredom during the press conference was significant. Their access to this space of official power exposed the everyday human character of what so often seemed otherworldly: the state, the media, and the charismatic force that was Hugo Chávez. In a historical context where Venezuela's vast oil wealth has been used by governing elites to make themselves and their institutions seem supernatural to many ordinary people, Catia TVe producers' access to the means of media production gave them new insight into the behind-the-scenes creation of state spectacle. Nestor and Jesica learned that the press conference was a carefully staged activity coordinated by ordinary people who made decisions about who should be permitted to ask questions, what camera angle to choose, and which dial to turn. The numerous espressos that Chávez requested with a subtle tap on his porcelain cup fueled his seemingly superhuman energy.

Just when it seemed that Chávez would talk straight through lunchtime, he opened the floor to questions. After calling on several reporters from international and national commercial outlets, Chávez turned to a woman from a community newspaper outlet. She was one of the few nonprofessional community media producers alongside Catia TVe at the press conference. The woman had dark-brown skin and looked to be in her late thirties. In a remarkably calm voice she asked the president to discuss the model of communication he thought was necessary to build twenty-first-century socialism. I had observed how this question had been carefully planned before the press conference began, when the director of a new bureau within the Ministry of Communications and Information devoted to community media asked the six representatives of community media outlets present that morning to agree jointly on a question for the president.

The community newspaper reporter followed up this carefully vetted question with a second query for Chávez that departed from the prearranged script. "Mr. President," she said, "if you'll permit me, knowing the freedom of expression that we enjoy plainly here in Venezuela when we are responsible with what we say, I'd like to tell you about an act of bureaucracy in our community." Given the way that select liberal notions of press freedom were so frequently used to delegitimize the Bolivarian Revolution, I was surprised to observe this community newspaper reporter invoke press freedom. She went on to describe how the government had stopped construction on a housing project in her neighborhood without offering her community an explanation. With all eyes in the room firmly resting on her, she launched a *denuncia*—a complaint or denunciation—about government bureaucracy and corruption. Chávez listened, his eyes narrowing. He made notes in pencil on a legal pad. When she was finished, Chávez restated his commitment to press freedom and turned briefly to her complaint. He asked the community reporter for more details and promised to have the corresponding minister look into the problem.

I never learned whether or not this community reporter received a response from the minister. But it was clear that the reporter transformed what could have been a tightly constrained performance of grassroots participation into an opportunity to raise a pressing concern for her community and hold Chávez accountable to rectify corruption. What was so remarkable was that, although a language of press freedom had become for many critics the go-to political grammar to discredit the Bolivarian Revolution, this community reporter mobilized this same discourse of enlightened liberalism in her denuncia to declare her solidarity with *and* criticism of the Chávez government in order to demand more commitment for social provisions from formal state institutions.

While community media producers like this reporter and Nestor and Jesica rejected a liberal ideology that prioritizes the press's independence from the state, they were also clear that they did not want to replicate historical socialist prescriptions for cultural producers to act as the vanguard of the party-state. Catia TVe producers were disillusioned by the failures of liberal capitalist democracy in Venezuela and wary of repeating the mistakes of previous socialist experiments. And yet both liberal democratic and socialist ideals shaped how Catia TVe producers developed and realized their community media project and how scholars, pundits, activists, journalists, and politicians evaluated their media practice. A central conceptual and political challenge for state-aligned community media producers has been to articulate media freedom in terms that build on and depart from the dominant Western liberal tradition of press freedom and experiments with socialist media. This book tracks this reckoning.

Through their participation in community media production in this and countless other moments, Catia TVe producers began to see not only the media but also the state as unstable projects of human construction. Their experience undermined the idea, reproduced by successive Venezuelan governments, that the state was something they could not participate in or change. Their participation in both the technological process of production behind media representations, and in the sociopolitical dynamics involved in the production of the state allowed them to challenge the dominant notion that the state was a magical monolith beyond the reach of human action that functioned apart from them. Their practice of media production encouraged Catia TVe producers to view the state not as a central headquarters of power or a chief threat to individual liberty but, instead, as a process they could shape.

Plan of the Book

Chapter 1, "State–Media Relations and the Rise of Catia TVe," charts the development of community media in the context of modern Venezuelan state formation. I describe Catia TVe's transformation from a film club formed on the heels of the 1989 popular uprising to a legal and well-funded television station by 2007. While Chávez's policies were often framed as a vast departure from previous relations between purportedly autonomous arenas of media and the state, this chapter places the Chávez government's approach to media within a long history of struggle, collusion, and compromise between commercial channels and Venezuelan governments.

Chapter 2, "Community Media as Everyday State Formation," examines how Catia TVe producers juggled multiple definitions of the state as they documented the formation of a communal council (an innovative local governance structure) and produced coverage of the 2006 presidential elections alongside ViVe TV, an official state television outlet. Catia TVe producers at times constructed and depended on notions of a reified state, autonomous and separate from society, to build their authority and engage in social activism. Nevertheless, in their everyday practice they defied the fixity of the boundary between state and society and advocated for activists to embrace statecraft.

Chapter 3, "Class Acts," analyzes the cross-class collaboration and conflict that emerged at joint training workshops between Catia TVe producers— the majority of whom lived in Caracas's barrios—and their allies at the official state channel, ViVe TV, most of whom were from middle-class families. I explore the problems that developed as community and official state media producers collaborated to create revolutionary television and used "popular culture" as a basis for the construction of Venezuelan socialism.

Chapter 4, "Channeling Chávez," explores the limits and possibilities of theories of populism, a heavily debated framework, to understand the Bolivarian Revolution. I assess how Catia TVe producers negotiated the contradictions of Chávez's centralized leadership and defined the concept of "the people" as working class and popular.

Chapter 5, "Mediating Women," highlights the connections between media production, public speaking, and gendered authority. While women producers at Catia TVe made remarkable gains in the field of media production, they nevertheless faced persistent gender-based oppression within the station. I argue that the distinction between democratic community and domineering state apparatus prevents scholars, methodologically as well as theoretically, from tracing the way that gender hierarchy was produced in Bolivarian Venezuela.

Chapter 6, "Reckoning with Press Freedom," explores how Catia TVe producers approached press freedom in the context of the Chávez government's controversial 2007 decision to remove RCTV, a commercial television station, from the public airwaves. Instead of approaching the state as a barrier to press freedom, community media producers in Caracas approached statecraft as a potentially liberatory process of collective engagement. The book ends with a glimpse of Catia TVe in 2015. I explore how community media producers have weathered the loss of Chávez and how a few of Catia TVe's founders understood their own missteps and the economic and political crisis they faced.

Channeling the State analyzes how people from Caracas's poor neighborhoods, together with their middle-class allies, used the process of media production to engage in forms of everyday statecraft with the goal of building an alternative to liberal capitalist democracy.

ONE

STATE–MEDIA RELATIONS AND THE RISE OF CATIA TVe

José, a twenty-seven-year-old taxicab driver, bounced his knee furiously up and down. "It's freezing in here," I whispered to him. José smiled nervously and steadied his knee. "It's not that I'm cold," he confided. "I've just never been on television before." José and I joined sixteen community activists, teachers, and community media producers in Catia TVe's heavily air-conditioned television studio. Luis, the host of that evening's show, settled into one of the mix-matched chairs arranged in a semicircle in front of two massive studio cameras. Catia TVe's founders acquired the cameras, cables, and microphones, and almost everything else in the station, through their publicity contract with the state oil company. Adeptly attaching a tiny microphone to the collar of his T-shirt, Luis warmly reassured his guests that all that was required of them was to continue the conversation they had been having for weeks about what kind of programming they thought should be broadcast on a new state-run television station. In a controversial move, President Chávez had announced just a few months before, in December 2006, that his government planned to replace a commercial television network staunchly critical of the government with a new state-run network. In the months following the announcement, Catia TVe organized a series of talks with local community organizers about how people from the barrio could participate in producing material for the new television state. "Why not broadcast our discussion?" Luis suggested at the close of the last gathering. So there we were.

My aim in this chapter is to understand the conditions that led to Catia TVe's founders to join forces with the Chávez government to remake Venezuela's media world. I briefly look back at the development of the television industry in Venezuela to unearth some of the alliances, tensions, and inter-connections between ruling elites who exercised control over state institutions, powerful business owners who held the monopoly over communications, intellectuals who sought to create a more democratic communications system, and activists who engaged the tools of community media to advance social justice.

Observers and activists have often framed the Chávez government's poli-cies as a vast departure from previous relations between media makers and the state, as if before the Chávez era, media producers and owners had ex-ercised full autonomy from official state actors. In fact, as I explore in the first half of this chapter, past interdependencies between state authorities and media makers have been multiple, significant, and, in many ways, taken for granted. Here I place the Chávez government's policy shifts regarding media within a long history of struggle, collusion, and compromise between commercial media and Venezuelan governments. I point to the roots of the contemporary community media movement in the 1970s debates about the need for a "New World Information and Communications Order."

In the second half of the chapter, I document how, under the Chávez government, barrio-based actors, middle-class allies, state employees, and international allies jointly produced new experiments in state and commu-nity television in Venezuela. In these projects, the interconnections between state, economy, and media were redrawn in ways that diverged markedly, although not entirely, from the patterns of liberal and neoliberal capitalist projects of previous administrations. This overview of state–media relations in Venezuela uncovers how marking borders between mutually constitutive social fields of state and society "generates resources of power," includ-ing "effects of agency and partial autonomy, with concrete consequences" (Mitchell 1999, 83, 84). Analyzing the Chávez government's approach to Venezuela's media world alongside those of previous administrations illus-trates how differently positioned social actors mobilize rhetorics of autonomy toward distinct political ends.

Setting the Scene

"Good evening." Luis looked steadily into one of the two studio cameras that encircled the group of invited guests. "Tonight we want to talk about the relationship between communal councils and the new television station. You don't have to be a filmmaker to create television. You may be a lawyer, a mechanic, a bus driver, or a housewife, but you have the responsibility to participate. And I think this is the moment. You, out there, spread the word! We need to discuss this on the corner, down your alley."

By 2007, when I observed the filming of this program, Luis had been moderating his studio talk show in one form or another for nearly ten years. Luis was full of a seemingly boundless energy; only his silver beard betrayed his almost fifty years. Over the course of my fieldwork, I heard Luis make a similar call for widespread participation in media production countless times. His list of professions—lawyer, bus driver, housewife, mechanic—was a way for Luis to index social class status and make clear that one didn't need elite professional training to be a media producer. Luis and his colleagues often expanded their call by noting that it didn't matter if people were "black, fat, or missing an eye." Luis and his Catia TVe colleagues' invitation for widespread participation challenged the racial, class, and gender hierarchy that characterized most television programming broadcast in Venezuela. They made a claim to transform their media world by changing who was in front of and behind the television camera. Community media activists at Catia TVe did so in close collaboration with the Chávez government, a fact that was evident in every corner of their television station.

Luis's composed demeanor betrayed no trace of the harried scene I'd witnessed just half an hour before. Luis had dashed around Catia TVe's two-story building trying to recruit camera operators for the program. His schedule had been irregular in the proceeding weeks and none of his colleagues remembered that they would be needed that evening to film his show. The guests on his program were already arriving as I followed Luis around the station pleading for camera operators. At our first stop in the production office, we found Douglas, a stocky man in his mid-thirties. He was one of the five Catia TVe staff members responsible for producing programming. Douglas was intensely focused; he was editing footage on a shiny new Mac computer the station had just purchased using funds from a publicity contract with the state oil company. Luis's effort to cajole Douglas into being a cameraperson for his studio program proved futile. Douglas scratched his short-cropped head of curls, explaining apologetically that he was about to leave to film a dance performance that evening at the National Theater.

I continued to follow Luis around the large rectangular atrium at the center of Catia TVe's headquarters, a sizeable building constructed in the late 1800s to serve as horse stables for President Joaquín Crespo.[1] The minister of the interior granted Catia TVe a rent-free fifty-year lease in 2003, providing a vital long-term subsidy to support their community television project. The building is located in the historic center of Caracas in a neighborhood

FIGURE 1.1. Catia TVe's television studio, August 9, 2004. Photo by the author.

called Caño Amarillo, named for the spectacular yellow flowers that once bloomed in the area. By 2007, the few remaining historic buildings were surrounded by poor neighborhoods. An elevated portion of the Caracas metro cuts through the densely packed houses of cement blocks and zinc roofing, noisily passing just twenty feet in front of Catia TVe's headquarters.

Luis led me to the station's transmission office, a dark, windowless room in the back of the building with the feel of an airplane cockpit. Edilson, a staff member in his late twenties, sat in front of two computer screens, three keyboards, countless knobs, and four television screens that were tuned to different channels. At the time, Catia TVe was on the air from 10 A.M. to 10 P.M. Edilson was responsible for organizing the day's programming schedule, which consisted of programs produced by Catia TVe's unpaid volunteers and paid staff, as well as documentaries made in Venezuela and abroad. Catia TVe also regularly broadcast Chávez's speeches. The station was under legal obligation, as were all media outlets based in Venezuela, to broadcast certain official transmissions. Catia TVe's staff regularly chose to broadcast many of Chávez's speeches that the Ministry of Information and Communication had not designated as obligatory. Between this lineup of programming, Edilson and his colleagues interspersed paid content, which consisted of official promotional segments produced by state institutions that celebrated the accomplishments of the Bolivarian Revolution.

"*Epa*, Harry Potter!" Luis shouted. Edilson's new round glasses had inspired his latest nickname. The glasses, like the braces that glinted in Edilson's mouth, were signs of his new access to steady income and health insurance as an employee at Catia TVe. "The show begins in twenty-five minutes," Luis informed Edilson and was out the door. He headed toward the front offices of the building. There on a balcony just outside the outreach department, Luis found just what he was looking for: Jesica, a staff member, and Rosemery, a volunteer, were sharing a cigarette. "Ay, mi amor," Luis enveloped Rosemery in a bear hug. "Mi vida," he kissed Jesica on the cheek. Luis had to wait a moment for a subway to blast by us before making his appeal for their help in the studio. With some coaxing and a promise that Luis would find the women a ride home to their respective barrios after the program was over, Jesica and Rosemery agreed to operate the cameras for his show. As a volunteer, Rosemery was not remunerated for her labor. Jesica earned minimum wage, as did the station's other thirty employees, which at that time included security guards, custodial staff, accountants, and media producers. The minimum wage was about $400 per month during my fieldwork, which was enough to cover Jesica's expenses in the household she shared with her parents.

Once the program began back in the studio, Luis held out a microphone to invite one of his program's guests to begin the discussion about how the local community organizations, known as communal councils, might influence the direction of the new state-run television station. Communal councils, legalized in 2006, allow groups of 200 to 400 families in urban areas (fewer are required in rural zones) to directly administer government funding for local housing and public works projects. A young man answered Luis's invitation, requesting the microphone. "Look, I'm trying to organize a communal council but I'm a bit stuck. I don't know how to proceed." Luis gestured for the young man to hold the microphone closer to his mouth so he could be heard over the air. The man overcompensated, pressing the foam of the microphone into his lower lip, his voice now painfully loud. "I saw a presentation from the mayor's office about communal councils," the man continued, tugging his T-shirt over his protruding belly, "but there's been no follow-up and I guess you could say that I'm looking for direction."

Lidice, a Catia TVe volunteer in her early sixties, reached for the microphone. "You need to consult the law about how to form a communal council," she instructed the young man. "There are books and PowerPoint presentations. The mayor's office can help you proceed." She paused and shifted in her plastic chair, sitting up a bit taller. "But what I want to say is this: the people who are going to organize the communal councils should be the inhabitants of that sector. This is the challenge that we all face in order to actually construct participatory and protagonistic democracy in concrete ways, and not reproduce representative democracy. You see, the idea of the communal council is to create a structure that will break with the old model of representation. You can't wait for the institutions to do things for you." Like other ardent activists, Lidice was adamant that they needed to assume leadership and initiative.

A skinny woman a few chairs away gestured for the microphone. As she started to speak, Rosemery tripped over a thick black cable connected to her camera, distracting several of the participants. After an awkward pause as Rosemery found her balance, the woman continued. "We need to appropriate the media so that we can inform people of their rights. Are the institutions really in favor of the people [el pueblo]? We have to remember that we still have structures of the fourth regime [the previous government] and to this date we haven't transformed them. So as we are transforming the media, we are transforming this structure. We don't need outside experts."

In many ways, Luis's program was what you might expect of community television: a barebones set with mismatched furniture, jerky camera movements, and uneven sound. The conversation was improvised; the participants immediately veered away from Luis's initial invocation to focus on what was on their minds. In the harsh studio light, faces were shiny and pockmarked. Stomachs spilled over tight waistbands. With its small audiences and low production values, community television might seem outdated, even comical.

And yet everyone in the room was riveted. Regardless of who was watching the broadcast over Catia TVe's airwaves, the space of the station's television studio became a forum for energetic debate, discussion, and information sharing. In the first few minutes of the program, the participants posed the central questions facing the Bolivarian Revolution. Could they and should they draw boundaries between their community activism and state institutions? Was the state a collective unfolding project of which they were a part, or was it an outside threat to community organizations? Could poor people's embrace of the tools to represent themselves allow them to transform, as one of the guests argued, the broader political and social structure?

Sitting in the back of the studio that evening, I noted the seemingly contradictory ways that Luis and his guests invoked the state. Throughout the program they spoke of the need to defend themselves from the impositions of *las instituciones*. They made clear that existing institutions, many of which had been formed under previous ruling regimes, were not necessarily on the side of "the people," by which they meant the impoverished majority. Yet in their conversation they described the state as both a set of institutions that might co-opt community organizations and, crucially, as a site of possibility, open to their involvement. The material reality of their surroundings—the flow of petrodollars that supported grassroots projects—provided evidence of the web of social relations that connected activists, official state institutions, and the global oil economy. Seizing the tools of media production made possible through these relations was a vital part of Catia TVe activists' efforts to challenge the historic processes of dispossession that left barrio communities impoverished and marginalized. Nevertheless, the ongoing question of how their reliance on "outside experts" and "the institutions" might compromise their ability to meet their goals and make local decisions worried Catia TVe producers and many of their pro-revolution allies who had adopted the challenge of building communal councils.

In the sections that follow, I place the conversation that unfolded that evening during Luis's studio program within the intertwined history of mass media and community media in Venezuela. The Chávez government and its allies' attempt to remake Venezuela's media world was not, in fact, as stark a departure from past practice as both left- and right-wing political observers have claimed. The Chávez government's close relationship with media producers, efforts to democratize access to media, and attempts to control what was sayable in the press had historical precedent.

Early Decades of Television

The modernizing dictator Pérez Jiménez (1952–58) welcomed television into Venezuela in 1952, following only eight other nations in the world (Mayobre 1996, 240). With the development of the oil industry in the early twentieth century, Venezuela had been transformed from an agricultural nation focused on coffee and cocoa production to one of the world's most important oil exporters, with close connections to American corporations (Tinker Salas 2009). Rather than building a state-run public model for media like that of Western Europe, Jiménez and later liberal democratic governments chose to follow an American commercial model. The new medium quickly became predominantly corporate-owned, advertising-supported, and dependent on U.S. programming to fill its program hours. Unlike many postcolonial

Third World nations, the aim of Venezuelan television was not educational uplift. In contrast with Egypt, for example, where Lila Abu-Lughod notes that television's "addressee was the citizen, not the consumer" (2005, 11), the ideal target of Venezuelan television was indisputably the consumer. The Jiménez government devoted little attention to developing public television networks. The state channel, Televisora Nacional de Venezuela, TVN-5, inaugurated in 1952, reached only parts of Caracas and was underfunded and little watched. A second state channel, Venezolana de Televisión or VTV, as it is commonly known today, was not launched until 1976. From the outset, then, a central goal of Venezuelan television was to deliver audiences to advertisers. Television enriched media and business owners, who were closely connected to state officials. While newspapers and radio continued to play a key role in Venezuelan politics and everyday life, television quickly became the most prominent means of mass communication (Bisbal 2005).

The type of democracy that political elites created in Venezuela in the late 1950s expanded some rights and access to resources to the broader population but did not significantly redistribute power. Venezuela's ruling elites signed a political pact in 1958 to share power between two parties under a representative liberal democratic system. Political organizations on the left, such as the Communist Party of Venezuela, were excluded from the institutional arrangements of the pact. Beginning in these early years of formal democracy, Venezuelan governments wrestled with the owners of commercial media outlets for political influence. Yet, despite this competition, media and state were far from mutually exclusive spheres. Media owners had intimate social and political ties with ruling elites, granting them privileged influence over decision-making within the two-party democratic system (López Maya 2005a). The absence of antitrust legislation allowed a few private corporations to exercise a virtual monopoly over media industries (Mayobre 2002, 180). A small number of companies grew to control not only nationally broadcast television networks, but also regional television stations, radio outlets, and newspapers. Scholars note that although Latin American governments have historically left private media officially unregulated, government actors have paradoxically tightly controlled commercial media (Fox and Waisbord 2002; Waisbord 1995). At times, governments have exercised their power over commercial outlets through overt censorship and suppression of information. More commonly, however, governments have exerted control through the extension of broadcast licenses, lucrative contracts to broadcast state publicity, and monetary exchange policy, which can make it difficult for media businesses to secure needed imports.

Although the 1961 constitution, ratified three years into the establishment of formal democracy, protected key liberal tenets such as press freedom, it left leeway for censorship by allowing for punishment of "statements that constitute criminal offenses" and by outlawing materials deemed to incite the public to disobey the law. At the outset of formal democratic rule, President Rómulo Betancourt (1959–64) put this flexibility to use, both by banning several small leftist newspapers and by shaping the coverage of mainstream media. When the leading national newspapers published articles exposing the government's brutality against the leftist insurrection, the Betancourt government moved swiftly to prohibit the dissemination of information about acts of violence that would affect Venezuela's "social tranquility" and "public order" (Botía 2007, 50). The commercial media vilified and excluded leftist voices, thus contributing to the absence of popular support for the armed struggle against the limited democratic system (Ciccariello-Maher 2013).

This competition, collaboration, and cross-pollination between media and governing elites in Venezuela took place against a backdrop of U.S. political and economic hegemony. In the 1950s, American networks ABC and NBC held partial ownership of two of the three television channels on the air in Venezuela, which came to be known as Radio Caracas Television (RCTV) and Venevisión. The third channel was the little-watched and underfunded state-run station. In the early 1960s, the prominent Venezuelan Phelps family purchased the majority of shares in RCTV, and the Cisneros group, a Cuban-Venezuelan industrialist family with strong ties to President Betancourt, purchased a portion of Venevisión. Even after Venezuelan businessmen purchased majority stakes in Venevisión and RCTV, these stations retained affiliation with American television networks and broadcast extensive American content that advanced U.S. corporate and political interests. Standard Oil, the U.S. oil giant, developed television programs for RCTV that emphasized the company's contributions to Venezuela (Tinker Salas 2009, 194). RCTV and Venevisión broadcast programming created by the U.S. government to influence Venezuelan opinion in favor of American-style capitalism, in an explicit effort to challenge the rising tide of communism elsewhere in the region (Tinker Salas 2009). At the same time, advertisements for Gerber baby food, Ford automobiles, and Avon lipstick encouraged consumer demand for American products.

Commercial television expanded its reach, proving to be both lucrative and politically influential. Between 1960 and 1970, the percentage of houses with television sets doubled to 47 percent (Bisbal 2005, 40). By the end of the 1970s, 79 percent of Venezuelan households had a television (Bisbal 2005, 45). Media owners and advertisers influenced not only consumption patterns, but also the continuity of the two-party political system. By 1969, President Caldera had allowed the return of the left to parliamentary politics, legalizing the Communist Party and the Movement of the Revolutionary Left, as well as granting amnesty to leftist guerrillas after they renounced armed struggle. The prohibitive cost of television advertising, however, undercut the ability of smaller parties to promote their candidates and mount presidential campaigns (Martz 1988, 163).

During the presidency of Rafael Caldera (1969–74), the government claimed the legal ability to interrupt all broadcasts, on public and commercial television, to air presidential speeches pertaining to "matters of public interest," whenever the president deemed it necessary. (Chávez's extensive use of a similar provision attracted widespread condemnation that almost exclusively overlooked the roots of this practice under earlier governments.) Caldera's efforts to expand the government's capacity to interfere with broadcasters signaled an ongoing struggle among the ruling classes to harness broadcast media toward different ends in different moments.

The Emergence of Anti-Imperialist
Cultural Nationalism and Internationalism

In the late 1960s and 1970s, during a period of intense anti-imperialist struggle in Southeast Asia, Africa, and the United States, revolutionary internationalist intellectuals, leftist activists, and elected and appointed leaders of Venezuelan state institutions began to address, from differing perspectives, the importance of local cultural production. In these debates, we can trace the roots of the contemporary community media movement in Venezuela.

By 1973, 50 percent of television programs broadcast in Venezuela were imported (Ewell 1984, 222). The majority of news, films, television, music, and magazines that circulated in Latin America during this period had origins in the United States (Beltrán Salmón 2008). Building on these findings, leftist intellectuals began to identify cultural imperialism as a central dynamic of neocolonial domination (Dorfman and Mattelart 1975). In Venezuela, the foreign origins of much television programming and the perceived low quality of the highest-rated telenovelas (Latin American soap operas) had begun to provoke much hand-wringing among Venezuela's educators and intellectuals over what they saw as the nation's cultural dependence and disintegrating moral fabric. The new influx of imported appliances, clothing, and food, as well as the prominent place of American music and film, stoked fears among some that Venezuelan culture was under attack. The consensus among most Venezuelan scholars was that television transmitted foreign values, encouraged social stereotypes, and was morally and aesthetically repugnant (Barrios 1988, 72).

In response to the perceived threat to what prominent thinkers and politicians labeled Venezuelan national identity, many argued for greater state regulation of television as a way to curb foreign influence. President Caldera, backed by one of the two major political parties, COPEI, put forth a resolution in 1972 to establish certain norms for television content. Resolution 3178 states, "Radio and television stations should foment moral and cultural values of the nation, strengthen democratic conditions and national unity, contribute to the development and improvement of education, and affirm respect for social morality, human dignity, and family institutions." Caldera also demanded that television outlets be fully owned by Venezuelans and that these owners assume greater responsibility for education and development. Caldera's government acted not only as if relying on "national" capital could ensure the defense of local norms and perspectives, but also as if that capital could be national and was not always already globally influenced. Politicians' and scholars' assertions that national ownership could challenge cultural imperialism ignored the interpenetration and symbiosis between the domestic bourgeoisie and global capitalists (Coronil 1997, 284).

Rather than highlight the need for national ownership, the conversation among anti-imperialist internationalist scholars, artists, and activists in Venezuela and beyond approached communications as a human right and a necessary component of democracy. The focus was not on defending the so-called values of the nation, but rather the need both to transform global flows of media products to ensure that the First World did not monopolize communications, and to assess the power dynamics underlying the production of media within individual nation-states. Brazilian political philosopher Paulo Freire's call (1970) for a "pedagogy of the oppressed" based on anticolonial horizontal communication energized the field of communications. The growing effort to challenge the imposition of First World values, habits, and perspectives on subaltern nations was part and parcel of a broader politics of international solidarity among oppressed peoples against the consolidation of capitalist class power. These calls for the autonomy of cultural industries, unlike President Caldera's resolutions, drew attention to class inequalities and sought to disrupt rather than simply to maintain these injustices. Thus, an anti-cultural imperialist nationalist discourse valorized

Venezuelan identity but largely sidestepped how the class interests of Venezuelan media owners and producers shaped media content. Alongside this discourse, an anti-imperialist *internationalism* focused not on reaffirming national identity but rather on challenging global capitalism.

The Call for a New World Information Order

The anti-imperialist impetus to rethink the global communications order found an institutional anchor at the United Nations. In 1974, the United Nations Education, Scientific and Cultural Organization (UNESCO), made up of a substantial number of Third World intellectuals, built on ongoing conversations to declare the need for what they called a "New World Information and Communications Order" (NWICO). These scholars argued that meaningful national independence was impossible without participatory national cultural production and news analysis originating in and focused on the Third World. Certain lines of discussion within this debate advanced a critique of capitalism, while others focused predominantly on a defense of national cultural sovereignty.

In line with the politics of NWICO, Venezuelan intellectuals participated in a commission that focused on the need to develop public service media. In 1974, under the leadership of prominent scholar Antonio Pasquali, a newly assembled National Council of Culture convened a group of academics and state officials, as well as representatives from the Church and the armed forces, to create the Project of Radio and Television in Venezuela, known by the Spanish acronym RATELVE. This project marked the first time a Venezuelan state institution sought to democratize access to the means of media production and characterized media as a tool for social change (Delgado-Flores 2007). Echoing the language the government had used to legitimize the 1976 nationalization of oil in Venezuela, the RATELVE commission's 1976 report argued, "Broadcasting is a public service and an instrument of development that should devote itself to national needs."[2] The author's report was careful to note that although the state should oversee communications, it should not do so in a "monopolistic sense." The question of whether privately owned for-profit media could contribute to the deepening of democracy was at the forefront of debate among scholars.

While fierce deliberation was underway among Venezuelan academics, media elites, and politicians about the need for public service media, in 1980 UNESCO commissioned a study, known as the MacBride Report, entitled *One World, Many Voices*. The report's recommendations were groundbreaking in their insistence that public and local media were vital for democracy. In a departure from the established approach to communications as the right of audiences to receive a "free flow of information," the MacBride Report instead declares that people have the right to bidirectional, horizontal, and participatory communication (Capriles 1996, 32). The report notes that the notion of the free flow of information, while seemingly democratic, disregards the context of extreme inequality of capital and technology between the First and Third Worlds. In practice, as the authors of *One World, Many Voices* make plain, a defense of a "free flow" worked to secure freedom primarily for the owners of international media corporations. The report encouraged the expansion of local and public service media. In line with the RATELVE proposal, the MacBride Report argued that communication is not a commodity and should not be subject to the logics of competition and profit. Given the national debate over the RATELVE proposal in Venezuela, Caracas was selected by UNESCO representatives in 1980 as the venue to present the findings of the MacBride Report.

Proposals for a new global communications order met harsh responses, which highlighted the political power of commercial media owners and their ability to shape government decision-making. The MacBride recommendations directly conflicted with U.S. foreign policy and the American telecommunications sector, which sought to remove any barrier to the spread of American cultural products. Through the prominent organizations that represented the private press in Latin America, media owners launched a smear campaign designed to taint the MacBride Commission as a pawn of the Soviet Union and to claim that UNESCO advocated for granting governments dictatorial control over the mass media (Capriles 1996). The Inter American Press Association, an advocacy group controlled by media owners in North and South America, immediately repudiated NWICO as an attack on press freedom destined to serve "the aspirations of fascists and Marxists" (Beltrán Salmón 2008, 146). Newspapers throughout Latin America reproduced the U.S. press services' damning reports about the MacBride recommendations (Capriles 1996, 32). Latin American media owners, international press organizations, and the U.S. government mobilized the repressive logics of the Cold War in their bid to undermine proposed changes to global media relations. The successful campaign to demonize NWICO was itself proof of the uneven flow of information that the MacBride Commission sought to expose and transform.

The U.S. and UK governments not only condemned the MacBride report, but also withdrew from UNESCO, taking with them their financial support for the international organization. Their withdrawal left little possibility for implementation of any of the report's recommendations (Tomlinson 1991, 16). Similarly, under considerable pressure from business interests, the Venezuelan government withdrew its support for RATELVE.

Thus, by the early 1980s, the private owners of commercial media in Venezuela, who rallied under the liberal tenets of freedom of speech and free trade, triumphed over those who proposed to decentralize and democratize ownership and cultural production. Their struggle was a sign of things to come (Aguirre 2005). With the growing global hegemony of neoliberal capitalism, calls for a new world communication order were relegated to the "attic of old utopias" (Roncagliolo 1991, 22). In the wake of the 1970s failure to implement RATELVE or the MacBride Report, Venezuelan state institutions retreated from challenging the corporate media monopoly of television. It would be three decades before the Venezuelan government would once again back aspirations for a new world communications order. Under the Chávez government, community media producers brushed the dust off of the 1970s proposals to advance arguments for a fair, participatory, and horizontal form of communication.

Oil Busts and Neoliberal Shocks

The late 1980s saw increased conflict between the Venezuelan media and the government (Rangel 2007, 143). When oil prices collapsed in the mid-1980s, everyday life for the majority of Venezuelans turned upside down. Caracas grew more unequal and divided; middle- and upper-class neighborhoods installed fences and bars and created new gated communities (Lander 2007, 22). The economic crisis violently ruptured a myth of class and racial harmony.

In the midst of the economic collapse in the early 1980s and the gradual loss of legitimacy of state institutions, the government of Jaime Lusinchi (1984–89) fiercely battled the private media. President Lusinchi attempted to contain escalating accusations of corruption by controlling the media owners' access to dollars through the state's exchange rate agency. Without easy access to dollars, media owners struggled to purchase paper, ink, and electronics from abroad. Opposition columns disappeared from newspapers (López Maya 2005a, 47).[3] Lusinchi suspended several prominent television opinion programs. However, even as Lusinchi proved intolerant of journalists who challenged his government, many media owners remained quiet both about government corruption and about the government's attacks on efforts to expose it. These outlets continued to do well financially, and some even maintained cozy relations with the president (Rangel 2007, 143). In 1988, his last year in office, Lusinchi began abundantly distributing new media concessions to politicians and businessmen friendly to his government (Mayobre 2002, 178).

Although Lusinchi's successor, Carlos Andrés Pérez (1989–93), was elected on an anti-neoliberal platform for his second turn in office, he imposed structural adjustment reforms with the firm backing of the owners of commercial media. RCTV's President Marcel Granier and the editorial board of the nation's most prestigious newspaper, *El Nacional*, championed a neoliberal approach of economic liberty and privatization of public goods (Ellner 2008, 84). The dominant discourse in the mass media delegitimized state distributive policies, portraying the state as corrupt and paternalistic. Gustavo Cisneros, a longtime close associate of President Pérez and prominent media owner, had much to gain from the increasing deregulation of the economy. With the decreased regulatory barriers, Venezuelan media giants further expanded their transnational reach; they developed extensive holdings in media companies throughout Latin America, as well as in the United States, and expanded investments in satellite technology. The business sector shifted its focus from appropriating oil rents through the state to privatization and control of the market (Coronil 1997, 382).

The anti-neoliberal urban uprisings that broke out in 1989 in response to structural adjustment and the intense violence that characterized the government's response made clear that a deep class and racial divide lay beneath a relatively calm façade of liberal democracy. Neoliberal reforms sharpened class distinctions in access to health care and education. Alongside mounting anger at unkept promises of redistribution, bus fare hikes brought people out into the streets for six days of uprisings known as the Caracazo. The poor burned property and looted stores. The government responded with unprecedented brutality against poor neighborhoods. The military murdered hundreds, perhaps thousands, of poor people.[4]

Out of this turmoil, in 1992, a little-known mid-level military officer, Hugo Chávez, led an unsuccessful coup attempt. Chávez built on ten years of clandestine organizing in the military. During Chávez's coup attempt, constitutional guarantees were suspended, including freedom of expression. The government carefully controlled coverage of the coup and temporarily shut down several newspapers that challenged the government's official narrative about the political turmoil (Botía 2007). The mass media largely sided with the government and defended the declining two-party system, and the major business organization representing radio and television did not complain, thus signaling its collusion with President Pérez's efforts to stabilize the government's hold on the political order (Rangel 2007). Nevertheless, the political turbulence exposed divisions among the elites. The Pérez government began to lose control over the dominant narrative explaining the rising rates of poverty and the spread of corruption. The government's embrace of the neoliberal agenda left it vulnerable to attacks from business owners who used evidence of corruption to push for privatization and limited government oversight.

During the second administration of Rafael Caldera (1994–99), the government continued to follow the emergent neoliberal orthodoxy. Changes were nowhere more visible, perhaps, than in the Venezuelan media world. Caldera's government relaxed the state's telecommunications laws, permitting U.S. cable and satellite television companies to partner with Venezuelan businesses. The Cisneros Group, owner of the prominent television station Venevisión entered a partnership with DirecTV.[5] This expanded access to international commercial television was accompanied by Caldera's 1998 move to privatize one of the two state television stations, La Televisora Nacional (channel 5), selling it to a group led by the archbishop of Caracas. Private control of television became almost total.

Over the 1990s, the commercial media eagerly filled the vacuum left by the increased loss of prestige of political parties. Print and broadcast journalists increasingly turned attention to printing and granting airtime to denuncias, complaints that accused public figures of corruption. The message was clear: state institutions and public ownership did not work and could neither protect nor adequately serve the population. The commercial media fanned the flames of the widespread dissatisfaction with the exclusive practices of the limited democratic order, creating openings for new political actors (Botía 2007; Samet 2012). Under neoliberal reform, owners of the commercial media expanded their profits and reinforced their political influence.

In what seems astonishing in hindsight, Hugo Chávez was able to amass considerable support from the commercial media when he ran for president in 1998. Amid "intra-elite conflict over access to the state," a sector of business elites calculated that they had a better chance of influencing state institutions and oil profits under Chávez than under his leading opponent (Gates 2010, 109). Their gamble proved incorrect.

Between 1958 and 1998, Venezuelan political leaders vied with owners of commercial media for influence. My aim has been to explore the evidence that the official arenas of state, economics, and media have been far from distinct autonomous fields, but instead have been deeply intertwined. In the next half of the chapter, I explore the rise of community media projects and the efforts of grassroots actors to reshape Venezuela's media world and the nation's broader political future. I lay the groundwork for an understanding of how and why state-aligned media activists engaged in a simultaneous and at times contradictory effort to challenge the central tenets of liberal views of press freedom and journalistic autonomy while also using liberal norms about the necessary division between social fields to define and defend their project.

Community Video in Latin America

In the 1980s and 1990s, social activists and leftist intellectuals across Latin America turned to grassroots video as a tool for social mobilization, self-determination, and resistance (Aufderheide 1993; Carelli 1988; Goldfarb 2000; Himpele 2007; Riaño 1994).[6] Early projects included Cine Mujer, a feminist organization in Colombia (Aufderheide 1993); Video nas Aldeias, a project that trained indigenous groups in Brazil to make video (Turner 1990); and La Escuela Popular y Latinoamericana de Cine, Televisión y Teatro, an effort to train peasants in rural Venezuela to make media (Deronne 2012). Many projects were "closed-circuit" rather than being broadcast over the airwaves; video productions were projected or played on televisions with a VCR for community associations, groups of workers, social movement organizations, churches, or cultural centers (Aufderheide 2000; Ranucci 1990).

While the immediate political context facing Catia TVe differed from that of their counterparts in post-dictatorship Latin America, the station's founders shared much with other emerging community, alternative, and grassroots video makers throughout the region. UNESCO's call in the 1970s for greater balance in global communications and its declaration of horizontal and participatory communication as a basic human right established an important framework for grassroots media producers to advance their projects. Experiments in community video throughout the region also drew heavily on the politicized New Latin American Film movement, which upheld film as a necessary component of social struggles of the colonized and oppressed people of the Third World (Aufderheide 2000). Central to the New Latin American Film movement were the ideas of a "Third Cinema," which aimed to mobilize audiences to take action to change the world, and an "imperfect cinema," which eschewed technical mastery and sought to engage the working class in every aspect of production in an effort to upend the class relations that ordered traditional film and society (Burton 1986; Espinosa 1979). Catia TVe's founders, like their community video counterparts elsewhere in the region, were convinced that without direct control of images and narratives about their own lives and struggles, broader efforts to challenge inequality and upend the social order were impossible.

Although there were early calls for government subsidies for grassroots video, most grassroots video projects solidified into nonprofit, nongovernmental organizations that depended on limited funds from unions and universities (Straubhaar 1989). Additional funding for infrastructure and equipment came from international foundations such as the American Ford Foundation, the MacArthur Foundation, the Inter-American Foundation, the Italian Centro Internazionale Crocevia, the World Council of Churches, and UNESCO (Aufderheide 1993; LaSpada 1992). These foundations saw funding for popular video projects as an aspect of their work of encouraging democracy and development (LaSpada 1992). The Mexican government's indigenous video program, launched in 1990, represents a rare effort on behalf of a government not only to fund but also to initiate video projects in marginalized communities (Wortham 2013).

Throughout much of the region, particularly in places marked by a history of violent dictatorship, video organizations prioritized independence from state entities. Venezuela's grassroots social movements and community media initiatives, including Catia TVe, have had a different trajectory. Shut out and violently repressed not by dictatorship but by liberal democracy, many on the left viewed liberal democracy as a mask for ruling-class hegemony (Levine 1973). This perspective encouraged social movement actors to search for alternatives and to combine formal and informal liberal and illiberal political practices, as well as relations of interdependency with official institutions and actors (Velasco 2015). Thus, Catia TVe's founders pursued funding from specific allies—elected officials and appointed functionaries in state institutions—while also engaging in informal and sometimes unlawful practices. Catia TVe sought to create not pure autonomy, but a form of radical interdependency with a diverse collection of allies.

Catia TVe: "Either We Invent or We Fail"

"We were just a group of crazy dreamers," Carlos always joked when he recounted Catia TVe's origins. Carlos and many of Catia TVe's founders enjoyed riffing on the name of their neighborhood, Manicomio—"insane asylum" in Spanish—to express how far-fetched their vision of a community television station seemed to their neighbors in the early 1990s. Their barrio's official idiosyncratic name, Las Barracas Simón Rodríguez del Manicomio or the Simón Rodríguez Barracks of the Insane Asylum, points to the improvised origins that characterize most poor neighborhoods in Venezuela's capital. Beginning in the early twentieth century, as the nation's burgeoning oil economy displaced agricultural production, Venezuelan peasants searched for new opportunities in the cities. Like many other rural migrants who settled in Caracas between 1940 and 1960, the first families of Las Barracas Simón Rodríguez del Manicomio left their rural homes in search of employment. The parents of Catia TVe's founders built their own houses and neighborhood on vacant government-owned land. In the late fifties, the Jiménez government evicted them in order to build a psychiatric hospital, referred to by locals as an insane asylum. The government relocated the families into unused army barracks adjacent to the hospital and pledged to build them housing.

Displaced in the name of progress and modernization, the families found that the promised apartment buildings never materialized.[7] Instead, over several decades, the inhabitants slowly converted the barracks into cement block homes. The growing neighborhood, now known as Manicomio, adopted the additional name of Simón Bolívar's most famous teacher and mentor, Simón Rodríguez, who introduced the young Bolívar to Enlightenment thinkers and liberal values. Rodríguez's phrase "O inventamos o erramos" ("either we invent or we fail") became a rallying cry for many in the barrio.

Wracked by violence and drug trafficking in the 1970s and 1980s, Manicomio had come to be known as "little Hong Kong," a reference to the spectacular violence portrayed in Hong Kong action films that were broadcast on Venezuelan commercial television.[8] In the wake of the 1989 popular uprising against neoliberal policies, the founding members of Catia TVe took over a building in Manicomio that had been looted and abandoned during the uprising. They wanted a practice space for their newly formed band, which played a genre of Venezuelan folk music known as *gaita*. In part to fend off local drug users who also made claims on the space, the young founders of Catia TVe, Luis, Carlos, and their friends cleaned and repaired the building and named it La Casa de Cultura Simón Rodríguez (Simón Rodríguez Cultural Center). They held band practice and began offering music lessons to other kids in the neighborhood. Like their comrades in nearby sectors of a famously militant neighborhood, known as the 23rd of January, these young men attempted to expunge the drug trade from their neighborhood by encouraging community ties and local pride, while also engaging in direct "para-police" action against criminals (Velasco 2015, 181).

Luis served as the wise elder of the group. In his mid-twenties at the time, he encouraged his fellow Cultural Center founders to reject alignment with the two dominant political parties, AD and COPEI, which competed for control over neighborhood political organizations. Luis was known around the neighborhood as a communist and a troublemaker. He explained that followers of liberation theology active in the local church and leftist groups in his high school first exposed him to radical politics. "I had resentment," Carlos, Catia TVe's future leader, explained when he recounted the influence of Luis on his childhood. "I'd ask, 'Why was my house made out of sheets of metal and the ones below us [down the mountainside in wealthier areas] were from cement blocks and had two floors?' I saw these differences. But Luis helped me turn this resentment towards the system. I wanted to know why and where this all came from. I began to see that the system was corrupt. We had a *democracia falsa*."

Carlos, Luis, and their friends from Manicomio experimented with different ways to draw young people away from the local drug trade and to encourage local activism, including folk music, street theater, and puppetry. Rather than reject state structures out of disgust with the betrayals of "false democracy," these young barrio activists selectively collaborated with a cadre of middle-class allies who were active in leftist political parties and employed by an array of state institutions in order to expand the activities of their cultural center. Carlos and Luis joined forces with militant leftist students at the Central University of Venezuela, some of whom were active in the Marxist–Leninist political party Bandera Roja (Red Flag), formed from the remnants of the unsuccessful guerrilla struggle of the 1960s. With the encouragement of their university and leftist allies, in 1991 the founders of Manicomio's Cultural Center sought support from the state-funded Venezuelan Federation of Centers of Cinematographic Culture (FEVEC), a group that had embraced the analysis of class oppression promoted by the New Latin American Film Movement. During the 1970s, 1980s, and 1990s, numerous leftist parties and organizations launched initiatives like FEVEC to support urban popular culture as a means to develop resistance against both the national ruling class and American cultural imperialism (Guss 2001, 98–99). FEVEC subsidized the purchase of a sixteen-millimeter film projector and, together with the National Commission of Culture, lent the group sixteen-millimeter films, making possible the launch of the Cineclub Manicomio (Manicomio Film Club).

Luis and Carlos explained to me how their early efforts at local political activism in Manicomio made clear to them that challenging the hegemony of the commercial media was absolutely foundational to any effort to enact political change. Luis noted that he and his comrades found that their attempts to counter crime in Manicomio were unsuccessful in part because young people were captivated, as Luis put it, by the images of capitalist consumption; young men in Manicomio, in particular, saw the drug trade as their only avenue to obtain the commodities and respect they saw on television. In order to organize for political change, Catia TVe's founders looked for a way to build on their neighbors' interest in mass media. While access to television was widespread, few in Manicomio had ever been to the movies. When Luis and Carlos set up a makeshift movie theater in Manicomio, turnout was good. With support from FEVEC, they screened films coming out of the New Latin American Film movement, which countered the mass media's erasure of poverty and its healing narratives of class harmony between elites and the poor. Such films, including Fernando Birri's *Tire dié* (*Throw Me a Dime*, Argentina, 1960) and Román Chalbaud's *Cain adolescente* (*Adolescence of Cain*, Venezuela, 1959) were marked by a concern with experiences of poverty and dispossession.

On the heels of Chávez's 1992 failed coup attempt, a leftist mayor named Aristóbulo Istúriz came to power in Caracas. Istúriz's administration granted the Manicomio Film Club the funds to purchase a VHS video projector. They shifted from screening sixteen-millimeter films to showing Hollywood films. Despite their criticism of mainstream commercial media, activists were strategic and flexible in their efforts to draw their neighbors out of their homes and get them talking to each other. Members of the Manicomio Film Club found they could easily purchase inexpensive pirated copies of *Titanic*, *Lethal Weapon*, and Walt Disney movies. They struggled to balance their desire to attract large audiences with their efforts to encourage viewers to reflect on the conditions of their lives. They attempted to draw their neighbors into discussions about the political messages of Hollywood films (Eekhout and Fuentes 2001).

Forming Interdependencies

Catia TVe's history and practice during the time of my fieldwork made evident how many social movement actors and certain representatives of Chávez-led state institutions had deep histories; they were connected by friendships, by kinship, and by political commitments, some of which crossed class lines.

These ordinary, and in some cases unusual, social ties and the interpenetration of grassroots activism and institutions would prove vitally important in advancing their community media initiative. In addition to cultivating allies in government positions, Catia TVe's founders began to form what would turn out to be a lasting and crucial friendship with a middle-class film student in her early twenties named Blanca Eekhout. Blanca would later become a prominent leader of a new state television station called ViVe TV, the minister of communication, and an elected member of the National Assembly. Originally from the small city of Acarigua in the central western Venezuelan state of Portuguesa, Blanca moved to Caracas to attend the Central University of Caracas. She became active in the leftist political group Bandera Roja and started to devote her time to community organizing. Blanca met the founders of the Manicomio Film Club in 1992. A short time later, she moved to their barrio, where she combined her research and activism. During the nearly ten years she lived in Manicomio, Blanca collected data for an undergraduate thesis about film clubs, which she eventually coauthored with another student, Gabriela Fuentes. Their principal case study was the Manicomio Film Club.

This relationship between Blanca Eekhout and the organizers in Manicomio proved crucial for the development of Catia TVe. As Carlos explained, "We had the practical things down, but Blanca understood the theory.... She kidnapped the knowledge from the academy and brought it to the barrio. This allowed us to begin to experiment." Blanca helped Manicomio Film Club organizers place their project within the broader context of Latin American media politics. She worked with them to craft proposals for funding that framed their project in politically and theoretically persuasive ways.

Although radio production and transmission was more affordable and required far less technical expertise, the tradition of social documentary film proved to be the inspiration for activists in Manicomio, encouraging them to turn to audio-visual production, and later television.[9] In the mid-1990s, Blanca helped them secure funds from a commission within the mayor's office to buy their own video camera. Carlos, Luis, and friends began to document life in their barrio. They recorded daily life, musical performances, Catholic festivals, and interviews with older people about the history of the barrio.

On the day of a much-anticipated baseball game between the rival Leones team of Caracas and the Magallanes from the city of Valencia, film club members organized a public screening of the game in the local basketball court. "We took advantage of our national obsession with baseball," Luis told me with a wink. During the commercial breaks between innings they surprised their neighbors by showing clips of their own footage of the barrio. Women, men, and children from the neighborhood crowded the cement bleachers, eager to see images of themselves projected on the white sheet that dangled from the rafters. After a few innings, people lost interest in the baseball game and demanded that film club members rewind and replay their own footage of the barrio. Most had never seen positive portrayals of poor neighborhoods on screen, let alone images of their own community. After hours of raucous cheers, laughter, and hearty applause, the founders of the film club knew they had discovered a powerful way to engage their neighbors.

It was through Catia TVe's founders' early experiences in recording and screening images of their neighbors and their collaboration with Blanca and other allies engaged in leftist critical studies of media that Carlos, Luis, and their friends developed a belief that media production by and for the poor was not ancillary but rather integral to progressive social change. This analysis, together with the intense enthusiasm their neighbors in Manicomio expressed for the opportunity to see and represent themselves in film, solidified Carlos, Luis, and Blanca's commitment to launching a local television station. They learned that a handful of community television producers around the country had been broadcasting clandestinely and sporadically on UHF signals since the 1980s.[10] At a conference on grassroots media, Carlos and Blanca met an engineer from Táchira state who had launched an illegal community television station in 1995. In a series of long conversations about the technological logistics of broadcasting and visits to the pirate Táchira station, Carlos and Blanca assembled concrete plans for a small television station in Manicomio.

Growing Pains

From the outset, the barrio-based founders of Catia TVe were not primarily focused on establishing self-reliance or autonomy from allies who worked in universities and official state agencies. Instead, they directed their energies toward assembling available resources and knowledge and cultivating various forms of support. Catia TVe's founders managed to avoid some of the pitfalls that plagued grassroots media production groups elsewhere in Latin America. Projects launched by middle-class allies in other contexts had little connection to the communities they ostensibly sought to empower (LaSpada 1992; Tomaselli and Prinsloo 1990). While some projects put video production in the hands of poor communities, enabling them to make their own media, others relied on intermediary NGOs that produced and screened videos for grassroots audiences, often assuming paternalist attitudes.

In contrast, Catia TVe founders worked closely with middle-class allies, who, like Blanca, proved critical in sharing their formal knowledge without undermining barrio-based leadership or participation. These connections between middle-class and barrio-based activists, while not always straight-forward or easy, relied on a basis of mutual respect. What proved crucial for Catia TVe's barrio-based founders and for other fledgling media projects in asserting their leadership was that local activists, who were already working to establish themselves as leaders in their community, approached media making as a process of political organizing, rather than as a means to an end.

As in many contexts, access to video production equipment accentuated the internal power hierarchies in the barrio (see Turner 1991). Blanca's reflections on her experience with Manicomio Film Club provide clues to some of the power relations and unstated rules that ordered the group. Blanca and her colleague Gabriella Fuentes noted, "In order to form part of the [Film] Club it is necessary to be approved through a series of 'tacit tests' of which nobody speaks, since their use is not necessary to mention between them. The right to participate is guaranteed by consistent attendance. In order to work [in the film club] and attend [meetings] it is necessary, above all, to be sufficiently cautious for a period of time, to not have a contradictory spirit, and to respect the line and strategy of the work of the collective" (Eekhout and Fuentes 2001, 255–56).

Given the unequal burden of family responsibilities in the barrio, the "tacit tests" of consistency would have been difficult for women to pass. Indeed, it is perhaps precisely these unspoken tests that explain why the Manicomio Film Club initially included few women from the barrio. The group struggled with ways to handle internal disagreement, rejecting those with a "contradictory spirit" who might have challenged their perspectives or ways of doing things. Carlos, who was charismatic, energetic, and confident, often monopolized decision-making.

However, as they converted their dream of a television station into a reality, participation expanded to include increasing numbers of barrio-based women activists, some of whom became central participants at the station. The film club founders met other activists, most notably Ana and Margarita, sisters from a nearby barrio. Blanca and Carlos invited the two women to join a discussion about the media. Ana recalled, "Commercial television spread information about our community when someone killed someone, and of course pornography, sexuality, violence. But it never spread information that our community was organizing itself, that it was transforming itself to change things. No one was seeing that. So we started analyzing and thinking. All the things we had accomplished and no one knew about them."

Like many others, Ana and Margarita were initially drawn into community organizing to try to meet the needs of their neighbors, friends, and family. At the time that they met Carlos and Blanca, they were organizing with neighboring communities to demand that the government build a hospital to serve their region. Ana explained that she began to understand how "television could be a tool to generate participation." Like her collaborators from Manicomio, she was hooked. As I recount in chapter 5, these women faced barriers in gaining the respect necessary to exercise leadership on- and off-screen. In ways that resemble the experiences of other grassroots media projects, Catia TVe has struggled with internal inequalities of resource allocation, intergenerational tensions, gender oppression, competition, and contradictory local and international expectations.[11]

A Greeting for Catia: Making Constitutional Reforms a Reality

When Chávez was elected president in 1998, film club members grew hopeful that they would be able to pressure the new government to expand opportunities for popular participation in media production. Ana explained, "Chávez was different. One identified with him. He was flesh and blood like us." Her sister, Margarita reflected:

> The [past] governments had nothing to do with me. Politicians would come to the neighborhoods, giving out things; maybe they would fix up a plaza before an election. They would say there was no money and they put the country in major debt. They said there was no petroleum and they went to the United States to ask for loans. But no, Chávez, he says, "Look, you need to study, you need to work hard, you need to develop yourselves, organize yourselves." This is totally different. The other presidents when they spoke they would just read from a page, probably something that they didn't even write themselves. No, Chávez talks to the people.

In Chávez, Ana and Margarita saw a community organizer who, they believed, had a genuine desire for poor people to become their own leaders, not subservient clients reliant on handouts. His ability to communicate in a seemingly direct manner with poor people, often via radio and television, helped widen his base of support.

The Chávez government quickly launched major changes, including the convocation of a constitutional assembly. The new 1999 constitution, approved by 71 percent of voters, proved one of the most progressive in the world. The 1999 constitution reaffirmed state ownership over petroleum as well as workers' rights and benefits. Unlike the 1961 constitution, in which popular sovereignty was limited to the exercise of voting, the new constitution emphasized the importance of what its authors referred to as "participatory and protagonistic democracy." The constitution establishes possibilities for active democratic practice in the form of referendums, constitutional and constituent assemblies, and open municipal councils. Over time, it became clear that many of the 1999 constitution's most progressive provisions, including those around gender equality and women's rights, remained difficult to fulfill because of contradictions with other new and existing laws, cost, or "lack of political will" (Rakowski and Espina 2011, 163).

In the arena of media, the new constitution expressed commitments to free expression and press freedom. For the first time, the rights of citizens to produce their own media were expanded. The constitution's provision that Venezuelans have a right to "timely, truthful, impartial, and uncensored information" raised concerns for some journalists, free press advocacy organizations, and media owners. Media owners had successfully rebuffed previous efforts by the Caldera government in the 1990s to include similar language in a revised media law. The Miami-based Inter-American Press Association and the Paris-based Reporters without Borders warned that the Chávez government could use this guarantee as a pretext to silence reporting and political analysis that it considered unsubstantiated. As was not the case in the past, however, media owners now had far less immediate access to government officials: only one member of the National Constitutional Assembly had direct ties to the media through a regional radio station he owned (Fox and Waisbord 2002, xxi). The Chávez government and the new constitution held enormous legitimacy and popular support.

Community media activists had to push new and old state institutions to fulfill the constitutional commitments to widened access to media production. Although the 1999 constitution included communication as a basic right and the 2000 Telecommunications Law granted community media stations the right to exist, community media producers needed a regulatory law that would fully legalize their practice. The National Commission of Telecommunications originally rebuffed Catia TVe's requests in the early 2000s to discuss their plans for a community television station. Catia TVe's founders pursued what would become a widespread strategy among activists and ordinary people: they took their proposal straight to government officials and Chávez, presenting their project to the president and his ministers at every possible turn.

In early 1999, Chávez was in west Caracas, the poor side of the city known as Catia, to inaugurate a new hospital. Alongside the usual mob of professional reporters, Blanca, Carlos, and several friends jostled to get a good position. Holding a microphone wrapped in their homemade logo, Blanca called out: "¿Presidente, un saludo para Catia?" (President, your greeting to Catia?). Chávez responded, curious to know what station was reporting for the barrios. After a short conversation about their proposal to build a community television station, Chávez asked one of his ministers to attend to the *chamos* (young people). Catia TVe's founders credit themselves with introducing community media to Chávez. Rather than seeing their need for a personal connection to Chávez as a threat to a fair democratic order, Catia TVe founders understood Chávez as their agent inside a hostile institutional structure, which together they sought to transform.

Despite the dialogue they began with Chávez and his ministers, the process of legalizing community media unfolded too slowly for Catia TVe's founders. They decided not to wait for legal permission to launch their station. Using small grants from the Ministry of Health, a social fund financed by the state oil company, and the American Inter-American Development Bank, they purchased an antenna and broadcasting equipment. In 2000, from a small office space that friends allowed them to use inside the Jesús Yerena Hospital adjacent to Manicomio, Catia TVe illegally launched their signal over the open airwaves.[12] Blanca assumed the position of director of Catia TVe with Carlos as assistant director. While not technically legal, their operation was far from clandestine. Their decision to go ahead despite lacking the necessary approval, served as a provocation to push state institutions to create the regulations needed to legalize community media.

Early programming included political debates, musical performances, and community events that they filmed in nearby poor neighborhoods. In theory, the station's UHF channel 25 signal was accessible to about a million people in the sectors of Sucre, El 23 de Enero, La Pastora, El Junquito, Altagracia, San José, and San Agustín (Eekhout and Fuentes 2001, 479). In practice, however, the signal was unreliable because of weather and the uneven terrain of the Caracas valley. Nevertheless, Carlos's vision was expansive. He told a journalist in 2000: "Let's be clear: our intention is not to remain a marginal initiative, but rather to compete with the commercial stations using a strategy that none of them have ever exploited and never can. Here, 80% of the production is in the hands of people of the community" (Duque 2000). From the outset, Catia TVe's leaders insisted that barrio-based nonprofessional producers would create the bulk of their programming.

In March 2001, after the station had already been on the air for several months, Chávez came to Manicomio to officially inaugurate Catia TVe. In a crowded assembly hall, Chávez declared that Catia TVe was "democratizing communications." From this inaugural moment, Catia TVe became an important symbolic counterpoint to commercial media, providing compelling audio-visual evidence that communications were being transferred to the hands of poor people. Chávez declared that Catia TVe was essential to the revolution. "The long hard battle is just beginning," he warned. At the end of his lengthy speech, Chávez congratulated Catia TVe for being wedded neither to political nor economic interests. The president celebrated the station's autonomy. In doing so he overlooked both the symbolic importance of his own presence that afternoon, and also the complex web of social relations connecting the realms of "state," "society," and "the economy" that constituted Catia TVe. Catia TVe's interdependencies included alliances with FEVEC and grants from various state ministries, as well as Caracas's mayor.

To be sure, not all community media projects have taken Catia TVe's founders' approach. Some community media projects in Venezuela rejected close collaboration with official state institutions (Fernandes 2010b). Fears of loss of local control and negative experiences with state bureaucracy and the middle-class leaders at the helm of state institutions turned many community media producers away from engaging with state media projects. Additionally, other community media groups embraced either anarchist or traditional liberal positions in regard to the state; for Catia TVe's founders, however, assertions of total autonomy and self-determination were neither politically viable nor ideologically coherent. Their strategy to advance revolutionary social change during this particular period in Venezuelan history was to embrace the possibility that the state apparatus and resources could serve as a weapon of the poor, rather than ceding the institutions and the oil dollars to the traditional ruling groups.

Liberal Alchemists

Catia TVe's founders not only depended on official state support to develop their station, but also ultimately worked together with other nascent community media groups to participate in the formulation of regulations for community media. Working closely with officials at the National Commission of Telecommunications (CONATEL), they helped craft the Regulation of Nonprofit Open Community Public Service Television and Radio Broadcasting, which was officially decreed in January 2002. "This was something totally new for us," Luis explained to me, "using the bureaucratic tools of the state."

Catia TVe's collaboration with official institutions was not without friction. CONATEL—which is the equivalent of the Federal Communication Commission in the United States—had little understanding of community media. As Blanca Eekhout noted in 2004, "The regulatory body, CONATEL is designed to regulate the corporate media. That was a major task for the [social] movements: to force compliance with the constitution. Of course, the managers of CONATEL, with their neoliberal idea of the state, their idea of 'neutrality,' just didn't get it" (Eekhout 2004).

According to Blanca, CONATEL remained wedded to a neoliberal vision of limited state involvement and liberal commitments to superficial parity. The vision of community media producers, who sought to represent the interests of only particular poor neighborhoods, contradicted CONATEL's liberal approach of pluralism, impartiality, and market rationality (Fernandes 2011). Community media projects did not claim to serve all audiences or create economic stimulus, as the existing commercial media did. As Fernandes (2011) notes, the struggles between CONATEL and community media producers signaled the inconsistencies between different state institutions under Chávez, some of which remained committed to a neoliberal agenda while others challenged this model.

Yet, despite their rejection of liberal and neoliberal tenets of impartiality and plurality, Catia TVe's founders also drew on liberal bedrock principles of press freedom in designing the organization of their new station. This is most visible in how they organized barrio-based producers. In formalizing the proposal for Catia TVe, Blanca and Carlos decided to divide participants at the station between a salaried staff and what they called Community Teams of Independent Audio-Visual Producers (Equipos Comunitarios de Producción Audiovisual Independiente), which producers referred to by the acronym ECPAI (pronounced eck-pie-ee). After participating in workshops, these new volunteer ECPAI teams were permitted to borrow Catia TVe video cameras, to use the station's computers to edit their material, to film programs in the station's studio, to broadcast their programs over Catia TVe's airwaves, and to participate in activities and meetings at the station. The staff was responsible for carrying out the day-to-day activities of audio-visual training and fundraising, while the ECPAIs were required to produce the majority of the station's broadcast programming.

Central to the creation of these ECPAIs was the impetus to establish their "independence." Catia TVe's founders formulated the status of the ECPAI based on the belief that they needed to shield the majority of media producers at the station from pressure the staff might impose, either directly or via the state institutions that funded the station. In other words, they adhered to a liberal belief in the necessity and possibility of the autonomy of media producers from the state. Although in the original plans for Catia TVe, ECPAIs were encouraged to look to local barrio-based businesses for financial support in exchange for advertising, this approach became untenable when fledgling ECPAIs had trouble demonstrating the reach of Catia TVe's broadcast signal and the size of their audience. The volunteer "independent" ECPAIs were thus left with no source of steady funding, a condition that later caused immense internal friction.

When the growth of community media organizations compelled lawmakers at CONATEL to draft formal legislation recognizing these new projects, Catia TVe's structure—based on liberal beliefs about the necessity of media autonomy from the state—served as the model. The figure of the ECPAI was codified into law in the 2002 Regulation of Community Media, encouraging community television stations throughout the country to replicate Catia TVe's approach.[13] During the course of my research, the liberal assumptions embedded in the foundational structure of Catia TVe increasingly clashed with the gradual efforts to move toward a state socialist model. Volunteers were caught in between; they faced a still-capitalist market system while at the same time negotiating the rise of socialist values that prized volunteerism and disavowal of material interests. In the long run, the liberal logic of independence left most of Catia TVe's volunteer producers—particularly women, who shouldered more domestic labor—without the funds necessary to remain consistently active at the station.

The World's First Media Coup

When Catia TVe first went on the air, producers entered a media world dominated by private television. That few voices on mainstream commercial media supported the Bolivarian Revolution left the government and its supporters vulnerable to attack. Commercial television held a monopoly over 81 percent of the open broadcasting spectrum (Hernández Díaz 2008, 69). The satellite and cable companies made possible by the neoliberal policies of the 1990s were enormously successful. Venezuela had the highest percentage of satellite and cable consumers in Latin America; subscription television reached between 20 and 50 percent of the population (Bisbal 2005). The vast majority of cable and satellite programming was from the United States (Bisbal 2007, 653).[14]

The national commercial media companies emerged as the most organized sector of the political opposition to the Chávez government (Hellinger 2007, 166). The most prominent daily newspapers, *El Nacional* and *El Universal*, and the major commercial television networks, Venevisión, RCTV, and Globovision, regularly included in their coverage racist and classist attacks on Chávez supporters. They portrayed the poor as dangerous, entitled, and unreasonable (Duno Gottberg 2004; Ferrandiz 2004). The commercial media were a formidable group. In 2002, Gustavo Cisneros, owner of Venevisión, was ranked fifty-fifth in *Forbes* magazine's list of the wealthiest hundred people in the world. The Chávez government began to threaten the economic interests of traditional business elites by passing major legislation that challenged private control of agricultural land, hydrocarbons, and fishing. The new laws were pushed through with little public discussion (López Maya 2005b). In response, the organized middle class, alienated by what they perceived as Chávez's creeping overreach, formed an alliance with powerful leaders in media and the oil industry.

When a massive opposition demonstration against the government confronted a progovernment rally in April 2002, protesters were shot and killed. Opposition forces, which included owners of the major television stations, aligned against Chávez and launched what some observers called the "world's first media coup." Using manipulated footage of the shootings, commercial media outlets blamed Chávez and his supporters for the deaths of nineteen people. Coup leaders also shut down the only state television channel on the air. The commercial media prohibited any news of continued support for Chávez; instead, as protest raged, they played American cartoons.

Fearing political repression by coup leaders, Catia TVe members quickly disassembled and hid the station's equipment. Catia TVe members took their camcorders into the streets, where they filmed the violent attempts of the metropolitan police to quell resistance to the coup. Catia TVe and other grassroots media producers spread the news that Chávez had not resigned as the opposition claimed, and that there was active resistance in the streets. On the third and final day of the coup, when military factions still loyal to Chávez regained control, Blanca Eekhout and several of her colleagues from the university and from Catia TVe helped relaunch the state channel, Venezolana de Televisión, lending critical support to the counter-coup. Pro-Chávez supporters in the military came together with large numbers of people from Caracas's poor barrios to demand that Chávez be reinstated. Thirty-six hours after being removed from office, Chávez reassumed the presidency.

Willing to risk their lives for the Bolivarian Revolution, Catia TVe producers renewed their dedication to the unfolding project of revolutionary state formation under Chávez's leadership. The events of the failed 2002 coup attempt made clear to Catia TVe producers the precarious human-made nature of the state and the pressing need to challenge the power of the commercial media (Schiller 2009). Seizing the tools of media production became an even more urgent task. Catia TVe producers' experiences early in Chávez's presidency helped cultivate their belief that the Bolivarian revolutionary state would allow not only them, but also Venezuela's poor, to gain access and agency in the process of state formation.

The Contentious Media World of Caracas

Following the 2002 coup attempt, the eminent Venezuelan journalist Elea-zar Díaz Rangel noted, "Never before have people discussed and questioned the exercise of media professionals this much, especially those of television, or demanded rectifications" (2007, 155–56). It seemed that everywhere activists, politicians, and pundits were discussing the role of media producers in the protection of democracy. The failed coup not only stimulated a boom in community media production, but also encouraged government officials to focus greater attention on how to expand and reorganize state-run media outlets. The Chávez government and its supporters began to speak of "la guerra mediatica" (the media war) that they claimed was being waged against the revolution (Britto García 2006). Chávez openly threatened to shut down commercial outlets and insulted individual journalists aligned with the opposition.

On terrestrial broadcast (non-satellite or cable) television, state and commercial channels broadcast profoundly different portrayals of everyday reality in Venezuela, equipped with their own competing narratives about the recent tumultuous past. While the Chávez government and its supporters

FIGURE 1.2. Catia TVe's microphone with those of other media outlets, February 1, 2007. Photo by the author.

claimed that the private media had launched a war against the revolution, the opposition to Chávez proclaimed that press freedom in Venezuela was on its last legs.

These divergent representations were strikingly visible in early 2003 when the commercial media helped support the political opposition's call for a national strike, which included a shutdown of the oil sector, in an effort to oust Chávez from leadership. The strike between December 2002 and February 2003 was the longest and largest in Latin American history (Wilpert 2003); it significantly reduced the flow of Venezuelan oil, costing the country billions of dollars in lost profits. During this period, the major commercial television stations suspended much of their regular programming to broadcast continuous footage of violent protests, with damning accusations against Chávez and his government. The strike finally faltered and resulted in a golden opportunity for the Chávez government to gain control of the petroleum industry and convert it into a key instrument for the implementation of the revolutionary project (López Maya 2005a, 274).

In the midst of this intense conflict, international press freedom organizations drew worldwide attention to the uncertain safety of Venezuela's private journalists. Less attention was devoted to the aggression that Chávez-aligned media producers faced. A scathing interview with three Venezuelan academics published in *El Nacional*, a major daily newspaper, compared Catia TVe's programming to videos produced by Osama bin Laden after the attacks on the World Trade Center in the United States (Meza 2002). Prominent scholars, including the influential communications scholar Antonio Pasquali (2004), who crafted the RATELVE proposal of the 1970s, argued that the government was producing "regime community media" wedded to what he called "ideological talibanism" (a reference to the Taliban, the fundamentalist movement).

The discrimination Catia TVe producers faced was not only class- and race-inflected; it also drew on a commitment to liberal norms about the necessity of media's autonomy from the state (Schiller 2011). Because they were not fully independent, critics claimed that state-aligned media could not exercise the kind of editorial objectivity traditionally understood to bolster democracy. Catia TVe producers and other state-funded community media makers were framed as subservient clients of the state. One prominent reporter at the commercial network RCTV called Catia TVe producers "the trash boot-licking network of the regime" (*bodrio comunicacional lamebotas del regimen*).[15] Catia TVe suffered not only name calling, but also physical aggression. In 2003, Alfredo Peña, the mayor of Caracas at the time, evicted Catia TVe from its original headquarters in the local Manicomio hospital. Peña, a former journalist and one-time Chávez ally, claimed that the broadcast waves of the station's transmitter were a hazard to the hospital's patients. Later, in July 2005, at an anti-Chávez student march, a reporter at RCTV assaulted a young staff member from Catia TVe, yelling, "Stop filming me, you spy, and tell your papa Chávez to buy you a new camera."

These attacks on Catia TVe helped the station gain recognition and support. Catia TVe received renewed funding from PDVSA, the state-run oil company. With PDVSA loans, the founders of Catia TVe were able to build their dream headquarters in an abandoned state-owned building in a poor neighborhood of Caracas, equipping it with classrooms, a post-production editing suite for volunteers, offices for staff, a small auditorium for film screenings, and a studio where they film live programs. In order to pay back loans from the oil company, Catia TVe broadcast publicity segments several times a day about the efforts of the state oil company to invest in public works and social programs. After these loans were paid off, Catia TVe renewed

FIGURE 1.3. Catia TVe's headquarters with banner that reads "Defend Your Television Station. Support Catia TVe," June 2003. Photo by the author.

their publicity contract with the oil company to purchase equipment and provide minimum-wage salaries for their growing staff.

Catia TVe producers rejected claims that their political alliance with the government and financial dependence on state institutions made them subservient to the state. But challenging the terms of liberal notions of press freedom was not easy. The producers struggled to explain their relationship to state institutions in alternative terms. In response to Peña's shutdown of their station and the RCTV journalist's assault on a Catia TVe producer, Catia TVe leaders turned to liberal principles of equality and liberty, even though they had been historically excluded on the basis of these same principles. While liberal norms provided some shelter, this protection at times proved stifling, as I explore in chapter 6. Liberal norms were the conditions of possibility for their claim to the right to broadcast, and yet at the same time these norms foreclosed Catia TVe's embrace of state formation as illegitimate.

Changing the Media Terrain

By the early 2000s, the 1970s utopia of a New World Information and Communication Order (NWICO) once again gained believers. Following decades of media concentration and monopolization of broadcasting by the private sector in Latin America, the 2000s found left-leaning governments in Bolivia, Brazil, Argentina, Ecuador, Nicaragua, and Argentina, as well as in Venezuela, making significant legal changes to their respective media systems (Becerra 2014; Segura and Waisbord 2016; Waisbord 2013). Returning to nationalist, internationalist, and anti-imperialist critiques of media systems articulated in the late 1970s, Chávez, members of his government, barrio-based community media producers, middle-class scholar-activists, and visiting international activists sought to remake Venezuela's media world.[16]

The unresolved questions about the NWICO proposals, in particular the limits of government involvement in shaping media content, surged to the forefront of debates. In 2005, Chávez signed the Law of Social Responsibility in Radio and Television after two years of discussion. The law forcefully asserted the government's role in mediating between national private media corporations and their intended audiences. Expanding the provisions of existing media regulations, the law prohibits material depicting sex and violence during daytime hours and requires media outlets to broadcast a certain percentage of domestically produced programming and advertising.[17] The most controversial aspects of the law imposed fines and revoked broadcast licenses if media outlets transmitted messages that were, in the view of the government, aimed at inciting violence or disorder. It also recycled provisions, first decreed in the 1980s, that granted the government uninterrupted access to the airwaves to make "announcements of national significance."

During the same period, the Chávez government launched ambitious new state-run media outlets that greatly expanded its communication capacity. The government created a new nationally broadcast state-run television channel, numerous regional outlets, and a Latin American international satellite channel, Telesur, modeled on the Arabic news channel Al Jazeera. By 2007, of the thirteen channels that reached television sets in west Caracas via the open air electromagnetic spectrum (public airwaves), three were state-run (VTV, ViVe TV, and Avila TV), seven were private commercial stations (RCTV, Venevisión, La Tele, Televen, Globovision, Meridiano, and Puma), two were under the joint control of the Roman Catholic Church and private funders (Vale TV and TV Familia), and one was a community-run state-funded channel (Catia TVe). In other parts of Caracas, additional community-run state-funded channels were accessible on the open airwaves.

In response to these changes, the government and its supporters faced international accusations that Chávez sought to shut down freedom of expression. Remarkably, there was little attention paid to the history of presidential decrees that included some of the same requirements. Few commentators, moreover, discussed how the Chávez government's new regulations took up the banner of UNESCO proposals for a new communications order and put into practice some of the recommendations of RATELVE by emphasizing the importance of democratizing access to media production. Critics maintained that the law would be used to implement "prior censorship" or prohibition of speech in the guise of protecting children and national security. The opposition and its allies argued that the government conflated "the public" with "the state." Rather than serve pluralistic, nonpartisan ends that included the perspectives of all Venezuelans, critics declared, new state-run media would privilege only government propaganda.

Venezuela's private media owners, neoliberals, and transnational corporations and policy organizations decisively shaped this debate. In the mix of detractors of the Chávez government's media policy were also some progressives who questioned whether poor Venezuelans would have access to participate in these new outlets as producers and critics. While the lives of the poor were undoubtedly the privileged focus of much of the programming, even committed supporters of the Bolivarian Revolution feared that their complaints and problems with state-run programs would not receive sufficient attention.

Expanding Catia TVe's Vision to Remake State Television

The government's experiments in state media drew heavily on the field of community television. Blanca Eekhout assumed national prominence in 2003 when Chávez appointed her president of a new television outlet, Visión Venezuela Televisión, known by its acronym, ViVe TV, which means "Live TV." Chávez's selection of Blanca as the station's president was unusual. In place of formal journalistic training, she had over a decade of experience as a community media activist with Catia TVe. Her appointment indicated the government's intention to reject Venezuela's existing model of state television. Although Blanca invited Catia TVe producers to accompany her to ViVe, most chose to participate in ViVe TV from their base at Catia TVe. Staff from the two stations closely collaborated during the time of my fieldwork.

Blanca built ViVe TV according to a vision for media that she had honed through her research on Latin American media, militancy in a leftist political party, and barrio activism. Integral to new state-run media experiments were local and international leftist activist networks that openly embraced the Bolivarian revolutionary state as a tool and process of social transformation.

Blanca's new position at the helm of this nascent television outlet instilled Catia TVe producers with confidence that areas of official state apparatus were being "taken," through gradual peaceful means, in the interest of the poor. Notwithstanding this perspective, as they sustained and leveraged the interdependency that their close relationship with official state actors entailed, Catia TVe producers faced the enormous challenges of ongoing class inequalities, gendered barriers to leadership, and concentration of power in the figure of Chávez.

Like socialist journalists of the twentieth century, Catia TVe producers often sought to "repair" the disjuncture between the revolution's political ideals and on-the-ground realities (Roudakova 2009; Wolfe 2005). Catia TVe producers faced concerns, as did journalists in the German Democratic Republic (Boyer 2005), that critical representations of leadership or government programs would fan the flames of the "counterrevolutionary" opposition at home and abroad. Unlike socialist journalists of the twentieth century, however, Catia TVe staff exercised significant local editorial control over their content. While state officials pressured Catia TVe producers to cover events that celebrated the revolution, there was no central party control over community media. Moreover, unlike the well-educated professional cohorts that staffed media outlets in the German Democratic Republic, the Soviet Union, and contemporary Cuba, Catia TVe producers were not for the most part formally trained professionals. They did not approach journalism as a professional vocation, but rather as an organizing strategy initially honed in struggles against the neoliberal capitalist state as a way to encourage local social action.

Conclusion

Catia TVe's founders came to political consciousness in the 1970s, 1980s, and 1990s, a period when Venezuela's liberal and neoliberal capitalist democracy had proven incapable of addressing the political, material, and cultural demands of the poor majority. Rather than dismiss the state as irredeemable, however, they rejected the political and economic system—liberal capitalism—through which the Venezuelan state had been organized. For them, the barrier to meaningful freedom and equality was not the blurred boundaries between media producers and governing leaders; it was instead the motivating principles of profit behind elite alliances and private ownership. Catia TVe's founders pursued a strategy of participation in the construction of a leftist state through cross-class collaboration and struggle and the intertwining projects of popular movements and official state institutions.

Debates about whether media should be controlled by "the state," "the market," "civil society," or some combination of the three obscure how these fields are, in fact, indivisible. The debate establishes the very boundaries it purports to examine. The history of broadcasting and journalism in Venezuela makes clear that widespread claims that the Chávez government uniquely violated liberal values of press freedom and the consecrated boundaries between state and civil society were both politically opportunistic and inaccurate. Venezuela's political establishment and the private media have been deeply intertwined since television was introduced in Venezuela in the early 1950s; at times the government and media owners have been at tense odds and at other times in lockstep. Throughout much of the history of relations between state officials and media owners in Venezuela, violations of the purported borders between state and media took place in the interest of national and global capital. In contrast, Catia TVe sought to cultivate linkages and mutual interdependencies with official state institutions and agents in the interest of the poor.

TWO

COMMUNITY MEDIA AS EVERYDAY STATE FORMATION

"Seven! Can you believe that? Seven invitations, all for this Sunday!" Celia waved a stack of papers at me and collapsed into a squeaky metal chair in Catia TVe's production office. She spread the invitations on the desk in front of her and exhaled loudly. In her early forties, Celia had a youthful face with round cheeks that flushed to a deep pink when she grew animated. Celia grew up in Manicomio, the poor neighborhood where Catia TVe was founded. As the director of the production department, she coordinated the work of the four staff members who filmed and edited short news segments to broadcast over Catia TVe's airwaves. Each month, the station received about fifty requests for coverage.

Standing beside Celia, I surveyed the letters requesting Catia TVe's presence that Sunday. Three were from community organizations inviting Catia TVe to document their local elections for communal councils, a new local governance structure that Venezuela's National Assembly had approved just seven months before, in April 2006. The remaining letters included a request from a local municipal official for coverage of a six-kilometer race in his district, an invitation from an organization of students and teachers to film their discussion about how to improve a new state program in higher education, and a solicitation from the mayor's office to document a meeting on environmental conservation in Caracas. There was also a handwritten note, in Celia's own neat lettering, with details about a dance festival that the Ministry of Communication and Information wanted Catia TVe to film at a central Caracas theater.

As Catia TVe grew and gained prominence, the station received an increasing number of invitations to cover events and pleas to document prob-

FIGURE 2.1. Catia TVe staff member filming, June 21, 2008. Photo by the author.

lems. Inundated by these requests, Celia had to constantly weigh the importance of numerous invitations. Reshuffling the letters strewn across her desk, she noted, "We need to cover the communal council elections. That's definitely the priority." Celia explained that she attempted to devote Catia TVe's limited staff's attention to requests that she viewed as coming from the "community" over solicitations from elected officials, state ministries, and other official state institutions. Marking certain invitations "community" and others "state," she upheld a belief that community and the state were well-defined and separate arenas.

Looking over the stack of invitations, I wondered how and why Celia drew this line. As Celia knew well, many official initiatives—like the proposal to build local communal councils—built on already existing social movement organizations first created in marginalized sectors, including community water committees, urban land committees, and health committees. Celia's insistence on neat categories conflicted with her everyday experience of the mutual constitution of many barrio-based organizations and emerging state institutions. I had observed for months how, in her work to document events and problems in poor neighborhoods and inside official state institutions, Celia encountered the state as an inconsistent, volatile, and shifting set of practices that extended far beyond the boundaries of the official halls of power. In fact, Celia and her colleagues not only witnessed but also contributed to the disunity and diffusion of state practices that the former governing elites often kept well hidden behind what Philip Abrams (1988) calls the "state-idea," the mystifying notion that the state was an independent, coherent, and omnipotent entity. With the growing overlap between the political agendas, personnel, and ideological formation of grassroots organizations and some official state institutions during the first decade of Chávez's rule, Catia TVe producers like Celia faced dilemmas about the boundaries of the state and the relationship between autonomy from and dependency on official institutions.

This chapter examines the participation of Catia TVe producers in the symbolic, ideological, and material practices that, on the one hand, eroded boundaries between the state and society, and, on the other hand, reaffirmed the distinction between these realms. I assess why Catia TVe producers often relied on and reproduced a conceptual duality of state and community despite the messiness of their actual practice. This analysis provides insights into how poor people who are engaged in struggles for revolutionary social transformation make strategic references to divisions between state and community, even as they fight to obtain access to forms of state power and make it their own.

As she reviewed the request from the Ministry of Communication and Information (MINCI) to cover a dance festival of barrio-based organizations, Celia's effort to demarcate state from community allowed her to resist what she felt was an unfair imposition from state officials. Celia complained of MINCI, "Just because they have a contract with us, they expect to get us to cover everything they want." In exchange for funding, Catia TVe broadcast informational segments produced by MINCI that celebrated government initiatives. The contract did not obligate Catia TVe producers to cover events to which MINCI invited them. Nevertheless, there was clearly an unspoken expectation that Catia TVe would show up when an official at MINCI requested their presence. Celia resented this relationship as one of obligation. In this moment, Celia positioned herself outside the state, asserting a desire to refuse its demands. She grudgingly assigned a staff member to film the MINCI-sponsored event.

To all appearances, Celia's capitulation to MINCI's invitation was an example of a state institution's "top-down" management of a popular movement, secured through the obligatory bonds of financial dependence. The very categories of state and community that Celia reproduced and affirmed certainly sustain such an analysis. I suggest in this chapter that Catia TVe producers' interactions with the Bolivarian state were far more fluid and uncertain than such an easy reading permits. For one, as the history I laid out in the previous chapter makes plain, Catia TVe has never been strictly independent, but has always relied on strategic alliances and funding from official institutions. To understand their seemingly incongruous efforts to be both dependent *and* autonomous, to embrace statecraft as a collective process and position themselves "outside" state institutions, we need to approach the state as many of Catia TVe producers have, in their practice if not always in their explicit analysis. That is, we need to consider the state as an unfolding process rather than a fixed entity with clear boundaries. Celia's depiction of the political order—her neat piles of invitations—was a tactic, honed over multiple and varied interactions, to guard their hard-won gains while continuing to participate in the uncertain project of revolutionary state formation.

Catia TVe producers' alignment with the Chávez government and their dependence on social and economic relations with state officials produced vulnerability. Coming mostly from poor neighborhoods, most Catia TVe producers had long been subject to precarity. But embracing an official state building project and the unpredictable process of change involved new risks, including the co-optation of their activism in the interest of a new rising power elite. At stake for Catia TVe producers and their allies was whether popular involvement in everyday statecraft would serve as window dressing to legitimize only limited gains in equality and social justice, or if such involvement would create the opportunity for the poor to radically reorder relations of power. As I argued in the introduction, grappling with Catia TVe's project requires understanding whether and how statecraft can be a weapon of the weak.

These debates about the meaning and boundaries of the state have intensified since the period of my fieldwork, as some social movement groups have worked to build what they call a "communal state" in the midst of an intensifying economic crisis (Ciccariello-Maher 2016). To understand more recent battles than those I document here, it is vital to understand this earlier phase of deliberation and rapidly shifting conditions and institutions. This phase in the Bolivarian Revolution highlights how debates over the relationships between popular movements and state institutions in times of revolutionary upsurge engaged competing liberal and socialist ideas of community, state, and autonomy.

Juggling Multiple States

Many of Catia TVe's producers grew up believing that the Venezuelan state was a distant and self-contained entity that ideally was responsible for using oil resources to benefit the population. They largely experienced state institutions, however, as the impenetrable enemy of "the people," inflicting untold violence on poor neighborhoods, squashing dissent, and diverting community organizing into the pacifying channels of political clientelism. To maintain their hegemony and resist radical movements for change, Venezuelan elites historically relied on the myth of the state as a magical standalone monolith (Coronil 1997). The authority of people in positions of official state power in Venezuela, as in many contexts, has derived not only from their control (be it partial or seemingly total) over violence and resources, but also from the idea that "the state" was a uniform, static, otherworldly thing set apart from "regular" people (Abrams 1988; Mitchell 1991).

The Chávez government and the Bolivarian Revolution explicitly sought to challenge this dynamic. State officials and allied community organizers encouraged the poor majority to see itself as capable of solving individual and collective problems alongside state institutions. Unlike the widely accepted self-understanding of liberal democracy, where community or society is supposed to be an autonomous force that monitors and influences the centralized governing practices of the state, the Chávez government, in line with historic projects of state socialism, openly celebrated the involvement of the government in sectors of "civil society" as well as the population's inclusion in processes that Foucault identifies as "governmentality" (1991). The Chávez government called upon the population to regulate their own conduct alongside allied state institutions through programs in health care, food distribution, schooling, and media production. These programs greatly improved the quality of life for most producers at Catia TVe and granted many of them new access to and recognition from officials in state institutions.

In the midst of their daily collaboration in the process of state formation, Catia TVe producers struggled with the globally dominant belief—enforced by liberal capitalist states—that their freedom as media producers required autonomy from the state and that their dependence signaled state domination and constraint. In contrast, in historic projects of socialism, such as Soviet socialism, proponents conceived of true autonomy as possible only through dependence, only by ceding control to central party actors who could synthesize diffuse understandings into an analysis of common interest (Yurchak 2006). Catia TVe producers diverged from both normative liberal and socialist perspectives. They juggled multiple competing and contradictory definitions of the state in their pursuit of radical interdependency.

Scholars have made strides in analyzing how social movement actors in Venezuela attempted to craft a "contingent autonomy, neither fully independent from nor fully beholden to the state" (Velasco 2011, 181; see also Ciccariello-Maher 2007; Fernandes 2010b). I extend and deepen this analysis by wrestling with what the state meant to Catia TVe producers in 2006 and 2007. How was being "beholden to the state" experienced in the multiple contexts in which Catia TVe producers lived and worked? Crucially, in contrast with the doxa of much contemporary social science, I do not assume that being obligated to the state in this context and historical conjunction was undesirable, that dependence means subservience, or even that subservience is the opposite of freedom. We require an empirical understanding of the specifics of place and time. In particular, we must understand the terrain and the dilemmas that Catia TVe producers faced in reckoning with liberal and socialist discourses of autonomy and dependence.

Hector, a Catia TVe assistant director in his late twenties, forcefully articulated the need to reject traditional categories of analysis of autonomy and dependency in order to understand Catia TVe's relationship with the state. From a middle-class family with left-leaning politics, Hector first met the founders of Catia TVe in 2002 when he was studying engineering at the prestigious Central University of Venezuela. Hector was a committed socialist, well versed in the history of socialist experiments worldwide. After producing several programs for Catia TVe about the student movement he had led against neoliberal initiatives at his university, he decided to drop out of school to devote his energies full-time to the television station.

One afternoon, I asked Hector how he assessed the importance of the autonomy of community media from the state. He noted,

> One understands that in other countries, or even here before the revolutionary process, to be dependent on the state was bad, to be connected to the state was bad. Now at Catia TVe we talk about *taking* the state. More than that, we are in the process of taking power and destroying the state to construct a popular one. To be independent of a state that is a revolutionary state is a right-wing position; it's a reactionary position, no? . . . The project of the revolution will last for many years and our position is to destroy this state and construct a popular state of participation. And we can't do this if we distance ourselves from the state. Instead, we have to enter and take the spaces that the revolution is opening inside the state.

Hector was adamant that independence from the state was impossible when they were revolutionizing the state from within. He didn't see the state as the central agent of power, and he didn't discard the state as an irredeemable instrument of the ruling class. Instead, Hector identified various institutional "spaces" inside an existing structure that could be transformed in the interest of the "popular" or poor people. For Hector, in other words, the state was not a monolith; it was permeable and processual. He refused the detachment from collective political commitments that classical liberal conceptions of autonomy insist is necessary for the exercise of freedom. To remain detached in the particular context in which Catia TVe producers found themselves, Hector insisted, would serve to maintain the status quo.

Hector acknowledged the difficulty faced by many observers of and even participants in the Bolivarian process in understanding his perspective. He explained, "A lot of people get confused because they have a manual in their head that does not allow another vision. We [at Catia TVe] also suffer from this confusion because we encounter problems in the revolution that aren't the same as other revolutions that have taken place." The manual—the conceptual tool kit that helps scholars and activists understand and act on the world—is shaped by globally dominant expectations that freedom requires individual and collective autonomy, particularly from formal state institutions. In place of a static understanding of states, Hector advocated for a strategy attuned to the possibilities of the specific projects and relationships they negotiated.

Hector's understanding of the state as made up of conflicting spaces came to the fore a few weeks after this initial conversation about autonomy. At a gathering at the station of community media producers and representatives from the Ministry of Communication and Information, Hector emphasized that while Catia TVe producers needed to embrace statecraft, they should be wary of official actors within state institutions who sought to undermine the revolutionary project. He warned that Catia TVe's reliance on state funding in the form of publicity contracts posed a risk, noting: "If we have a denuncia [a complaint] and we take a political position against some functionary, they could block us saying, 'Cut their publicity.' And we could say, well, we'll continue functioning or we can continue with the denuncia. How can we make a participatory budget [where viewers fund the station] that guarantees our independence, independence as a media outlet, independence from the bourgeois state, from the old state?" Here, Hector warned that Catia TVe's editorial independence was undercut by "functionaries" or state officials who propped up the "old" "bourgeois" state and were not genuinely committed to remaking the state in the interest of the poor through popular participation and leadership. Hector insisted that the revolutionary state was a project in motion that would unfold over many years. "We have a state that is incoherent in the sense that many institutions that defend imperial interests remain," he declared. "Institutions that defend the interests of the pueblo are just being born."

For Hector, there was no clear once-and-for-all strategy to negotiate the relationship between community media producers and state institutions, given the inconsistent and rapidly changing political conditions. This was a sentiment that I heard repeatedly. Hector's colleagues at Catia TVe rejected the idea that they needed to cede independence to centralized party control, as had previous proponents of state socialism in Germany and the Soviet Union. Yet, crucially, Catia TVe producers embraced the notion that close accompaniment, support, and interdependence of radical forces in the places of "constituted power" (state institutions) were necessary to create any kind of meaningful creative nonbourgeois autonomy.

Carlos, Catia TVe's thirty-four-year-old founder and director, avidly embraced the state as a collective work in progress. He was the primary decision maker and most prominent public voice of the station. A skilled speaker and community organizer, Carlos was granted respect and deference, even as many volunteers at the station were critical of his hierarchical leadership style. Carlos's close friendship with Blanca Eekhout, Catia TVe's former director and then president of the state channel, ViVe TV, granted him direct access to government decision-makers and expanded his familiarity with state institutions. As I highlighted in the previous chapter, alongside Blanca and his Manicomio comrades, Carlos had contributed to shaping the state laws that govern community media.

Carlos welcomed opportunities for Catia TVe to collaborate with state institutions. Sitting in his quiet office, which was decorated with the many awards Catia TVe had won from state agencies, Carlos explained,

> I understand that there are many groups and social organizations that try to demarcate themselves from the state or from the government. But I believe that really in this moment, that's not the correct thing to do. I believe that what should be more important is how we contribute to the construction of the new state of the future. . . . Of course there are many revolutionaries that dreamed of armed struggle, of a guerrilla fight with the execution of traitors. But in Venezuela we are creating a historic process via an electoral path, with a military guy at the head, with a process where the people have come out to defend the institutions, and it was the people that maintained those institutions in power. This, all of this, one has to know how to interpret and manage things.

Carlos argued that the "correct" action for social movements' actors was not to assert autonomy but rather to contribute to the construction of a new state. Like Hector, Carlos emphasized that the Bolivarian Revolution had not emerged through the violent overthrow of the central government and state institutions but instead aimed to transform those institutions over time. For Carlos, the ideal type leftist Latin American revolutionary was not the *guerrillero* of the Cuban Revolution but the social activist who worked in cooperation with state actors and institutions, along the lines of Chile's process of social transformation under Salvador Allende. Carlos's comment that "one has to know how to interpret and manage things" suggested his belief in the need to rethink basic ideas about revolutionary strategy and to create new ways of practicing politics.

The competing logics of liberal autonomy and socialist relatedness, and the departure of the Bolivarian Revolution from the established scripts for revolutionary socialist change, contributed to the complexity of how Catia

TVe producers approached the boundary of the arenas of state and community. Even while Catia TVe producers embraced the task of building what they called a "popular state"—a state that would not only serve the interests of the poor majority but also be governed by it—they struggled to reckon with the belief that the state was irrevocably a separate and hostile monolith that would ultimately squash dissent. Although many of my informants, like Hector and Carlos, analyzed and experienced the state as divided, uneven, and dispersed, they nevertheless often spoke of it as a real, concrete object and stand-alone entity, as Celia did in my description at the outset of this chapter. At times, in the same breath, they demystified the state as a porous and diffuse human project and reified it as a stand-alone solid object. The ethnographic accounts that follow explore the micropolitics of everyday statecraft, the unclear boundaries between state and community, and why Catia TVe producers and their allies at times reasserted state and community as mutually exclusive entities.

Everyday Statecraft in the Barrio

Despite historic efforts by Venezuelan ruling elites to make the state appear as an entity beyond the reach of everyday actors, nonelites have always participated in the production of both "the state" as an abstract idea and the material practices of official state institutions. People shape the state in their everyday lives through mundane actions like singing the national anthem, following laws, and interacting with state employees and officials inside formal institutions or even over a family meal. More explicit efforts at state formation involve participation in organized social movements that affirm or challenge the power of central state institutions. To recognize the dispersed everyday nature of state formation is not to suggest that power is distributed evenly or that influence over official state structures is allocated equally (Joseph and Nugent 1994). An approach to statecraft as a commonplace diffuse practice instead focuses our attention on how ordinary people contribute to the creation and development of the state as both an idea and a set of concrete institutions. Through Catia TVe's participation in the process of media production inside barrios and official halls of power, community media producers shaped ideas about and practices of the emerging revolutionary state.

Catia TVe producers' involvement in processes of everyday state formation were visible one Sunday afternoon when I accompanied nineteen-year-old Nestor to document a meeting to organize a communal council in a poor neighborhood of west Caracas. We took the metro from Catia TVe three stops farther west to Plaza Sucre, emerging from the cool and quiet metro into a hectic tangle of informal vendors selling huge hunks of red meat, knock-off designer jeans, and pirated DVDs. After stopping several times to ask for directions, we finally found the departure point for a four-wheel-drive jeep taxi that would take us to our destination, a poor neighborhood nestled in one of the many steep mountains of Caracas's periphery. The jeep protested the nearly vertical incline of the street, stalling several times en route. When the driver deposited us on a hot concrete street, we stretched our cramped legs and surveyed the breathtaking view of the buildings below.

A similar view first drew Nestor to Catia TVe when he was just thirteen years old. From his bedroom window, high on a hillside adjacent to the neighborhood where Catia TVe had its original headquarters, Nestor had a direct sightline to Catia TVe's first broadcast antenna. One evening he noticed that the red light at the top of the transmitter tower had burned out. Nestor searched out Carlos, Catia TVe's director, to let him know. Carlos, in turn, invited Nestor to enroll in a video production workshop. Nestor spent the next six years working as part of a volunteer team of producers. In 2006, Nestor was asked to join the production staff.

Walking in the direction the jeep driver had pointed, we found a street blocked off with rope. Salsa music blared and people milled around in small groups. In place of cars, empty plastic chairs were assembled in tight rows. Massive steel lattice towers that supported electric cables nestled incongruously between the three-story houses of concrete and terracotta blocks. Inhabitants had built the neighborhood decades earlier on land the Ministry of Energy cleared for electricity towers.

A man named Douglas, who looked to be in his forties, approached us with a handshake and a wide grin. He had extended the initial invitation to Catia TVe to cover that afternoon's communal council event and seemed relieved that we had made it. Douglas wore a red shirt—the official color of the government—emblazoned with the slogan, "All elevens have their thirteens," a reference to April 11, 2002, the day that Chávez was unseated from power in the ill-fated coup attempt, and April 13, 2002, the day he was reinstated. The slogan attributed the coup's failure to the power of the masses that had surrounded the presidential palace to demand Chávez's return. The slogan suggested that any attempt to stall the revolutionary process would be met by similarly swift mass defiance. The back of the T-shirt read, "The people [el pueblo] continue in the street, now on the path to socialism." The T-shirt built on the memory of the 2002 rebellion to suggest that the project of building socialism was a similarly spontaneous activity that happened in the street. Earlier that week I had seen government workers distributing the T-shirt for free at a march to celebrate the fifth anniversary of the coup's reversal. This official embrace and insistence on what had begun as a rallying cry of the masses was the first example of many that I observed that afternoon that pointed to the complex interplay between official state institutions and urban barrio-based activism. The possibility for radical structural change coexisted with the threat of co-optation.

Douglas explained that he was part of the group trying to promote the construction of a communal council, a legally recognized local governance organ designed to bring together several hundred families from the same neighborhood. Once it was established, a council would formulate proposals for funding from state institutions and oversee the budgeting and implementation of community development projects in health, housing, communications, and water. State-hired community promoters worked closely with neighborhood groups who were interested in forming a council to certify the local election of council spokespeople and to ensure the consistent application of the procedures set out in the communal council law. The Chávez government characterized communal councils as central to its program to redistribute economic resources and decision-making in order to advance participatory democracy and create what it called a "new geometry of power."[1] Over the previous year, 2006, the National Assembly had spent $1 billion to finance projects presented by communal councils (López Maya and Lander 2011a, 74). As with many initiatives of the Bolivarian process, there was little consistency in how different councils managed their relationship with official state institutions: some councils fulfilled their mandate to democratize participation and reorder power, while others reproduced traditional forms of hierarchical administration (McCarthy 2012).

Douglas took us on a quick tour of the street, pointing out problems that he hoped the communal council would one day address. The boys needed a place to play basketball. The garbage was rarely collected and contributed to flooding when it rained. Part of the street was crumbling and needed to be rebuilt. As we slowly made our way down the street, Nestor's camera and microphone attracted considerable attention. A group of small girls tugged at his pant leg, wanting to know what television station he was from. A group of young men around Nestor's age with his same brown complexion, baggy jeans, and sneakers studied him with more guarded enthusiasm. Douglas seemed quite pleased at the notice Nestor attracted. He introduced us to as many people he could. He insisted on taking us up several flights of stairs to a house where women from his street ran a government-funded soup kitchen that provided free lunch to people living in extreme poverty in the neighborhood. Like many of the Chávez government welfare programs, the soup kitchen was state-financed but depended on local participation and initiative for its implementation and daily management.

Douglas introduced us to a young man who was there as a representative of the Ministry of Participation. He was tasked with offering support to the local community organizers and certifying that they were adhering to the procedures prescribed in the communal council law. This young man was the only official from a state institution present at the event that afternoon. He explained that he was studying social work at the new Bolivarian University of Venezuela and was new to the job. Although he was far from being a formidable figure, his involvement signaled how the communal councils were ultimately subject to the approval and centralized funding mechanisms of official agencies over which the local population had little direct control.

Many of the people we spoke with registered no familiarity with Catia TVe but were excited to be interviewed by Nestor and pose for the camera. Douglas explained that Catia TVe's signal was only sometimes accessible on the higher floors of the homes on his street. Despite the improbability that Catia TVe's coverage of the event would be widely viewed by members of the neighborhood, Nestor's presence had great importance. As I would learn many times throughout my research, it was during the process of media production, rather than through the effect their finished programs had on audiences, that Catia TVe staff and volunteers had the most impact in encouraging their interlocutors to actively embrace statecraft.

Nestor's presence validated not only Douglas's aspirations to local leadership, but also the legitimacy of his community's initiative to form a communal council and, by extension, the state institutions that propelled and validated the councils. In every house we visited, and with every person we interviewed, there was a blurring and interpenetration of community with state. The organizational rubric that Celia attempted to establish with her neat piles, described at the opening of the chapter, did not hold up. That afternoon, Nestor and I encountered multiple manifestations of official and unofficial efforts to create a just and equal collective sociality through the idea and the institutions of the state. Concrete manifestations of the mutual constitution of state and community included the T-shirts that celebrated the construction of socialism in the street, the locally run soup kitchen, and the law of communal councils that guided the day's events.

FIGURE 2.2. Catia TVe's microphone against backdrop of west Caracas, November 6, 2006. Photo by the author.

Douglas and his fellow neighborhood activists agreed that it was time to begin the meeting. Nestor hurriedly slipped on his headphones and began filming. Most of the red plastic chairs assembled in the middle of the street remained empty. A woman who ran the soup kitchen took the microphone on the small stage and urged her neighbors to join their discussion. She noted, "Many times we have said that we'd like to see the problem of the crumbling street fixed, the trash collected, transportation to our sector improved. Well, this is your opportunity to be involved directly in solving these problems. This isn't just one more meeting. We want to see these chairs full, with you raising your hand saying, 'I want to participate in the decisions that are being made here.'" As she spoke, Nestor panned the camera away from her to the half-filled seats and then up the façades of the houses that faced the street. He filmed several people who were leaning out their windows, seemingly unsure if they wanted to participate in the meeting. One woman in a window on the third floor of a narrow house quickly retreated inside.

Seeing her recoil from the camera, I realized that Nestor's documentation of the meeting not only validated the event as "newsworthy" and signaled Douglas's skill at gaining attention for the neighborhood, it also potentially worked as a mechanism to govern members of the community. I recalled how one regular volunteer producer at Catia TVe, Javier, explained to me that his neighbors often requested that he film their meetings so that members of their community would know who participated in meetings and who did not. The presence of the camera, according to Javier, encouraged his neighbors to come to meetings and defused conflict, as people were less likely to act inappropriately when they knew they were being filmed. The camera, in other words, exerted a disciplinary presence. It had the potential to encourage participation and expose nonparticipation. While there were no clear or immediate sanctions for nonparticipation, other than perhaps social stigma from the organizers, access to resources in the long term was contingent on people's involvement in councils, organizations that were explicitly aligned with the Chávez government.

Perhaps the woman who hastily retreated inside her house had been called away by a family member. I wondered, nevertheless, whether Nestor's camera was perceived by members of that neighborhood as a form of coercion, and if that coercion was experienced as coming from their allied barrio activists or official state bureaucrats. While local barrio leaders issued the call for participation in constructing the communal council based on their estimation of urgent collective and individual needs of their neighbors, the day's activities were simultaneously supported and propelled by official state actors. To be sure, Javier, the volunteer at Catia TVe, saw oversight via the camera as a social good, one that encouraged widespread participation in the political process in order to challenge the injustices of the "old" bourgeois state.

Catia TVe's camera was not the only mechanism encouraging people to participate in the day's events. A performance by a local children's dance troop, organized by Douglas and his co-organizers, had immediate success in drawing many people out of their houses. Most of them remained afterward to hear Douglas and others speak about how the communal councils worked and why they were important.

With his mini DV tape almost full and the camera battery running low, Nestor thanked our hosts and we packed up the camera and microphone. As we were leaving, three national guardsmen approached Douglas. They had come to investigate whether the community had formal permission to close the street. As a replacement for the much-despised Metropolitan Police, the National Guard had, at the time, a growing presence in poor communities where they set up checkpoints, ostensibly as a way to curtail the drug trafficking and violence that plagued many barrios. Douglas showed the guardsmen the necessary permissions and the guardsmen prepared to leave, taking their large semiautomatic weapons with them. In this instance, the presence of "the people in the street" building socialism required paperwork and was subject to oversight by armed guards.

Much to my surprise, Nestor approached the guardsmen and displayed his Catia TVe identification card; he asked for a ride back down the mountain to the metro. One of the guardsmen, a stocky young man, hesitated for a moment and then agreed. "I wouldn't normally do this," he said, "but we saw you two filming." We climbed into the jeep and began the steep descent. After a minute of silence, the guardsman noted, "You, as professionals, as journalists who are not from areas as insecure as this one, don't know. But these people can really be abusive. They can really treat us badly and get out of hand," he said. Nestor and I laughed nervously. After an afternoon listening to inhabitants of this neighborhood extol the importance of popular empowerment by embracing new laws backed by state institutions that declared their interest in asserting popular power, it was jarring to hear this guardsman portray poor communities as criminal. The discrepancy between the guardsman's comments and the broader official state discourse powerfully highlighted another incoherency of state institutions. At every turn, the inconsistencies we encountered challenged received understandings of states as fixed "things" with clear interests.

The guardsmen dropped us at the nearest metro station. When they were out of sight, Nestor began laughing. He explained that just a few days before, as he was running home from a nearby bakery with a loaf of bread, a national guardsman had briefly detained and questioned him. Because he was running late at night through his poor neighborhood, the guardsman had profiled him as a drug dealer. With the video camera in his hand, press credential around his neck, and accompanied by me, a light-skinned woman, the national guardsmen assumed he was a middle-class professional. Despite his experience of harassment, Nestor nevertheless had felt emboldened to ask the guardsmen for a favor, signaling an expectation of recognition and respect. His silence in the face of the guardsman's derogatory portrayal of Douglas and his barrio neighbors was a blatant reminder of the unequal relationships of force that characterized the unfolding revolutionary state.

The next day Nestor edited a ten-minute segment from his footage that was broadcast over Catia TVe's airwaves several times over the next two days, sandwiched between similar short segments produced by the staff, programs created by volunteers, and official propaganda by state institutions lauding the accomplishments of the Bolivarian state. The impact the segment had on Catia TVe's audiences was unclear to me. Observing the process of production, however, I uncovered how Nestor's presence at the neighborhood meeting that Sunday contributed to legitimizing the unfolding political process. He had participated in shaping how life was lived and imagined. As a newly empowered media producer from a barrio not unlike the one he was documenting, Nestor embodied the social changes that he and the barrio leaders wanted to advance. As Nestor, Douglas, and others from poor neighborhoods worked alongside official power brokers to engage in everyday state formation that advanced official projects of popular empowerment, they rendered the lines between state and community indecipherable. The means of violent force and power over decision-making was far from evenly distributed. Nevertheless, Nestor's work as a community media producer, Douglas's labor as a neighborhood activist, and the barrio participants they interacted with that afternoon all contributed to a process of state formation. Together they legitimized a belief that people from poor neighborhoods could participate in creating state institutions in which they held some degree of power, including the ability to redistribute resources.

An approach to the state that recognizes it as an effect of everyday processes extending throughout society necessitates concomitant scrutiny of the popular or grassroots actors as practitioners of state formation. In this vein, the division between popular and state perspectives and forces in Venezuela, insistently repeated by scholars, the government, and barrio-based activists through their use of the spatial metaphors of "top-down" versus "bottom-up" social change, cannot account for the blurred boundaries between some government and community action. Nor does it recognize the possibility that top-down management may be choreographed by and for the poor.

Making and Unmaking the Divide between State and Community

Most Chávez supporters were confident that Chávez would easily be reelected for a second term. Nevertheless, an air of tense uncertainly hung over Catia TVe in the buildup to the December 2006 presidential election. With the experience of the failed 2002 coup attempt still a recent memory, Catia TVe producers—like many supporters of the Bolivarian process—were concerned that the groups that opposed Chávez would use the elections to foment chaos and uncertainly in order to oust Chávez by extralegal means. The government, together with Chávez-aligned community producers, went to great lengths to prevent a repeat of the virtual media blackout that opposition forces had imposed during the 2002 coup attempt when they gained control of the only government-managed television channel then in existence.

The election period made vivid how Catia TVe producers not only depended on official state institutions, but how actors working within state institutions also looked to Catia TVe for legitimation, support, and fortification. The material aspects of this codependence were never more visible than the lead-up to the 2006 election. The location of Catia TVe's headquarters, a poor neighborhood just blocks away from the presidential palace and steps away from famously militant pro-Chávez neighborhoods, provided an ideal site to create a backup transmission point for official state media in the event of an attack on state networks. The National Commission of Telecommunications (CONATEL) temporarily installed a large satellite dish on the roof of Catia TVe that could transmit state channels. The state oil company, PDVSA, loaned Catia TVe a power generator to ensure that if electricity to the neighborhood was cut, Catia TVe and the backup satellite transmitter for official state networks would continue to operate. Catia TVe staff and volunteers expressed pride and excitement at this collaboration.

State institutions depended on Catia TVe not only for material support but, perhaps more crucially, to legitimize the claim that the revolution was succeeding. Catia TVe offered a "from below" authenticity that state-run media projects, no matter how much they attempted to reflect popular voices, did not grant. State officials relied on "outside" voices to legitimize a call to unity at this critical moment in the formal political process. Despite the reality of blurred boundaries, a range of actors disseminated the idea of a clear divide between the community and the state.

Nestor's participation in documenting the organization of a communal council in a poor neighborhood underscored how state and community were mutually constituted. At the same time, the explicit collaboration between official state institutions and Catia TVe during the 2006 presidential elections revealed how Catia TVe staff and volunteers both activated *and* disassembled the divide between state and community in order to manage their pursuit of radical interdependency. This dynamic was made particularly clear in a series of meetings that I observed in the weeks before the presidential election.

The Delicate Screen: Planning Coverage
and Identifying as the State at ViVe TV

As the December 2006 presidential election approached, Catia TVe's leadership together with their contacts at ViVe TV organized a meeting of community media producers to plan how community media producers could contribute to ViVe TV's official coverage of the election. Twenty-two people—seven women and fifteen men—assembled in one of ViVe TV's spacious production studios in the station's headquarters at the National Library of Venezuela in central Caracas. In addition to representatives from seventeen community television projects from twelve different states, the meeting attendees included two men from a pro-Chávez website and representatives from ViVe TV, the Ministry of Culture, and the Ministry of Communication and Information.[2] Blanca Eekhout, ViVe TV's president, joined the meeting midway through.

Many of the representatives from community television projects had traveled great distances—ten to fifteen hours by bus—to join the meeting. These media activists were eager to participate for several reasons. They wanted to be involved in representing what they characterized as another historic step in the peaceful process of revolutionary change. In addition, many of these community media activists were in the midst of the lengthy bureaucratic process of seeking legal recognition from the National Commission of Telecommunications, the state institution that licenses broadcasters. They were keen to form alliances with employees at ViVe TV and other state institutions that might offer future political and financial support. Moreover, they expressed a belief that the participation of community media outlets in the official coverage of the presidential elections would legitimize and normalize the participation of nonprofessional popular media producers in the production and representation of national news.

The collaboration of nonprofessional media producers and activists in the coverage of the elections also met the strategic needs of officials in state institutions. The Chávez government relied on community media makers to display how the state–society relationship was being redefined. Community media institutions assumed a critical function in creating representations of mass participation that legitimized Chávez's claim that he ruled in the interest of empowering the poor to be the central protagonists of the political processes.

Official state actors and barrio-based organizers relied on the aura of nostalgia, authenticity, and homogeneity that the concept of community held (Creed 2006; Ferguson 2004) in order to legitimize the claim that the revolutionary state was a project being advanced "from below." Throughout the meeting, Carlos, Catia TVe's director, paradoxically asserted his and Catia TVe's status as outside the official realms of power and of state institutions in order to legitimize his call for Catia TVe and other community media producers to see themselves as part of the process of state formation. The differently positioned actors at the meeting had distinct motivations in reifying the state. Together they reinforced a belief in the purity of community media and its direct connection to grassroots organizing.

"Should we begin?" ViVe TV's head of public relations asked Carlos, a question that established his status as the leader of the group. Carlos easily embraced the role. He explained how many of the community stations outside Caracas had not been able to resolve their technological and financial needs in time to broadcast coverage of the election. Of the thirteen stations represented at the meeting, only eight had the capacity to broadcast. Carlos proposed a strategy for how they could all, nevertheless, participate in the election coverage. He suggested that community producers use cell phones to take photographs of the voting process in their neighborhoods and towns and digitally send them to ViVe TV. ViVe TV could then broadcast the photos, Carlos explained, while the community media producers who sent the photographs could describe over the phone what was taking place at the voting center, all on live television. The other producers in the room responded positively to Carlos's suggestion, and with palpable excitement discussed how to coordinate logistics.

This inclusion of untrained disparate producers in official state media presented risks for a unified line and narrative for ViVe TV's election-day coverage. Carlos played a critical role in communicating to his fellow community media producers the stakes of their involvement and the responsibility that it entailed. Making eye contact around the circle, Carlos spoke confidently. His voice easily filled the oversized room. "The opposition is determined that there be a bloodbath, that there be problems, that there be a death. . . . We have to fight and work so that this electoral process is impeccable, clean, that we win with huge numbers, and that there isn't one single thing to lament about. Why am I saying all this?" Carlos took a deep breath and continued, "Because, perhaps we have to manage ourselves in double time. One thing, when we are on the air, when we make a phone call, we can't spread any information about anything negative." Carlos switched to a high-pitched voice, mimicking the voice of a nervous caller: "'We don't have electricity! They haven't opened the voting tables! The people are starting to fight! The opposition is taking the streets!'" Returning to his normal register, Carlos continued, "This can't go out on the air, you know, but we *can* communicate, send a text message, '*Compañero*, there's an irregular situation here, please call me.'"

Carlos gave explicit directions for what community producers should communicate, making clear how reports of chaos might play into the hands of the opposition. Carlos's message revealed the depth of concern about the damage that community media's participation could potentially cause the "delicate screen," as one representative of ViVe TV referred to their televised broadcasts. Looming in people's memories were both how the 1989 urban uprising in Caracas spread throughout the country—encouraged in part by the few televised images of protest that made it through government censorship—and how the commercial media had legitimated the coup against Chávez in 2002 by broadcasting misleading footage. There was a palpable sense that televised images could quickly and uncontrollably influence political outcomes.

Carlos presented his fellow community media producers with a way to understand the constraints on their inclusion in ViVe TV's broadcast. Given the history of liberal expectations that the state would threaten press freedom, his message needed to recast the stakes and reposition the players. He noted,

> We, in a certain way, this third of December, subordinate ourselves in this case to a person in whom I trust completely and who I'm sure would never try to mess with us or implicate us in a problem: Blanca. She has a direct link, we can say, with the high government [*el alto gobierno*]. . . . But we aren't going to approach this as our adventure. . . . That would mean not only getting ourselves into trouble but also getting this television station [ViVe TV] in trouble when they are providing us with a communication platform. They are giving us support. And it's true that all of this is ours, but the fact that it is ours also means that we have to follow lines [political directives]. This is part of a revolution. . . . These are the lines that they are giving us. I think that it should be like this, not simply because they have told me so, but because I think that logically we can resolve problems only when we stop to analyze the situation. . . . At Catia TVe we can say whatever occurs to us; we wouldn't do it because we are responsible. But we could and it's not going to have the impact that it could have on ViVe, which covers 80 percent of the country. . . . It's not that we have to wear a straitjacket. Rather, we are assuming this responsibility as the state because I believe that the state is not just the government, you know. Really, we are all responsible for what happens election day.

Carlos performed his allegiance to a state that, he asserted, belonged to the people. He pledged his trust in his long-time confidant, colleague, and president of ViVe TV, Blanca Eekhout, and encouraged the other community television producers to see the state as a collective project for which they, too, were accountable. Carlos characterized self-discipline and constraint as a revolutionary act. Community spokespeople had to exercise their judgment, as Carlos had, about what was the best way to proceed, but within a preordained set of parameters that he argued was necessary to defend the revolution.

From his position as a community producer "outside" state institutions, Carlos made the official call for unity and subordination not simply as a state directive, but also as the position of an organic social movement. His identification of Blanca was a crucial aspect of his message. Rather than a faceless, abstract "state," they could be confident that someone who was known and trusted by community media producers—who had once been a community media militant—was working alongside them to advance their interests. Carlos's claim to be outside the state granted him persuasive force to convince other community media makers that he was not commanding them to fall in line because he was ordered to do so by the government, but because, as a longtime community activist, he believed that following official directives was part of the revolutionary process, at least for that moment.

Several community producers asked a few logistical questions about transmitting the photographs to ViVe TV. No one challenged or questioned the "lines" that Carlos suggested for the content of the community reports, nor did anyone express doubts about self-censorship or subordination to the government. The representative from the pro-Chávez website reiterated Carlos's perspective, noting that "The most important thing is that we can coordinate ourselves, and as you say, each person should not go out there saying whatever they wish." In the ensuing conversation, these community media makers from across the country reflected that they were in the midst of a political struggle shaped, in large measure, by the messages transmitted on television. They described the careful management of national broadcasts as a way to control the efforts of the groups that opposed the Bolivarian Revolution to incite chaos. A producer from a community station in Guárico state exclaimed excitedly, "We are starting the motor of revolution!" They echoed Carlos's message that they were engaged in a struggle to defend what they called "their government" and to build what they referred to as "the revolutionary state."

Like Carlos, Blanca maintained that the serious threat involved how the opposition might seize and manipulate popular mobilization and communication through the spreading of destabilizing rumors. She noted, "Our networks demonstrated the 13th of April [the day the 2002 coup was reversed] that in spite of everything, the immense power of communication via telephone, human communication between people, *radio-bemba* [word of mouth] . . . toppled a coup d'état. Then we, we have a power that is unlimited. If *we* don't channel it we can be a field of resonance for anyone." Blanca aligned herself with the community producers ("we") against the opposition. Blanca suggested that the opposition's only real power lay in their ability to provoke confusion among chavistas. This power of the popular masses—the common people—to assume the responsibility of the state, Blanca made clear, was a double-edged sword; she depicted the popular mass subject as both invincible and uncontrollable. Popular strength could also become a devastating weakness. She encouraged community media makers to manage the impact of informal mechanisms of communication and to recognize the importance of their subordination to the central coordination by official state decision makers, and she relied on Carlos's opening address to legitimize this message.

Blanca and Carlos emphasized that community media producers were part of the process of state formation. They did so in terms that would encourage the community media producers to stick to a unified message on election day. Rather than simply creating a superficial staging of popular participation predicated on top-down control, Carlos and his colleagues saw themselves as taking, remaking, and maintaining a revolutionary state alongside activists in positions of official state power who sought to build a popular state. Key to legitimizing the assertion of unity was the divide between state and community.

The meeting itself conspicuously demonstrated to all those present that state processes were disorderly, ad hoc, last minute, and very much a product of human design. Blanca repeatedly answered her cell phone. ViVe TV staff members rushed in and out of the room. Blanca ceded the floor to representatives of various state ministries who provided updates on their plans for election day, which reflected a lack of coordination. For community media people from far-flung regions of the country, their presence at this meeting enabled them to witness how the state was far from a cogent, distant, or all-powerful actor.

Popular State Spectacle on Election Day

At 3 A.M. on election day, Ana, one of Catia TVe's assistant directors, screamed into a bullhorn, "Wake up, wake up! Long live Chávez!" She blasted a digital recording of a military bugle call at full volume through the bullhorn to awaken the few people who had managed to fall asleep in makeshift sleeping areas in the classrooms and production studios of the station. As if the trumpet's call was not enough to raise the dead, firecrackers exploded in the surrounding barrios. Jesica, a twenty-four-year-old staff member, excitedly grabbed a camera and stormed into Catia TVe's basement classroom, where six volunteers of the station were sleeping. As during previous elections, teams of Catia TVe volunteers and staff had assembled at the station, ready to document the voting process at dozens of voting centers in the poor neighborhoods of west Caracas from the moment they opened. Jesica filmed one volunteer struggling in a dazed state to put on his socks. Next, she raced to film one of Catia TVe's security guards who was distributing cameras to groups of volunteers. Each group was assigned to film the voting process and interview voters at polling stations in and around their neighborhood. Cristina, who had been up all night coordinating routes for different teams of producers, snapped into action, directing Jesica to bring the fifteen minutes of footage she had just filmed to ViVe TV just over a mile away. Jesica excitedly hopped on the back of a motorcycle taxi and sped off into the darkness.

About half an hour later, around 3:30 A.M., ViVe TV broadcast the shaky footage of the tired Catia TVe volunteer pulling on his socks. Blanca was hosting a live round table in one of ViVe TV's studios. She interrupted the conversation to comment on Catia TVe's footage, expressing how beautiful it was to see the passion with which community media producers embraced their role in documenting the election. Blanca drew on the "home-cooked realism" (Aufderheide 1993) of Catia TVe's wobbly footage of the sleepy-eyed volunteer to convey the seemingly spontaneous, untrained nature of popular participation in the political process. The unpolished "outsider" quality of the footage was essential to the narrative that Blanca related about the expansion of enfranchisement. Not all ViVe TV staff, however, saw the footage in this way. An employee at ViVe TV later told me that several producers inside ViVe TV's transmission room had fiercely criticized the amateur quality of Catia TVe's sound and lighting, arguing that ViVe TV should have better broadcast standards. "Blanca's comments shut them up immediately," he chuckled. His remarks made clear how even within a state institution ostensibly dedicated to expanding access to the means of media representation, there was disagreement about including nonprofessionally produced media.

Throughout the day, under Blanca's direction, ViVe TV broadcast reports from several other community television stations from across the country. The commentary of the media producers closely followed the lines Carlos suggested during the planning meeting. Over blurry cell phone photos of voting centers and seemingly endless lines of people, spokespeople from community stations described the joy with which their neighborhood had turned out to exercise their right to vote. If community media makers encountered any problems at voting centers, such as obstruction, violence, or technological failures with the voting equipment, none were reported over the airwaves.

I accompanied several Catia TVe producers throughout election day. Rosemery, a Catia TVe volunteer in her late thirties, was at the time unemployed and suffering frequent bouts of depression. Whizzing through different barrios on the back of a motorcycle, Rosemery looked happier than I had ever seen her. Like the other Catia TVe producers I followed that day, Rosemery did not encounter any violent or unusual activity at the voting centers where she filmed. Instead, she found long lines of remarkably patient people waiting to vote. With her Catia TVe shirt, hat, and large plastic press credential dangling around her neck, Rosemery boldly approached strangers waiting in line to interview them.

At one polling center in a local elementary school, the line snaked around the building and extended several blocks down the street. Rosemery walked to the head of the line, announcing to the military sergeant stationed at the polling center that she was from a television station and she intended to enter the voting center to film the process. Easily gaining access, she joked with the volunteer poll watchers inside about how she had been up all night; there had been so much to do. Everywhere we went in the poor neighborhoods of west Caracas, people treated Rosemery with respect. They were thrilled to be filmed, eagerly asking when and where they could watch themselves on television. Her presence and visibility at various voting centers generated palpable elation and pride in the people she interviewed. Rosemery brought to life the slogans about popular empowerment.

The presence of community media producers on ViVe TV throughout the day provided visual evidence for the narrative that popular forces were central participants in the process of revolutionary state formation. Even while this participation hewed closely to preestablished protocols, the process of producing the narrative of widespread participation in politics and media production made this participation a reality. Community media makers from across the country contributed to ViVe TV's coverage. Poor and rural populations historically overlooked or denigrated by the exclusionary practices of both commercial and state media outlets had the opportunity to speak for themselves.

FIGURE 2.3. Catia TVe crew conducting an interview, August 15, 2004. Photo by the author.

Conclusion

In their interactions with state institutions, Catia TVe staff and volunteers developed multiple conceptual and practical definitions of the state. For many community producers, the station's participation in government projects has contributed to the formation of an experiential understanding of the state, not as a distinct conceptual or empirical object standing above them, but rather as a set of institutions made up of social relationships that include or exclude them (Sharma and Gupta 2006; Steinmetz 1999). Catia TVe producers at times constructed and depended on barriers between state and community to build their authority and engage in social activism. At the same time, they defied the fixity of the boundary between realms of state and society in their everyday practice and advocated for social movement actors to embrace the state as a collective project.

Government officials depended on Catia TVe producers as representatives of the "authentic popular" to embrace and justify the call to unify with official state actors and institutions. The social actors, such as the Catia TVe leadership, were understood as "outside" the official realms of power of state institutions; these people could most effectively encourage other social movement actors to see themselves as part of the process of state formation. Catia TVe producers were constantly negotiating relationships that were potentially co-opting. Yet it is important to note that they did not uniformly understand top-down orchestration as stifling their goals and their potential to struggle for a better world.

Catia TVe's participation in the developing political process involved constant calculation and flexibility as they moved in and out of different institutional arrangements, dealt with different state actors with distinct commitments, and sought to build the necessary unity to deflect powerful opposition forces. In their work to produce a new belief in the state's unity—not separate from community but at one with it—Catia TVe producers did not simply create yet another mask that would obfuscate the reality of actual political practice. Instead, in their effort to produce a "future imaginary" (Coronil 2011a) of a just and equal popular state, they pushed state actors to fulfill their commitments.

Catia TVe staff and volunteers continuously weighed the mixed results of compromise, and whether positions taken at heightened moments of threat to the Chávez government needed to be sustained in other contexts. In their daily work and during tense political contests, Catia TVe producers were part of the practice of reorganizing life. Together with official state actors, Catia TVe's leadership encouraged and attempted to regulate other emerging media makers in the name of advancing the Bolivarian project. In this way, Catia TVe was both the producer and the product of an emerging form of governmentality that managed the conduct of newly trained media producers. They collaborated in the formation of a diffuse web of relations—some of which remained under the control of actors who did not intend to redistribute power. For many Catia TVe producers, the manifold and incongruous experiences and ideas about what the state means in theory and practice created confusion, apprehension, and hope.

To recognize that people can experience the state as an uncertain process undermines abstract expectations of what the state represents and allows us to set aside normative analytic frameworks to search for better-fitting understandings. To acknowledge the state as a process rather than a thing allows us to account for the history of the material and ideational unfolding of the state-idea and the social relations that constitute it in particular places and times. Most crucially, perhaps, a processual view of the state signals that there were and are many possible futures (Hartsock 2006).

THREE

CLASS ACTS

At 9:30 A.M. Catia TVe was slowly coming alive. A small television in the corner of the kitchen area was tuned to Venezolana de Televisión, the officially state-run television station. A series of short public service announcements celebrated Chávez's announcement of a cable car service that would connect several poor neighborhoods to mass transit. Jesica, a member of the production staff, passed through the kitchen, greeting me with a quick peck on the cheek. She made a beeline for the large metal coffee thermos. Finding it empty, her mood darkened and she retreated to the production office down the corridor from the kitchen, letting the door bang loudly behind her. Antony, a staff member, walked by clutching his toothbrush and towel. He kept his distance, muttering "Good morning." Antony often slept at Catia TVe to avoid the two-hour commute to his neighborhood on the outskirts of Caracas. He had half an hour before he was scheduled to begin work in the transmission office broadcasting Catia TVe's programming to the surrounding neighborhoods.

Pilar, Clara, and Gregorio arrived one after another. They dragged over three plastic armchairs to join me at a small round table. Our agenda that morning was to discuss proposals for the content of a new state channel that was set to replace a long-established commercial television station (a case I discuss in detail in chapter 5). The Ministry of Communication and Information, together with media activists, had launched several weeks of open discussion about the future of this station. Just a few minutes into our conversation, the debate grew heated.

"The middle-class [television] producers are idiots and capitalists," Pilar complained. In her early thirties, light-skinned, and petite, Pilar grew up in

Spain but had spent much of her youth living in the United States, where she was politically active in leftist social movement organizing. About a year earlier, Pilar had relocated to Venezuela to participate in the Bolivarian Revolution. She volunteered at Catia TVe, helping to produce a weekly talk show discussing theories of socialism. Pilar argued: "If they [the middle class] get control of the new channel, the pueblo will never get that space." She was vehement that those who she identified as middle-class television producers should not be allowed to dominate the new television channel. Instead, poor people—who she referred to as el pueblo (the people)—needed to assume control over the new station. "The middle class," she noted confidently, "should step aside."

By many measures, Pilar would certainly be considered middle class. She was internationally mobile and highly educated. Although she didn't have a steady income at the time, she had access to what Pierre Bourdieu (1984) calls elite "cultural capital," which includes the skills, knowledge, and tastes of an economically privileged class. In some ways, she had more in common with the middle-class television producers whom she derided as enemies of the people than she did with the brown and black inhabitants of Caracas's barrios, to whom she referred as el pueblo. Yet Pilar aligned herself politically with oppressed groups and had committed her life to participating in social justice organizing.

Clara, who also volunteered at Catia TVe, exhaled in frustration at Pilar's comment about middle-class television producers. "You can't count all those [middle-class] people as useless," Clara argued. Clara grew up in the same poor neighborhood as the founders of Catia TVe. She was in her mid-thirties and had light-brown skin and thick curly black hair. Clara tapped on the faux wood tabletop vigorously, noting, "A lot of middle-class people are very supportive of el proceso [the Bolivarian political process] and committed." Over time, I had learned that Clara's husband was from a more upwardly mobile family than she was. She and her husband owned a car and lived in a worn high-rise apartment building in the center of the city. She often joked with me about the oddities of Americans whom she had observed when she and her husband spent a year living in the United States. Clara straddled different class environments.

Clara's voice grew tense, "Look, I'm middle class. We're all middle class here. I've fought for what I have and I come from the barrio. In this country, the middle class isn't like it is in the United States or Spain." Clara paused, resting her eyes on Pilar and me. She took on a didactic tone, noting, "Here there were five families who had the money. Everyone else in this country comes from the barrio. Our middle class isn't like it is in other places. We're unique because we're an oil country."

Gregorio, who was sitting beside Clara, weighed in. "Well, I don't consider myself middle class. The middle class comes from the east," Gregorio explained, referring to the largely affluent eastern end of Caracas. A Catia TVe staff member in his mid-twenties, Gregorio lived in the poor neighborhood where he grew up. He was soft-spoken and lanky, with light-brown skin and thinning curly hair. "But," Gregorio wondered, "I guess the middle class in the west [a poor region of Caracas] is different?" Trying to quell the tension between Pilar and Clara, he smiled and noted, "Anyway, I've been learning that it's always the middle class who starts the revolutions. Wasn't Marx or Engels a factory owner or something like that?"

We had met that morning to generate ideas about programming content for a new television station; instead, we found ourselves debating the meaning and role of the middle class in the Bolivarian Revolution. New experiments in community and official state media created the opportunity for people from different class backgrounds—like Clara, Pilar, Gregorio, and me—to exchange knowledge, make social connections, and struggle over leadership. Informed by their various life experiences and ideological commitments, this group of Catia TVe producers was divided over whether certain sectors of the middle class formed part of what Gramsci termed the "power bloc"—the economically, politically, and culturally dominant sectors—or if they were they part of "the people," a multivalent term (which I analyze in the following chapter) that often refers to the oppressed majority. Which groups and individuals would and should assume leadership of the revolutionary state project? Who had the authority to determine what revolutionary television looked like?

New state and community media projects formed an important battleground for class conflict and formation. Class antagonism and collaboration were at once symptoms and catalysts of the effort to remake state institutions. Catia TVe producers were for the most part (although, crucially, not entirely) from poor neighborhoods. The people I came into contact with at ViVe TV, the official state station, were generally (although, again, not entirely) from middle-class backgrounds. Both cohorts viewed television production as the central instrument to create the socialist values necessary to challenge elite hegemony and capitalist culture. In conversation with the philosophy of Paolo Freire and media theory first elaborated in the 1970s under the broad aegis of the New Latin American Cinema Movement, Catia TVe's and ViVe TV's leadership held that challenging the traditional class division of labor between elite media producers and impoverished media consumers was part and parcel of their broader project to overcome capitalist class relations. Drawing on a blend of Marxist and Gramscian ideas, together they embraced the notion that in order to produce socialist men and women, they needed to create television content—and culture industries more broadly—capable of generating socialist hearts and minds. Even while, as I have been arguing, Catia TVe producers were often focused on advancing social transformation during the process of production rather than through the effects of programming, they nevertheless saw both their process and their products as part of a battle for cultural hegemony.

Catia TVe producers argued that the knowledge and culture of the poor—known in Latin America as the "popular class"—was central to creating this new anticapitalist cultural hegemony. They sought to valorize poor people's culture as providing the necessary authentic foundation to advance what they saw as genuine Venezuelan socialism. The symbolic centrality of popular culture to the Bolivarian Revolution afforded Catia TVe producers an opening to assert their leadership and exercise leverage over their allies in state institutions. This dynamic contributed to the growth of interdependencies between community and official state projects. Yet community and state media producers aligned with the Bolivarian Revolution had multiple, at times inconsistent, understandings not only of what it meant to be middle class but also of the meaning of "popular culture" or the "culture of the poor."

Catia TVe producers' attempts to define and validate the culture of the urban poor as the foundation for Venezuelan socialism overlapped in significant ways with their allies' efforts at ViVe TV, the official state channel, to promote national popular cultural forms. What often emerged through their joint efforts to characterize the poor as the keepers of Venezuelan authenticity was a version of poor people's culture and social existence that little resembled those people's everyday lives, pleasures, and aspirations. At times, producers at both Catia TVe and ViVe TV advanced a limited understanding of popular and poor people's culture. This limited portrayal of popular culture undermined barrio producers' equality with their middle-class counterparts. In certain moments, a reified notion of national popular culture worked to marginalize blackness, hybridity, and internationalism, and ultimately bolstered middle-class leadership. Yet I found that in other moments, barrio-based producers challenged such a limited notion of their lives and ways of being and were able to upend—if only briefly—traditional power hierarchies.

The Class Heterogeneity of Chavismo

The questions Clara, Pilar, and Gregorio raised about who counted as middle class underscored the complexity of class relations among supporters of the Bolivarian Revolution. Social class is a complex puzzle in Venezuela, as elsewhere.[1] Rather than a fixed identity or unchanging social position, social class is best approached as a relation of ownership, authority, taste, and accumulation of resources, always simultaneously interwoven with other hierarchies of power, including race, gender, and sexuality. The categories of middle class, upper class or affluent, and the poor or popular class that I use in this chapter are rough approximations meant to draw attention to broad patterns of access to income, wealth, living and working conditions, prestige, and privilege. My approximate characterization of the people I observed and interacted with as "middle class," and others as "barrio based," "poor," or a member of the "popular class," is based on my best assessment of an individual's access to economic and cultural resources.

The conversation between Clara, Pilar, and Gregorio at the outset of this chapter highlights some of the dilemmas in identifying people in terms of class categories. Clear definitions of the middle class, as Miguel Tinker Salas points out, are particularly tenuous (2009, 11). Many in the professional and managerial middle class do not control the means of production, but rather often control and manage the labor of others (Portes 1985, 9, cited in Tinker Salas 2009, 11). Middle-class cultural producers—academics, artists, and media makers, for example—occupy ambiguous positions, often producing systems of representation that maintain and mask class inequality, while not directly managing the poor. While life experiences are more complex than these class categories allow, it is nevertheless vital to name and analyze class locations because they broadly indicate unequal power, inherited privilege, wealth, and access to institutions. The Venezuelan middle class has historically dominated the Venezuelan poor by managing their labor, extracting profit, and participating in the production of ideas and representations that legitimized class inequality. These power inequalities shaped Catia TVe producers' interactions among themselves and with producers at other stations.

Chávez, his supporters, and detractors often depicted *chavismo*—the political alliance formed under Chávez's leadership—as uniformly poor and working class. In turn, most observers and participants described the political opposition to Chávez and the Bolivarian movement as almost entirely middle-class and affluent, with greater economic wealth and a historic claim to social esteem. While these generalizations certainly had some merit, the reality on the ground was far more complex.

Beginning in the early 2000s, many in the Venezuelan middle and upper sectors rejected the Bolivarian Revolution and viewed Chávez as a rising dictator. They saw Chávez as an impediment to their ascent into the safety and security of modern First World existence (Ellner and Hellinger 2003, 225–26). As I outlined in previous chapters, the Chávez government's efforts to reorganize the oil industry and advance agrarian reform, as well as Chávez's increasingly hostile posture toward the previous governing elites, alienated business groups and the established middle and upper classes. Class conflict had an obvious and overt racialized dimension. Some affluent and middle-class people disdained not only Chávez's policies, but also his colloquial speech, his use of song and narrative, and his informal manner, which many upper-class sectors associated with the darker poor majority. Their intertwining class and racial prejudice solidified into a visceral rejection of Chávez and chavismo. While Chávez's critique of class inequality, his reference to his poor, black, and indigenous roots, and his embodied performance alienated affluent Venezuelans, these same qualities appealed to and inspired the poor, the majority of whom shared Chávez's mixed-race ancestry.

And yet the broad brush strokes that depict chavistas as poor and black and the opposition as middle-class, affluent, and white conceal not only the heterogeneity within each sector, but also the cross-class alliances and conflict that I observed to be vital in shaping the emerging state. Rather than being forged exclusively by poor and historically marginalized Venezuelans, a diverse group of differently positioned actors, including those from the Venezuelan middle class, international intellectual elites, the upwardly mobile poor, and the most marginalized embraced the process of revolutionary state formation under Chávez.[2] While most, but significantly not all, Catia TVe staff and volunteers grew up in poor neighborhoods, middle-class participants, as I described in the previous chapter, were vital to the creation of Catia TVe, lending technological knowledge, grant-writing skills, and fluidity with the history of socialism, Marxism, and media theory. Even while these differently situated actors had unequal access to resources and privilege, they had a joint interest in challenging global capitalism. Nevertheless, their shared political and ideological commitments did not erase inherited patterns of privilege. Moreover, my interlocutors' analyses of the class domination of capitalism often overlooked how racial and gender oppression are integral to the accumulation of capital.

In what follows, I focus my analysis on the cross-class collaboration and conflict that emerged at joint training workshops between Catia TVe producers—the majority of whom lived in Caracas's barrios—and their allies at ViVe TV, most of whom were from middle-class families. As Catia TVe producers joined forces with their counterparts at ViVe TV, they struggled over ideological orientations, organizing symbols, and legitimizing logics. Joint workshops were marked by class distrust and injustice, as well as by cooperation and dialogue. Before I present this ethnographic data, I will first expand on the history of class formation in Venezuela.

Inequality and Class Formation in Venezuela

Changes in the national and global economy over the course of the twentieth century shaped the complex class relations I witnessed in 2006 and 2007 in Caracas. As Clara noted at the outset of the chapter, Venezuela's class history is indelibly shaped by its role as a major exporter of oil. Beginning in the 1920s, the oil industry generated a massive influx of foreign capital. The former agrarian elite, which was predominantly of European descent, monopolized control of this capital to build a commercial base focused on the importation of commodities. As the burgeoning oil economy began to displace agricultural production in the 1920s and '30s, massive numbers of peasants—the descendants primarily of African and indigenous populations—migrated to Venezuela's cities. Although oil workers were successful in demanding high wages through labor unions, only a small percentage of the Venezuelan workforce labored in the oil industry, as oil extraction (as compared with the coal industry, for example) does not require a large workforce (Tinker Salas 2009, 11). Rather than becoming an urban proletariat, by the 1950s rural migrants had shifted from the category of peasant to "other" (Roseberry 1994, 65). They worked short-term jobs in construction, commerce, and service (Roseberry 1994, 69).

A sector of the population grew into a middle class by gaining positions in the private arena of petroleum-related commerce and in the growing state bureaucracy. Given their new roles as technicians, managers, and bureaucrats, this growing middle class exercised a relatively large degree of political power as "upper- and middle-level managers" (Tinker Salas 2009, 11–12). With close ties to American oil companies, this middle sector developed tastes and aspirations for American culture and commodities. The business-owning elites and the middle class saw Caracas's explosive population growth and the self-constructed housing—the *ranchos*—that the new urban poor created as a threat to order and modernity (Velasco 2015, 28–34).

The two major political parties in Venezuela that dominated politics between 1958 and 1999, Acción Democrática and COPEI, mobilized heterogeneous groups of supporters by using oil profits to subsidize food, education, and transportation, while funneling massive resources to the business sector (Roberts 2003, 56–57). Democratic leaders created stability and quelled class conflict by serving both "the consumption demands of the majority and the accumulation demands of private capital" (Smilde 2007, 21). Between the 1950s and the early 1980s, minimal concessions to social and economic equity improved the quality of life in many barrio neighborhoods. The 1970s oil boom expanded job opportunities, and public services improved across classes (Buxton 2003, 115). Middle-class and elite Venezuelans increased their consumption of luxury items, ranging from imported foods to houses in Miami. The poor experienced lowered infant mortality rates, improved access to health care, and higher rates of immunization (Smilde 2007). The poor continued to labor mostly in conditions that some scholars describe as "informal": cleaning middle-class and elite homes; selling food, clothing, and trinkets on the street; and running small, non-capital-intensive businesses out of their homes.

Orthodox Marxist understandings of class as one's relationship to the means of production have been ill-equipped to analyze conditions in Venezuela, where, as in many places, the impoverished and marginalized have not had a straightforward or singular relation with processes of material production and the uneven distribution of profit generated from that production. This is not only because, as feminist scholars have long pointed out, conventional understandings of production exclude the labor of social reproduction, but also because the vast majority of Venezuelan workers have not been industrial workers. Instead, they have been service workers, self-employed merchants, and small entrepreneurs. These groups have formed part of what historian Steve Ellner (2013) calls the "traditionally unorganized and unincorporated sectors" of Venezuelan society.

As I explored in previous chapters, the Venezuelan government's massive development projects of the 1970s fueled widespread expectations that wealth would find its way to all Venezuelans (Ewell 1984, 193). These expectations were quickly dampened by the debt crisis of the early 1980s, which hit the poor the hardest. The turn toward neoliberal austerity and privatization in the 1980s and 1990s undermined what was left of the agricultural base and the fledgling efforts at expanding national industry. A service-based economy solidified as the primary source of employment for the vast majority (Roberts 2003, 60). As the national and international elite imposed structural adjustment policies that made the poor even poorer, the shallow veneer of class harmony and inclusivity violently and vividly dissolved. The bloody Caracazo—the anti-neoliberal uprising of 1989—was perhaps the most blatant expression of the period's class-based violence and injustice.

In Caracas, an already highly class-segregated city, the disparity between the rich and the poor had grown even more pronounced by the end of the neoliberal 1990s. The vast majority of the urban poor remained without legally recognized property, well-resourced schools, or regular municipal services such as water, electricity, or waste collection. The poorest built their homes out of sheets of zinc on squatted hillsides of Caracas, derisively called *los cerros* (the hills). This majority, which included the families of most of the staff and volunteers at Catia TVe, had little access to formal higher education or steady public-sector or private-sector employment. At the same time, encouraged by fear of the growing impoverished masses, middle- and upper-class neighborhoods installed fences and gates around their modern highrises built on more geologically stable land, reverentially referred to as *las colinas* (the hills) (Lander 2007, 22). These fortressed neighborhoods enjoy regular access to electricity, water, and waste management.

While poverty statistics are notoriously politicized, concrete improvements in the quality of poor people's lives under Chávez have been well documented.[3] Many non-cash benefits in health care and education are excluded from standard measurements of poverty, but played a fundamental role in improving quality of life for Venezuela's poorest. Urban and rural social movements advanced initiatives, which were regularly taken up by the Chávez government, to challenge structural inequalities. For example, urban land committees fought for legal title to the government-owned land where barrio inhabitants had built their own homes (Antillano 2005). The poor gained increased access to primary health care and secondary education (Briggs and Mantini-Briggs 2009; Buxton 2011; Cooper 2015). Between 1999 and 2007, the number of primary care physicians working in the public sector increased from 1,628 to 19,571, a rate of more than twelve times (Weisbrot 2008). During the same period, enrollment in higher education increased 86 percent (Weisbrot 2008).

Nevertheless, even while the organized poor joined forces with middle-class and some elite allies to make inroads in challenging structural inequality, capitalist relations of production and dispossession continued to produce economic, social, and political marginalization of the poor. During the time of my research, the professional managerial middle class who remained in control of many official state institutions under Chávez resisted worker control; some of this opposition involved the immense difficulty of such a process, while much of it stemmed from the enormous private appropriation of public finances that continued to occur under Chávez (Azzellini 2015; Hetland 2015; Purcell 2015). Caracas's urban poor continued to work mostly as service workers, self-employed merchants, small entrepreneurs, and, under the social welfare institutions created by the Chávez government, low-paid participants in participatory governance and service-providing programs (Smilde 2011, 5). Many continued to lack social security and labor legislation benefits that accompany formal employment. Millions of people lived in self-constructed concrete and zinc homes on dangerously unstable land.

In other words, the "roofs of cardboard" that the famous leftist Venezuelan singer-songwriter Alí Primera sang about during the oil boom of the 1970s in order to expose the hypocrisy of Venezuelan progress remained. And yet the Chávez government's political discourse made it impossible to continue to sideline the urban and rural poor from political discussions or to perpetuate a myth of class or racial harmony (Coronil 2008). During the first decade of the twenty-first century, activists and allies opened a deep breach in the staid façade of social harmony that created revolutionary optimism about the possibility of change through class struggle.

Joint Catia TVe–ViVe TV Workshops

At the time of my field research in 2007, I found Caracas to be intensely class segregated, more so than New York City, which I call home. Many people from long-established middle-class families have limited experience interacting with people from poor neighborhoods apart from the domestic laborers who work in their homes. For the most part, the middle-class people I met had spent very little time—if any—in barrios. On a number of occasions, they were appalled to learn that I was living in a barrio; many middle-class people were terrified of entering poor neighborhoods, convinced that to do so would put their lives at risk.

Joint television production workshops for state employees at ViVe TV, the newest state channel, and Catia TVe were rare occasions when people from poor and middle-class neighborhoods worked together to collaborate in conditions where they were ostensibly framed as social equals. Although ViVe TV's leadership had made efforts to recruit staff from poor neighborhoods, the majority of ViVe TV's staff continued to be from more privileged middle sectors. Their life opportunities and class habitus differed markedly from those of most of their Catia TVe counterparts. While ViVe TV's middle-class staff learned the principles of television production in traditional film and television schools and on the job working for commercial outlets, most Catia TVe producers first gained access to media production as a tool to engage in political activism.

Joint video production workshops were an explicit attempt on behalf of ViVe TV's leadership to instill revolutionary commitment in their predominantly middle-class staff through their contact with community media producers from poor neighborhoods. Daniel, a video production teacher who led one of the joint workshops that I observed, noted, "The idea is for ViVe TV staff to absorb the vibe [*la nota*] of Catia TVe." In line with tactics employed under previous socialist projects, the masses—in this case Catia TVe producers—were supposed to reeducate ViVe TV's staff.

Cross-class collaborations between ViVe TV and Catia TVe produced some lifelong friendships. ViVe TV attracted a cadre of young middle-class activists from Europe and Latin America, many of whom took up residence in poor neighborhoods, where they formed unusual cross-class neighborly bonds. During the period of my research, members of Catia TVe and ViVe TV staff regularly socialized at a handful of bars, where they shared beers, danced, and gossiped. Although I observed several long-term romantic relationships develop between colleagues, these intimate bonds never crossed class lines, drawing my attention to the enduring limits of cross-class sociality.

As I recounted in the introduction, one of ViVe TV's founding goals, first articulated at the time of its 2003 debut, was to produce educational and cultural programming that highlighted historically disenfranchised populations. Under the leadership of Blanca Eekhout, Catia TVe's original director, and Thierry Deronne, who had been active in community media since the early 1990s, ViVe TV aimed not only to make marginalized sectors the subjects of the station's programming, but also to train the rural and urban poor to make their own media. Eekhout and the middle-class colleagues who joined her in building ViVe TV explicitly privileged a notion of "popular knowledge" as fundamental to the advancement of their state media project. In order to break with the traditional model of dominant television, Thierry Deronne, ViVe TV's vice president, argued that it was necessary to encourage "ongoing socio-political training so that a team of media producers is a revolutionary group at the service of the people, acting as 'organic intellectuals.' A team well equipped in history, economics, sociology, philosophy, etc. would be able to cross their scientific knowledge with popular knowledge in order to generate transformative action before, during, and after a program" (2009, 2–3).[4] Deronne's approach here reflects the broader discourse of the Bolivarian Revolution, which valorized popular knowledge, prioritized nonelite experiences and perspectives, and sought to encourage the development of leaders from the popular class. President Chávez, for his part, insisted that knowledge and culture did not entail "only classroom study in high school or the university, or in the [educational] missions." Rather, he argued that revolutionary knowledge and values involved "the search for knowledge from the countryside, the cerros [hillside shantytowns], the street, and in books" (Chávez 2007, 12). He challenged the privileging of elite formal education as the only legitimate knowledge. This represented a significant departure from established practices in Venezuela, where to be considered a journalist, for example, one needed to be officially credentialed and licensed by exclusive institutions.

What Deronne's vision of integrated multi-class teams that incorporated multiple forms of knowledge overlooked, however, was the difficulty of encouraging traditional middle-class intellectuals to cede power and authority to the "organic" intellectuals of the urban poor. The joint Catia TVe–ViVe TV video production workshops that I observed provided ample material to examine the class conflict over authority and the meaning of popular culture that took place among revolutionary allies. What was immediately clear was the palpable mistrust between class actors and the historic injustices that class inequality had inflicted.

On the second day of a joint video production class held at Catia TVe in October 2006 for ViVe TV staff and Catia TVe producers, Daniel, the workshop leader, was over half an hour late. An event at the presidential palace, located a half mile down the road, left traffic congested for blocks. Cars and crowded buses honked angrily outside Catia TVe's door. Six ViVe TV staff squeezed into Catia TVe's small reception area and patiently waited for Daniel to arrive. They entertained themselves by reading the bulletin boards of Catia TVe's reception area. A flier with a menacing caricature of George W. Bush denounced the neoliberal North American Free Trade Agreement. Another poster advocated solidarity with the people of Bolivia and Palestine. A third celebrated Chávez's presidency with the phrase, "Eight years . . . for now!"

Catia TVe's security guard, a bald man in his early fifties and the father of one of Catia TVe's founders, made conversation with Viviana and Talia, two employees from ViVe TV. Both women were in their mid-twenties. Observing the traffic outside, they speculated about what Chávez might be up to that morning. "Poor thing, he looked exhausted on television last night," Talia said, fidgeting with a long string of colorful wooden beads around her neck. Her jewelry, which looked like it was made by local artisans, was in style at the time among middle-class young people who were aligned with the Bolivarian Revolution. In place of gold or silver accessories, the humble material and local origins of her wooden necklace, just like her presence at Catia TVe that morning, signaled a commitment to a certain understanding of an authentic autochthonous culture.

Rosemery, a Catia TVe volunteer in her early forties, and Jesica, a Catia TVe staff member in her mid-twenties, arrived next with a burst of laughter. They abruptly ended their conversation when they saw that the workshop participants from ViVe TV were already there. After a tepid set of greetings, Rosemery and Jesica scribbled their names quickly on a sign-in sheet. While the ViVe TV staff had to wait to be invited past the reception area, Rosemery and Jesica breezed past us and headed upstairs to Catia TVe's small cafeteria. Before they slipped out of sight, Rosemery turned and beckoned me to follow her, claiming me and granting my passage as a further show of her authority. Rosemery and Jesica's confident display of access and belonging momentarily upended the historic hierarchies between people from the barrios and middle-class employees of state institutions. The poor are usually the ones made to wait (Auyero 2012).

Leaving the ViVe TV staff downstairs, Rosemery, Jesica, and I settled into the plastic chairs in the cafeteria upstairs. After helping ourselves to the pot of hot sugary coffee brewed by one of the two women who work as custodians at Catia TVe, Rosemery turned to discuss the events of the previous day, the first day of the joint ten-day workshop. She rolled her eyes, "*La gorda* from ViVe TV thinks she's so superior, no?" Jesica and I nodded our heads, agreeing that Viviana, a plump woman from ViVe TV whom Rosemery had bitingly dubbed la gorda or "the fat one," seemed to have an air of entitlement.[5] "They don't even recognize that Catia TVe is the mother of ViVe!" Rosemery complained. Her kinship metaphor, which referred to Catia TVe's role in the creation of ViVe TV, expressed her view that Catia TVe should not feel beholden or inferior to middle-class media producers employed by central state institutions; rather, from Rosemery's perspective, the state channel and its employees should pay deference to Catia TVe. Her discussion of Viviana's sense of entitlement and the lack of respect that she felt ViVe TV staff had extended to Catia TVe producers served Rosemery as an "alternative vocabulary" to discuss the class tensions that emerged on the first day of the workshop (Walley 2013, 8).

Rosemery's criticism of Viviana and her defensiveness at any perceived slight were shaped by her many experiences of social exclusion. In the previous few months, I had spent several evenings with Rosemery in the tiny apartment that she shared with her two daughters in Manicomio, the neighborhood where Catia TVe got its start. In her late thirties, Rosemery was unemployed at the time. She explained to me that her sporadic participation at Catia TVe was a welcome distraction from the depression she had suffered since her husband was killed five years earlier in a random shooting in the barrio. Rosemery recounted several times to me how the commercial media misreported her husband's murder as an *ajuste de cuentas* (a settling of accounts), suggesting that her late husband was a participant in gang warfare. Rosemery insisted that his murder had been random and unprovoked. The social stigmatization of the poor who inhabited Caracas's barrios as criminals usually served to justify relations of domination (Antillano 2013, 589). The commercial media's narrative deeply upset Rosemery. While I often heard people at Catia TVe identify commercial media as the "enemy" and complain about its discriminatory coverage of poor neighborhoods, Rosemery's anger toward the private media had a particular kind of intensity. The media workers who had once stigmatized Rosemery and her family were part of the same middle-class social milieu as many staff members at ViVe TV. Her experience of the loss of her husband, compounded by its misrepresentation, informed her distrust of ViVe TV staff members.

Class Injuries and Performances

In Venezuela, as in many contexts, distinct knowledge, skills, and tastes produced through access to wealth have helped to legitimize economic inequalities by making it appear that power hierarchies are based on merit. To be sure, the middle class do not stay middle class only because they have particular kinds of cultural capital. But elite knowledge and skills help to justify their leadership and grant them insight into how to best benefit in the shifting symbolic and material economies that order life. At joint workshops, I observed how Rosemery and her Catia TVe colleagues' lack of middle-class cultural capital inflicted what Richard Sennet and Jonathon Cobb (1993) call the "hidden injuries of class." These injuries included a "feeling of vulnerability in contrasting oneself to others at a higher social level, the buried sense of inadequacy" (Bettie 2003, 43). Catia TVe producers at times defended themselves from these injuries and, at other times, uncomfortably tolerated the reassertion of class-based stigma and hierarchy.

It fell to Daniel, the workshop facilitator, to bridge the gap between Catia TVe and ViVe TV producers during the weeklong training for new television producers. Daniel was a documentary film professor in Belgium in his early forties, whose family had fled Pinochet's Chile when Daniel was four years old. He had light skin and fine light-brown wavy hair. This was his fourth trip to Venezuela at the invitation of ViVe TV's internal filmmaking school. As he explained to the workshop participants, "I'm here to support the Venezuelan process and pick up a thread broken in Chile." Daniel saw his engagement with ViVe TV as a way to contribute to the long struggle to build socialism in Latin America. Initially, Daniel's outsider status as a foreigner seemed to exempt him from the dynamics of class tension apparent between Catia TVe and ViVe TV producers. Daniel's passionate embrace of the Bolivarian Revolution allowed him to establish rapport quickly with both cohorts of students. Aspects of Daniel's relatively privileged upbringing overlapped with the Venezuelan middle-class folks from ViVe TV, while his leftist militancy created affinity with Catia TVe producers. Daniel's international mobility and access to formal documentary film training granted him authority over both groups. Yet, despite the camaraderie he established, Daniel struggled to maintain favor with both groups at once. The histories of class injury and disparate access to cultural and financial capital proved to be formidable challenges to easy collaboration.

Early in the weeklong workshop, we assembled our metal chairs into a semicircle around a twelve-inch television in Catia TVe's windowless basement classroom. Unforgiving fluorescent lights glared down from a low ceiling. Daniel screened short clips from an eclectic film oeuvre. He urged the class to establish intimate relationships with their subjects as French ethnographic filmmaker Jean Rouch had done, to grapple with revolutionary contradictions following the model of Mikhail Kalatozov's 1963 Soviet–Cuban film *Soy Cuba*, and to be attentive to details of frame composition in the tradition of British filmmaker Alfred Hitchcock. Viviana—whom Rosemery from Catia TVe had dubbed "the fat one"—made a show of taking feverish notes of Daniel's lecture, loudly turning the pages of her notebook. The Catia TVe producers in the room, none of whom had finished high school, did not take notes.

We watched a long clip from Hitchcock's 1960 film *Psycho*. "Notice," Daniel instructed, "not a single camera movement, cut, or frame is gratuitous. Everything is well thought out. It all builds to tell a story." Augosto, a Catia

TVe volunteer, repositioned his chair to have a better view of the small television screen. In his mid-forties, Augosto's many years of heavy smoking and drinking made him look far older. Augusto was just completing his high school diploma through one of the government's new educational programs. We watched several minutes of an early scene in Hitchcock's film, which included some quick dialogue. "*Coño,*" Augosto muttered, "it's too quick." It took me a moment to understand that Augosto was having trouble reading the subtitles. While he was certainly literate, Augosto did not read quickly.

When the clip ended, Harlan, a ViVe TV staff member in his early twenties who had studied communications at the Central University of Venezuela, raised his hand and asked Daniel his opinion about a different Hitchcock film, *Rope*. Rosemery from Catia TVe sighed loudly, making no effort to disguise her boredom. She conspicuously pulled out the cell phone she had lodged in her cleavage and began to compose a text message. Even while Daniel insisted that they use the tools of film to upend historic inequalities, his teaching style and materials often favored the middle-class people in the room—the ViVe TV staff—who were highly literate and familiar with the film canon he introduced. The ViVe TV staff's skill set and tastes, honed in middle-class households and institutions, made them comfortable and well equipped to participate in the conversation. Rosemery and her Catia TVe mates were subtly disqualified from aspects of Daniel's lesson. Rosemary's disinterest was a symptom of class injury; she was bored because she was excluded from the conversation. Her explicit performance of apathy and disrespect—the loud sigh and text messaging—was a way for Rosemery to reject this marginalization.

Daniel briefly addressed Harlan's question about Hitchcock, but, sensing that he was losing some of his audience, he moved on to express his passionate vision for revolutionary television. He noted, "You see, we can't reproduce what already exists! We have to reinvent our language, our values, with our ideas. We can't simply make an RCTV [the prominent commercial station] of the left. That's not what we're about. . . . We need to invent a new language, reappropriate the media and revolutionize it!" Daniel challenged his students to think more boldly about how to rework established approaches to television production. Reinvention was a central concept for Daniel, as for many advocates of the Bolivarian Revolution. Yet even as he pushed for new ways of thinking during his video production class, he subtly reproduced long-standing class hierarchies. At these cross-class workshops, middle-class participants subtly enacted and legitimized their power.

FIGURE 3.1. Catia TVe video production workshop, April 1, 2007. Photo by the author.

Popular Class Stigma

Catia TVe producers' authority was undercut not only by the ViVe TV's staff performance of competency, but also by how Daniel approached popular culture and knowledge. This became clear when Daniel shifted gears to involve the students in hands-on filmmaking. He sent the class into the streets with small camcorders, asking each of them to tell a story in three long film takes. When we returned, sweaty from the blazing Caracas sunshine, we spent several hours reviewing the footage.

We began by examining the scene that Jesica, Catia TVe's newest staff member, had shot. Jesica was the daughter of Colombian migrants to Venezuela. In her mid-twenties, she had brown skin, jet-black eyebrows, and straight dark hair. Although she explained to me shortly after we first met that her minimum-wage paycheck was a much-needed addition to her parents' household, she sheepishly confided that she had devoted much of her first earnings to a new MP3 music player, which she loaded up with salsa, some reggaeton (a musical genre that combines reggae, dancehall, and hip-hop), and a smattering of American pop music.

Daniel lavished praise on Jesica's footage. She had filmed a long line of people waiting for public transportation on the side of a street that was densely packed with vendors hawking inexpensive clothing made in Asia, fried foods, phone services, and pirated music. Daniel's discussion of Jesica's footage celebrated what he deemed authentic representations of the lives and experiences of the people (el pueblo).

Daniel paused the playback, freezing the film on the image of six women grasping multiple shopping bags, with several children in tow. He asked Jesica, "What do you see?"

"Well, people [*gente*]?" Jesica responded hesitantly.

"But they are just any people [gente] in any place?" Daniel encouraged Jesica to continue.

"No, they are going to my community," Jesica answered, referring to the barrio where she lived in the west of the city.

"What do we learn about these people [gente] by how they look?" Daniel prodded. "Are they middle-class people?" His question hung in the air. All eyes in the room rested heavily on Jesica. She laughed awkwardly and pulled down on her tight black T-shirt, which read in English "The Night Queen: Fashion Girl." After a moment of uncomfortable silence, Agosto intervened to ask Daniel a technical question about the camera. The question of Jesica's class status was left unanswered. The conversation moved on.

Although Catia TVe leaders and producers often celebrate their popular class perspective and belonging (as I explore in the next chapter), Jesica, clearly embarrassed, refused to answer Daniel's question concerning the class status of the people from her neighborhood. While she referred to them as *gente*, literally people, Daniel invoked the term *el pueblo*, which, as I explore in depth in the next chapter, means "the people" and often connotes the oppressed, noble, united majority. As I understood it, Daniel was encouraging Jesica to characterize her neighbors as representatives of the popular classes—objects of reverence, for sure—but also distanced ideal noble types, the perfect material for revolutionary television. His explicit attention to Jesica's popular barrio origins in "mixed" class company was potentially a stigmatizing practice, given that barrios were so often equated in mainstream discourse with violence and disorder. Many view poverty as a sign of inferiority, not structural inequality. Jesica, in other words, had much to lose in being classified as poor. Moreover, she had aspirations to leave behind the poverty of her community. Being forced to endure long lines to catch a crowded bus in order to make her way home from a harried experience of bargain shopping, all the while weighted down by several children, was an experience Jesica wanted to escape, not celebrate.

Daniel and the workshop participants did not address the interrelationships of racialized, gendered, and class oppression, or the practice of shaming that often accompanies poverty. Instead, Daniel promoted a symbolic economy that privileged the heroism and authenticity of the revolutionary urban poor. His approach existed alongside a long-standing symbolic order that associated the barrios with depravity. Neither set of symbols provided Jesica a solid foundation to assert her own authority and knowledge.

While I have highlighted moments of class conflict that emerged during the workshop, I would be remiss if I did not also point to moments of collaboration and mutual recognition. A mock dialogue that participants in the workshop produced between a Catia TVe producer assuming the perspective of a chavista and one of ViVe TV's staff pretending to be a member of the political opposition to the revolution proved particularly unifying as it highlighted their shared commitment to the Bolivarian Revolution.

Informal conversations that unfolded outside the classroom were perhaps the most successful in building trust between some ViVe TV and Catia TVe producers. One woman from ViVe TV, named Talia, joined Daniel and the group from Catia TVe in celebrating the end of the workshop with a long evening of drinking beer at a local barrio bar. Talia complained that she was disappointed by her ViVe TV colleagues' lack of political commitment. Daniel echoed Talia's observation, adding that he thought that Catia TVe producers were more dedicated to the revolution. He noted that ViVe TV workers were just in it for a paycheck. "That's right!" Rosemery cheered, raising her beer, happy to celebrate her Catia TVe colleagues' revolutionary commitment.

Daniel and Talia affirmed the importance of Catia TVe's work and held up Catia TVe staff and volunteers as models for their middle-class counterparts. Yet this reverence over-idealized Catia TVe producers, misrepresenting them as untroubled by internal struggles for power and unmotivated by individual economic need or desire for upward mobility. Catia TVe producers were, in fact, divided by unequal access to resources and control. Although Catia TVe's claim to be the authentic foundation of the new officially sanctioned approach to revolutionary televisual culture was a way to challenge the experience of degradation and the hidden injuries of class, this romanticized portrayal of Catia TVe producers left little room to explore the problems and power struggles within Catia TVe. The story of the purity of Catia TVe producers' political commitment denied the complexity of their motivations and their equality with their middle-class counterparts.

Defining Popular Culture

In her 2001 coauthored undergraduate thesis, Blanca Eekhout observes, "Television has displaced most activities that make up people's pastimes in the communities [poor neighborhoods]. Traditions, customs, meeting spaces, identities, and belonging have been replaced by mass culture" (Eekhout and Fuentes 2001, 479). Global mass media, according to Blanca and her coauthor Gabriela Fuentes, had all but destroyed traditional culture in Manicomio, the barrio where Catia TVe originated. Although they acknowledge the complexity of popular culture, noting that "We do not intend to sustain an idyllic vision of the popular" (Eekhout and Fuentes 2001, 34), their analysis of the impacts of global mass media on poor communities contains certain blind spots. Notably, they overlook not only how barrio inhabitants themselves understand mass commercial media, but also how the traditional Venezuelan cultures that Blanca and others lament as having been lost were, in fact, themselves products of colonial histories, capitalist relations, previous nation-building projects, and deep inequalities of race and gender (Garcia Canclini 2001; Martín-Barbero 1993; Yúdice 2003).

As a founding member of Catia TVe, president of ViVe TV, and later minister of communications and National Assembly member, Blanca's analysis represents an important strain of thinking among middle-class intellectuals involved in the Bolivarian Revolution. State officials and barrio-based organizers veered between what Stuart Hall has identified as the two poles of "pure 'autonomy'" from the degradation of commercial mass culture industries and "total encapsulation" of local culture by foreign influence (1998, 447). Despite Blanca's radical leftist political orientation, her inclination to define authentic or pure popular culture as an ideally local and autonomous form of national culture reproduced historic efforts by the middle-class sectors and elites to summon an authentic basis for their political projects and leadership.[6]

As early as the 1920s, young Venezuelan elites involved in an incipient student movement for democracy argued that the true essence of "the people," and the foundation of genuine Venezuelan identity, could be found in the popular masses, the poor, indigenous, black, and mixed-race groups that populated the countryside (Skurski 1993, 180). As elsewhere in Latin America, elite nation builders and folklorists invoked popular culture as a nostalgic marker of an imagined tradition uncorrupted by urbanization, colonialism, and imperialist modernity (Abercrombie 1998; García Canclini 1995). In fact, far from being "precapitalist," large sectors of the Venezuelan peasantry had long been engaged in coffee and cacao economies and were affected by fluctuations in the world market (Roseberry 1994, 60). Nevertheless, ruling elites have approached popular culture as if it had a "primordial solidity" (Joseph and Nugent 1994, 16) that developed unconnected to dominant cultures. This search for a national authentic subaltern culture ultimately bolstered existing hierarchies of class, color, and nation.

Delineating who had authority to define and identify the culture of the poor or popular class proved to be central in the struggle for power over the Bolivarian Revolution's new experiments in television. At stake in the collaborative workshop between Catia TVe and ViVe TV producers was whether the valorization of popular knowledge and culture would produce a romanticized objectification of the poor or would account for their complex and contradictory social existence.

The effort to identify, salvage, and celebrate traditional subaltern culture emerged repeatedly during the joint Catia TVe–ViVe TV workshop. When we reviewed footage shot by Agosto, a Catia TVe volunteer, Daniel, the workshop instructor, was adamant about defining popular culture. Agosto had filmed a street performer in the Plaza Bolivar who remained eerily still until someone placed a bill in his bucket, which was labeled with a hand-printed sign that read "popular artist." Pausing the tape, Daniel scoffed at the notion that this man was a popular artist, noting that he had seen similar performances in several European cities. His comment highlighted not only his own social mobility and class privilege, but also his assumption that popular culture was national culture. In contrast to the street performer, Daniel praised footage one group had taken of a stooped elderly woman who was making *arepas* out of a cart on the street. These small corn cakes are a staple in the Venezuelan diet. "*This* is the popular," Daniel declared. He encouraged the group to understand popular culture as national in origin and seemingly uncontaminated by mass mediated international flows. "Does popular wisdom [*sabiduría popular*] exist?" Daniel asked. He quickly answered his own question, "Yes, it exists. We have to evaluate it. We have to learn how to see it, detect it." Despite his invocation of "we," Daniel positioned himself as having the necessary expertise to "detect" popular culture and knowledge. He did not create space for anyone in the room who enjoyed Agosto's street performers to express their own "wisdom."

For Daniel, popular culture and wisdom encompassed practices and traditions that seemed firmly rooted in Venezuela's rural past. He also celebrated the gritty everyday experiences and related knowledge of the urban poor, insofar as those experiences did not betray too explicitly the influence of globalized mass culture. Daniel's approach to popular culture as the authentic culture of the poor was undoubtedly part of a broader effort to challenge historic patterns, shaped by racism and classism, which dismissed the poor as abject and vulgar. Daniel's veneration threatened to solidify into a form of invention and idealization that dismissed the complexity of people's lives and relegated them to the past. For one thing, this celebration of popular culture overlooked popular forms of racism, sexism, homophobia, and nativism (Mukerji and Schudson 1991, 36). Daniel's approach reproduced a binary opposition between "pure autonomy" from mass culture industries and "total encapsulation" of local culture by foreign influence.

Rejecting Reggaeton and Telenovelas: The Dubious Strategy of Cultural Essentialism

It is important to note that Daniel and his middle-class counterparts at ViVe TV were not alone in drawing a stark boundary between mass mediated capitalist culture and popular national culture. An effort to jettison poor people's engagement with globalized media formed an important part of Catia TVe producers' discourse. During Catia TVe's frequent outreach campaigns at crowded high schools, noisy barrio patios, carpeted international conference rooms, and at their own television station, Catia TVe staff and volunteers underscored how community media made it possible to revive their cultural mores and learn their own history after decades of capitalist mass media indoctrination. They consistently emphasized the importance of "rescuing their culture" from elite and foreign domination. Carlos, Catia TVe's director, often spoke passionately about how Caracas's urban poor had been taught to see elite culture and foreign commodities as superior, drink Coca-Cola, desire straight hair and light skin, and watch Latin American soap operas that denigrated or whitewashed the experiences of the poor. This critique was rooted in a rejection of the racism and classism that barrio inhabitants constantly faced. Yet Carlos's description of the poor overlooked important complexities.

Even as Carlos lamented the impacts of capitalist culture on the lives of the poor, Carlos insisted that unlike the Venezuelan elites who—buoyed by oil wealth—had forever traded their authentic national identity for Western values, consumerism, and modernity, the poor remain rooted in their authentic traditions. Producing their own television, Carlos explained, would allow people to reclaim their "true" identities. He argued for attention to specific dances like the joropo, foods such as *papelón con limón* (a drink of raw sugar and lemon), and music for the *cuatro*, a Venezuelan musical instrument similar to a ukulele. These cultural practices, associated with the rural countryside, served as an invaluable touchstone for Carlos and for many barrio inhabitants, particularly the older generations. Declaring that the urban poor had their own authentic cultural practices was a way to assert the worth and creativity of the barrios outside the oppressive logics that valued middle-class consumption and whiteness. Nevertheless, many of the cultural practices they upheld as pure and autonomous were themselves formed in the crucible of European settler colonialism and capitalist expansion. The characterization of the authentic practices of the poor as pure and original denied acknowledgment of how oppressed peoples have long adopted, modified, and blended different traditions and influences, generally not in conditions of their own choosing.

The particularly strenuous rejection of two particular forms of mass mediated culture, reggaeton and telenovelas, highlighted the pitfalls of an approach to popular culture that excludes such negotiations and hybridization. During the same Catia TVe–ViVe TV joint workshop that I have recounted above, Jhonny, a long-time Catia TVe volunteer in his mid-forties from a poor neighborhood, harshly criticized the material that one participant from ViVe TV had shot of young black men on a nearby basketball court dancing to reggaeton. "Listen, we shouldn't be promoting that crap music," Jhonny insisted. He argued that reggaeton did not represent Venezuelan culture or popular art, asserting his authority over that of his middle-class ViVe TV counterparts to detect and define popular culture. Jhonny maintained that reggaeton encouraged violence and depravity. He dismissed the pleasure and identification that many young people experienced with reggaeton. Jesica, who I knew listened to some reggaeton and enjoyed it, did not contribute her perspective to this discussion.

Although scholars and many fans approach reggaeton as a "trans-Caribbean" genre "whose history and aesthetics do not abide by nation and language as chief organizing principles" (Rivera, Marshall, and Hernandez 2009, 11), many Catia TVe producers saw reggaeton as a symbol of "Yankee" domination. They disliked the overt sexuality and its close relationship to American rap and hip-hop, which they associated with celebration of the drug trade. The vehemence with which Jhonny and many producers at Catia TVe rejected reggaeton was striking. For them, the sudden ubiquity of reggaeton's throbbing beat in Caracas's barrios in the mid-2000s signaled the total saturation of poor communities by an immoral capitalist culture that promoted the depraved values that, many in the middle and elite classes claimed, originated in poor neighborhoods. Their experiences in poor neighborhoods, where drug wars and addiction have taken many lives and disrupted the ability of the poor to organize their communities, shaped their fervent rejection of these new musical genres and youth cultures. Nevertheless, Catia TVe producers' disdain for reggaeton unwittingly reproduced middle-class and elite discourse that poverty and delinquency among young men was attributable to "vulgar" cultural forms rather than to the structural inequalities of classism, racism, and patriarchal heterosexism. There was little exploration of how globalized cultural forms combine complicity with and resistance to capitalist commercial forces and domination.

While I understood Catia TVe producers' rejection of reggaeton as an effort to escape the stigma of criminality, it also signaled their disidentification with diasporic black culture. While Catia TVe producers dismissed traditional understandings of Venezuela as a harmonious *café con leche* mestizo nation, the blackness (and Indianness) that they embraced was largely historical, tied to saints and historic black heroes. Catia TVe producers were eager to document and broadcast urban fiestas and religious celebrations that activists explicitly linked to their black and enslaved ancestors. The recreations and interpretations of traditional celebrations and religious fiestas, such as the celebration of San Juan in the Caracas parish of San Agustín, allowed the urban poor to connect contemporary antiracist and classist struggles to the past (Fernandes 2010b, 125). These connections, as Fernandes has described, serve as a foundation from which to make claims for resources (Fernandes 2010b, 158). But while Jhonny and the leadership at Catia TVe often expressed pride in how traditional Venezuelan culture was influenced by their African ancestry, they rejected links with a kind of "modern blackness" (Thomas 2004) that a genre like reggaeton makes possible for many enthusiasts.

Catia TVe producers' embrace of what they understood as their authentic culture was an effort to reject intertwining class and race domination, yet it paradoxically reproduced nationalist and racist logics. Ultimately, their rejection of reggaeton and suspicion of rap and hip-hop culture compromised their success in sustaining the participation of young people at Catia TVe, particularly young black men, who form the most marginalized sectors of the urban poor. Catia TVe's leadership often labeled young people who adopted reggaeton and hip-hop clothing and hairstyles as *marihuaneros*— pot-smoking stoners who lacked a revolutionary commitment and analysis. During the time of my research, they regularly discouraged Catia TVe staff and volunteers from including rap and reggaeton music in their productions. I observed Catia TVe leadership exclude young people who displayed such styles from one of the station's free video production classes.

Telenovelas were another favorite target of disdain for Catia TVe producers. Telenovelas are melodramatic serial programs much like soap operas in the United States, but with some key differences. Most telenovelas in Venezuela and elsewhere in Latin America are broadcast during prime-time evening hours and are often the highest-rated programming among both women and men. Middle-class and elite intellectuals have long scorned the popularity of telenovelas in ways that indicate a paternalistic air of superiority. Although Catia TVe producers' condemnation of telenovelas focused predominantly on the genre's celebration of elite lives, consumerism, and its class-harmonious conclusions, their approach also contained traces of a condescending dismissal of the tastes of the masses. Despite this open disdain, many chavistas I knew were ardent telenovela viewers.

The gap between their harsh analysis of telenovelas and the ongoing pleasure that people experienced watching them came to the fore one afternoon in early 2007. At a meeting held at Catia TVe for about fifty people from the surrounding poor neighborhoods, Hector, Catia TVe's assistant director, expressed his disgust for the ongoing popularity of telenovelas. He noted,

> There are still a lot of the people who see Chávez and scream in excitement who also scream for nightly telenovelas on some of these [commercial] channels. They are *still* watching telenovelas. So we [Catia TVe] provide a type of education where we begin to tell people, "Look, pull yourself away from there," because they [the telenovelas] have a certain intention. There's always the story about the poor girl who gets married to the rich guy. So there's always that hope and there's no need to fight for the revolution or anything like that. You can just wait for your prince. They always repeat the same story.

Hector's contempt for telenovelas included the assumption that poor audiences—particularly women—are passive receivers of telenovelas' messages. Echoing the critique of cultural imperialism first advanced in the 1970s (Dorfman and Mattelart 1975), Hector assumed that televisual messages have direct and obvious effects.

As Hector finished his commentary against telenovelas, a woman sitting behind me in Catia TVe's small auditorium whispered to another woman sitting beside her, "Did you hear that *la negrita* [the little black woman] died last night on *Blessed City*?" Her seatmate whispered in feigned shock, "No!"

Both women chuckled quietly. *Blessed City* (*Ciudad Bendita*) was a telenovela broadcast during evening prime time on Venevisión, a commercial television station. In one of the telenovela's many subplots, a character played by an Afro-Venezuelan actress had met her untimely end during the previous evening's episode. The few black characters who appeared in telenovelas always seemed to make an early exit.

The women's exchange about this juicy plot development on *Blessed City* contradicted Hector's assertion that women who enjoyed telenovelas would be lulled into waiting for a wealthy man to solve their problems rather than participating in local politics. Although Hector argued that support for Chávez and interest in telenovelas were contradictory, the experiences of his audience did not sustain this critique. These women were devoted community organizers and telenovela viewers. Hector's assessment overlooked how media reception is a field of ideological struggle. His analysis was disconnected from the complexity of people's experiences as audiences.[7]

Although Catia TVe's leadership approached the process of media production as a weapon for barrio producers in the ongoing political struggle, they dismissed poor people's enjoyment of commercial television as a symptom of ruling-class domination. Alongside their deep belief in the creative forces of the poor, they held an abiding assumption that barrio inhabitants were passive viewers of elite and foreign media. And like Catia TVe producers' dismissal of reggaeton, their analysis of telenovelas did not account for the ways that most people's lives are characterized by an eclectic blending of cultural material drawn from a wide variety of sources. Hector himself was an avid consumer of commercial satellite television and Hollywood films, as well as the collected works of Marx and Lenin. By overlooking their own day-to-day practices that included contradictory desires and pleasures, Catia TVe producers and their middle-class interlocutors obscured how meaning is a product of struggle shaped by people's experiences and perspectives. Moreover, their nationalist framework for popular culture and their rejection of what they understood as foreign influences cut them off from global solidarities.

Catia TVe's leaders' assertion of the essential or primordial nature of popular culture recalls the dilemma that Beth Conklin (1997) observed in the late 1990s, wherein indigenous groups in Latin America employed a "pragmatic politics" that relied on reproducing an essentialist understanding of their culture in order to gain the visibility and support necessary for survival. Cultural essentialism is sometimes an expedient path to win resources and rights. But it portends further marginalization by reinforcing ideas that indigenous peoples are non-modern, homogenous, and outside of history. Catia TVe's leadership posited a primordial culture of the poor as a way to resist the racism and classism of dominant cultural forms and to claim authority. Although cultural essentialism had short-term rewards, it provided a dubious foundation for the poor to assert themselves as leaders in the long-term struggle for equality and justice.

Struggling for Authority over Popular Communication at ViVe TV

"I remember when this place had just a few walls and chairs," Margarita commented to me, as we arrived at ViVe TV's headquarters. The station was housed on the fourth floor of the National Library, a vast modernist structure of poured concrete nestled at the base of the Avila mountain range just a few blocks north of Caracas's Plaza Bolivar. Margarita and I arrived at ViVe TV that afternoon to attend a weeklong joint workshop for ViVe TV and Catia TVe staff members. Unlike Daniel's workshop, which I described above, this collaborative workshop prompted Catia TVe and ViVe TV producers to address the class inequalities that boiled just beneath the surface. This workshop provided an opportunity to assert barrio-based leadership and allowed Catia TVe staff to define popular culture as everyday practice, rather than as a revitalized authentic tradition.

Margarita invited me to accompany her to the workshop that week, and I eagerly accepted. In her early forties, Margarita was an ardent community activist and one of Catia TVe's first volunteers. She lived with her extended family, many of whom also participated at Catia TVe, in a barrio high in the hills of west Caracas. At ViVe TV's reception desk, a young man inspected our identification cards and gave us ViVe TV visitor passes to hang around our necks. We passed through a metal turnstile and entered the station. Margarita paused just outside a glass-encased television studio, where a live news program was being filmed, to chat with a ViVe TV staff member whom she knew. Having only been inside ViVe TV a handful of times, I was mesmerized by the behind-the-scenes labor of the news program. Margarita was nonchalant; the inner workings of the state station were, by this time, familiar to her. The ease with which she moved through this official state television station reminded me that despite the challenges that arose in Catia TVe's collaboration with ViVe TV's staff, the political changes created by the Bolivarian Revolution granted unprecedented openings for popular participation in the production of nationally broadcast state-run media.

Margarita led the way to a cavernous television studio where Gregorio and Antony, two other staff members from Catia TVe, and seven ViVe TV staff were already gathered. Unlike Daniel's workshop, which was pitched at beginners, the aim of this workshop was to train already experienced television producers to lead their own workshops. All of the participants had years of experience producing television at their respective stations. Margarita's younger Catia TVe colleagues Gregorio and Antony had not yet led their own workshops for new volunteers. Margarita had over five years' experience leading training workshops in poor urban communities.

In his late twenties, Nicholas, the workshop leader and ViVe TV staff member, had moved to Caracas from Paris five years earlier. He was among a cadre of young women and men from Europe and Latin America who had initially traveled to Venezuela to learn more about the Bolivarian movement. Finding new state institutions eager to hire trained professionals who were sympathetic to the leftist project, many of these young people found employment and decided to stay. Unlike Daniel, the Belgian-Chilean workshop leader described above, Nicholas lived year-round in Caracas, where he rented a small apartment in a poor neighborhood. In his previous few years of work with ViVe TV's internal filmmaking school, Nicholas had given countless media training workshops not only to the staff at ViVe TV, but also to groups of community organizers across Venezuela. ViVe TV's effort to spread or "massify" community media practices was thoroughly shaped by the presence of these international socially mobile immigrants. Nicholas's long-term engagement with ViVe TV allowed him to become privy to the complex negotiations around class privilege that the new state project entailed.

Class tensions between Catia TVe staff and ViVe TV staff surfaced at the outset of the workshop. A young man from ViVe TV spelled a word incorrectly on the dry-erase board at the front of the room. Quickly erasing his perfect handwriting, which was one of the many embodied signs of middle-class privilege that ViVe TV producers possessed, he made a joke that he was a student in Misión Robinson, the government program that teaches basic literacy.[8] In response, a woman from ViVe TV turned toward the Catia TVe staff and remarked apologetically, "People from Catia, ignore this! This is what we are like at ViVe." Her declaration indicated an awareness that his joke could be interpreted as a sign of elite disparagement of the uneducated poor. Her command to ignore her colleague's comment was meant as an apology and an indictment of the class chauvinism of ViVe TV workers, but it served to draw attention to the class lines between the two stations.

Margarita, who at the age of thirty-nine had finished her high school diploma through the Chávez government's program in secondary education (Misión Ribas), noted in response, "No one should be embarrassed. We all make mistakes." Margarita's comment momentarily eased the tension by excusing the ViVe TV employee's flippant remark as a cover for his insecurity. The class tension between the two cohorts remained a steady feature of the weeklong workshop.

Nicholas broke the participants into groups to discuss how to create a lesson plan to teach different filmmaking concepts, including narrative structure, sound, and editing. I joined Margarita's group of four, which included her and three ViVe TV staff members, in their discussion of how to teach narrative structure. Carolina, a ViVe TV employee, suggested that they begin by explaining the various components of a narrative, which, she confidently noted, included "main characters, an objective, an obstacle, conflict, and a resolution." Margarita interrupted Carolina mid-sentence: "You can't just begin that way because people won't understand what you're talking about." Carolina disagreed. But rather than backing down, Margarita quickly responded, "Look, have you ever given workshops in popular communication? It's really not that easy."

Carolina froze, taken aback. She paused to study Margarita. Her eyes traveled up Margarita's forehead to the gray roots peeking through her magenta-dyed hair. Margarita wore a tight synthetic pink T-shirt, matching beaded earrings, and a headband. Her eyebrows were drawn with a dark-red pencil. In contrast, Carolina's hair was arranged in a perky bob of what seemed like professionally dyed chunks of blond and brown locks. She had on minimal makeup and a tailored cotton blouse. Carolina's skin was several shades lighter than Margarita's. Roughly the same age, their different styles indexed their differing class-based tastes and disposable income. Carolina backed down, "Well, it's you who knows; you obviously have the experience."

Margarita assumed leadership of the discussion. She insisted that rather than teach abstract categories, they should instead invite people to tell their stories about struggles in their communities. As an example, she recounted how her neighbors had cleaned up an area that had become an informal trash dump in order to create a basketball court for their sons. "See how there's a beginning, middle, and end? There's conflict and then there's what you called a 'resolution.'" For Margarita, teaching popular participation in media production demanded focusing first and foremost on people's experiences with community organizing rather than on the technical components that make up narrative structure. Margarita claimed that people like her, who have dealt with and challenged oppression, would be brimming with stories to tell. Moreover, these stories, she argued, would contain the necessary narrative components and analytical perspective. Margarita insisted on replacing Carolina's formal approach to narrative not with traditional folktales or other widely accepted representations of static popular culture, but with the experiences of everyday life in poor neighborhoods, which included a globalized pastime, basketball, that many in Caracas associated with African Americans. Carolina nodded her head in agreement and took notes in a small spiral notebook.

Margarita's knowledge and familiarity with teaching media production to poor and oppressed communities emboldened her to object to Carolina's approach and take charge of the discussion. Their interaction was influenced not only by their individual personalities and experiences but also by the power hierarchies and changing institutional structures in which they were embedded. The broader political environment of official and activist projects to assert the centrality of popular knowledge bolstered Margarita's authority. While the class and racial differences were stark, they shared the position as students in the context of an officially sanctioned workshop to teach popular methods of media production. These factors contributed to Margarita's ability to challenge Carolina's authority and the historic privileging of elite knowledge as naturally superior. For Carolina's part, her acquiescence to Margarita signaled a willingness to retreat, at least momentarily, from a position of privilege and to respect Margarita's leadership. It was a brief but nevertheless significant moment of confrontation over authority and class power. Their dialogic development of ideas represented precisely the kind of collaboration that ViVe TV and Catia TVe leaders hoped to stimulate through their joint workshops.

As the workshop drew to a close, Nicholas asked people to reflect on what they had learned. First he shared that he thought that Catia TVe's staff was more politically engaged than ViVe TV's, echoing what I heard in the first workshop I described in this chapter. Turning to the ViVe TV staff in the room, he noted, "You have to insist on the commitment with all your colleagues." A young woman staff member from ViVe TV noted, "The comrades from Catia have allowed us to see that there are many alienating things at ViVe. Everyone is here to get paid. They are far from being politically committed." Margarita, Gregorio, and Antony remained silent about the ongoing conflict at Catia TVe between volunteers and the paid staff about how resources were distributed.

Nicholas steered the conversation to address the problems that shaped ViVe TV's commitment to challenging class exclusion at the television station. He noted,

> At least now there are more people working at ViVe from the communities [poor neighborhoods]. But it's hard to employ people from the communities because the schedule is really demanding. If people have kids or lots of family, it's difficult to travel or work fifteen hours a day. But also there are a lot of class issues. People who have come here from the barrios have had a difficult time fitting in and haven't been integrated well. They've been ostracized or ignored because of their style or the way they speak. And they leave because they aren't integrating socially.

Gregorio from Catia TVe immediately responded, "Or people from the barrios [who begin working at ViVe TV] simply change their style and how they are to fit in here." Gregorio's comment acknowledged that most often, rather than middle-class people at official state institutions changing their practices to sustain widespread participation, the few people from poor neighborhoods who worked at ViVe TV had to adjust their lives to adapt to the demands and ways of being of their middle-class colleagues as best they could, or leave their positions.

Nicholas concluded the workshop by stating, "We all need to be aware of these problems so that we keep working hard to not reproduce old ways. This is a historic thing that we are building." Unlike the experience of Daniel's workshop at Catia TVe, which I recounted above, Nicholas explicitly highlighted that addressing class inequalities within the Bolivarian movement was fundamental to their effort to collaboratively produce television and to advance the creation of a revolutionary state.

Success Stories

The Bolivarian movement's success in redistributing resources to poor communities had some troubling consequences: new inequities emerged as some barrio-based activists gained greater upward social mobility than others, a change which, in turn, created conflict. Catia TVe producers found themselves negotiating historic class injustices while simultaneously coping with the emergence of these new imbalances among barrio-based activists and between some barrio-based activists and their middle-class counterparts.

These struggles were often invisible to their middle-class interlocutors, as I have indicated above, who projected a vision of an autonomous barrio subject with pure revolutionary commitments and culture, unsullied by capitalist values, global cultural flows, and the desire for middle-class comforts. The reductive schema of autonomy or encapsulation, which Catia TVe staff and volunteers themselves advanced, made it even more difficult for Catia TVe producers to address their internal hierarchies, aspirations, and contradictory desires. In fact, many committed revolutionaries aspired to the middle-class lives that they so vehemently critiqued. As I have been suggesting, many people's stated values about commercial television and capitalist consumerism often did not correspond with how they lived. This dynamic is certainly not unique to Venezuela, but it did create particularly marked tensions within the context of the Bolivarian Revolution. These conflicts proved significant as anger over unequal access to resources among chavistas fractured precious alliances and solidarities.

Catia TVe became a path of upward social mobility for several of its staff members and volunteers. Many volunteers were frustrated that Catia TVe did not pay them for their video productions. A small group built on the video production skills they learned at Catia TVe to find better-paying jobs at ViVe TV and other professional media outlets. Several staff members supplemented their minimum-wage incomes at Catia TVe by filming weddings and parties or by selling programming to media outlets. I found it difficult to evaluate exactly how far the minimum wage of $400 a month could stretch in Caracas in 2007. Some producers at Catia TVe rented their homes or living spaces. Others lived in homes they or their parents had built on squatted land and did not pay rent. Only some paid electricity bills. Food prices varied widely, even in 2006 and 2007, depending on where one shopped: private grocery stores, informal open-air produce markets, or government-subsidized food stores. While gasoline was incredibly inexpensive, people at Catia TVe spent at least a dollar a day on buses and the metro to commute to work. While employment at Catia TVe provided much-needed stability, most of my interlocutors at Catia TVe found that it was difficult to support their families on one or even two minimum-wage salaries. Many tried to supplement their Catia TVe salaries with other employment.

One morning, on our way to the ViVe TV workshop described above, Margarita confided in me about her frustration with the unequal access to additional income that she saw among her colleagues at Catia TVe. "You know what really bothers me, Naomi? So many people use what we have taught them to get jobs or make money elsewhere. I know that we have [video production] skills and that people will work on the side but, honestly, I feel frustrated that I dedicate all my time to Catia. I'm feeling very frustrated that some people spend so much time doing these other projects. Sure, I know that they need money. We all need money." Margarita's comments made clear that some who worked at Catia TVe were taking advantage of new opportunities for income far more than others. For Margarita, these side jobs compromised the amount of time and energy that her Catia TVe colleagues devoted to their work at the station. She felt increasingly angry and resentful of her colleagues who capitalized on their new skills for their individual economic advancement.

The differences between the lives of barrio-based participants at Catia TVe that I have uniformly glossed as "poor" were, in fact, striking. The lives of two Catia TVe staff members, Jesica, a young and fairly new staff member, and Carlos, the director of Catia TVe at the time of my research, capture the complexities of class experiences and the sharp internal differentiation among people from poor barrios.

Jesica

When I first met Jesica shortly after she joined the station's staff in 2006, she did not strike me as particularly passionate about organized or formal politics. Unlike her colleagues, she did not engage in debates at the station about how best to reorganize the media world of Caracas or how to apply existing theories of socialism to the Venezuelan context. When I accompanied her around Caracas to film events, she rarely expressed interest in discussing with her colleagues or me the dynamics we observed. She did, however, communicate a deep commitment to the importance of the fair and equal distribution of resources, regularly referencing a quotation, widely attributed to Che Guevara, that many of her colleagues at Catia TVe also frequently invoked: "If there isn't coffee for everyone, then there isn't coffee for anyone."

I recounted earlier in this chapter how Daniel, the leader at the workshop held at Catia TVe, had encouraged Jesica to claim her status as part of the popular class and how she had demurred, rejecting his invitation to make herself or her neighbors into representatives of "the people" or "the poor." A visit one evening to Jesica's cousin's home perched high on the hillside above Catia TVe focused my attention on the different levels of poverty that barrio inhabitants endure and the folly of overlooking these differences.

We boarded a crowded microbus that Jesica hailed with an expert flip of her wrist. After fifteen minutes on the stifling minibus, Jesica loudly commanded, "La parada, por favor!" (Stop, please!), and the bus driver came

FIGURE 3.2. View from a west Caracas barrio, November 5, 2006. Photo by the author.

to a sudden halt. We squeezed our way off the bus and headed for a nearby bodega where Jesica bought a three-liter bottle of pineapple soda for her cousin Angelica's household. As in many poor neighborhoods, the barrio where Angelica lived had only intermittent access to running water. Jesica explained that she always tried to bring something to drink when she visited. We descended a long flight of steep cement steps hemmed in by two-story houses. Some had neat patios bordered with cement blocks that were plastered with stucco and painted bright colors. Others, like Angelica's, were roughly finished with dirty gray cinder-block walls. Jesica rapped on a thin metal door. As we waited for Angelica to answer, we took in the view below. Caracas's aging skyscrapers, middle-class apartment buildings, and winding highways spread out in the distance.

Angelica appeared, wearing a sweatshirt embroidered with a picture of Mickey Mouse. She welcomed us in. In her late twenties, she had light-brown skin and curly brown hair dyed with streaks of blond. Jesica introduced me as the American ambassador, pointedly acknowledging my status difference. "I was just cleaning," Angelica remarked as she ushered us onto a small couch draped with a worn sheet. The small sitting room smelled of bleach, and the cement floors and walls were bare except for a calendar with images of Jesus. Jesica asked how Angelica's mom, who had diabetes, was feeling. "The same," Angelica sighed, looking upward from where we could hear the familiar tune of the seven o'clock telenovela on Venevisión, one of the commercial television channels.

Angelica recounted how the previous week she had taken her mom to the nearby Barrio Adentro clinic in her neighborhood, one of the thousands of free primary health clinics built in poor neighborhoods by the Chávez government starting in 2003. Angelica noted that they had received medical attention there before. But that night, she explained that although she could see the doctor sleeping inside, the woman who answered the door claimed that the doctor was not there. "I said it was an emergency, but they didn't pay any attention." We empathized with her frustration. Angelica exclaimed, her anger rising, "I should denounce that doctor!" Jesica suggested that Angelica come to Catia TVe to record a complaint on television. Angelica raised her eyes, intrigued by the suggestion, but quickly changed the subject and disappeared, reemerging with large plastic glasses filled with the pineapple-flavored soda.

While Angelica was out of the room, Jesica explained that Angelica's furniture had once belonged to her parents, making clear that the poverty of her cousin's household was much more extreme than that of her own. While Angelica was a single mother of two with a disabled mother to care for, Jesica's family was far more secure. Her father had steady employment as a bus operator, and Jesica's regular income and health benefits at Catia TVe were sufficient to cover her own needs.

We drank the sugary soda and played with Angelica's two sons, two and eight years old. The older boy begged Jesica to let him play with her digital music player. Angelica was eager to learn English and asked me to teach her some curse words. I obliged and we spent the next half an hour giggling as Jesica and Angelica awkwardly insulted each other in English. Before we left, Angelica pleaded with Jesica for 250 bolivars (about ten cents) to buy a cigarette. Her work washing and ironing clothes for households in more affluent neighborhoods had been slow. Jesica replied that she had little money. I knew that Jesica was saving up for an expensive pair of hiking sandals. The day before we visited a shoe store in central Caracas and she had carefully inspected the nylon, rubber-soled shoes designed by an American company and made in China. Jesica handed Angelica a 1,000-bolivar bill. Angelica sent her eight-year-old son to the house next door, where an old woman sold loose cigarettes and cold beer through a barred window.

Angelica and Jesica directly experienced the failings as well as the benefits of new social programs initiated by the Bolivarian movement. The conditions of Angelica's life help place in relief the opportunity that Catia TVe afforded Jesica. Like Angelica, Jesica had not finished high school. Angelica remained, as far as I could tell, unincorporated in the new structures of political participation, which also served some as a path to greater income. Catia TVe offered Jesica steady employment doing something creative and prestigious. Jesica had new, if limited, purchasing power for a wider range of imported commodities, like the music player and the American sandals she coveted. Her passion for fairness and equality existed alongside her desire for commodities and enjoyment of global mass culture.

Carlos

The additional income some staff members at Catia TVe generated outside of their work at the station allowed them access to upward mobility far beyond that which Jesica experienced. This was most visible to me in Carlos's household. Although they lived in a poor barrio, over time I observed how the inside of their home began to include many of the accoutrements of a middle-class household. Although Carlos's salary as Catia TVe's director was only marginally larger than the minimum wage earned by the station's staff, the job had come with other perks, including collecting rent from me and traveling internationally. Carlos's wife also held a salaried staff position at Catia TVe. Their two steady salaries made them comfortable enough that they could use my contribution to the household budget to send their older child to a private college, where she gained skills to enter a middle-class profession usually far out of reach for most young people from the barrios. On weekends at home from college, Carlos's daughter spent hours surfing the Internet while simultaneously flipping between telenovelas on Venezuelan stations and American programming on *Fox and Friends* and the Discovery Channel, accessible through the family's satellite subscription to DirecTV.

Carlos's access to upward mobility was paradoxically predicated on the political clout he gained as the leader of a barrio-based popular organization. Activists, politicians, and university groups regularly invited Carlos to travel internationally to speak about the emergence of Venezuelan community media and the Bolivarian Revolution. In his first five years as director of Catia TVe, he visited South Korea, Spain, Bolivia, and the United States. During his travels, Carlos often took advantage of the comparatively low prices of consumer goods outside of Venezuela to stock up on electronics and other commodities. His trips abroad exposed him to new tastes, middle-class knowledge, and new allies. Carlos's household boasted several computers and cameras that he had purchased abroad. After he returned from his trip to Spain, Carlos insisted that his wife buy olive oil, declaring it far superior to the corn oil that is a staple in most barrio homes. Over the months and intermittent years I spent in Carlos's household, I watched his wife redecorate their kitchen and living room. She installed an oven in their kitchen, an unusual luxury in barrio homes, which typically use one or two burners to cook. Relationships Carlos formed with visitors like me and through his travel abroad linked him to a middle-class network of international activists and scholars that he continued to draw on long after his trips.

One afternoon, I accompanied Carlos and his family on a short trip in their uncle's car to a massive supermarket called Éxito, which means "success" in Spanish. The shopping trip exposed the incongruous desires and commitments that shaped Carlos's life. Unlike the small supermarkets near Carlos's barrio in west Caracas, Éxito had clean wide aisles abundantly stocked not only with a wide variety of food products, but also with appliances and electronics. Éxito was known for its discount prices, but because it was in a wealthy area of the city and easily accessible only by car, the clientele appeared predominantly affluent.

Carlos, his wife, his wife's uncle, and I waited outside the massive supermarket for Carlos's brother-in-law to finish his shopping. Conversation turned to a recent march in support of Chávez. Carlos's wife's uncle, Jorge, noted that he had been impressed with the turnout. Carlos responded, "That was nothing, you should see the marches they have in Cuba." Jorge responded, "The Cubans are not joking around; they take their marches seriously." They discussed how the U.S. blockade had crippled the Cuban economy and the political righteousness of the Cuban people. Many chavistas I encountered, including Carlos, had gained firsthand experience of Cuba, traveling there for medical treatment. Carlos glowingly affirmed the Cuban people's dedication to their revolution, their unity, and their lack of compromising desire for meaningless possessions. The conversation turned lighter, and Jorge and Carlos began trading jokes.

"An egg gets out of a plane in Cuba," Carlos began, "and the Cuban people go crazy. They're hungry; they've never seen an egg quite this nice. The crowd goes after the egg, chasing him down the street." Jorge listened attentively, seemingly ready for a good laugh. Carlos had a remarkable gift for oratory. His memory for details, his persuasive delivery, and his energy made listening to him a treat. "So the egg is huffing and puffing, just fifty meters out of the crowd's hungry reach. The egg makes a sharp turn to hide in an alley and he encounters a big juicy steak that is casually leaning against the wall, smoking a cigarette." Carlos drew two fingers to his lips and dramatically exhaled make-believe smoke. "The egg says to the steak: 'Damn, brother, let's get out of here! They're going to get us!' But the massive steak remains calm. After taking another leisurely puff of his cigarette, the steak says to the egg, 'Me?! They're chasing *you*, my friend. Around here, they don't even know me!'"

Jorge erupted in laughter. We all joined him, slowly grasping the meaning of the joke. People in Cuba were so poor they wouldn't even recognize a succulent piece of beef.

Although Jorge and Carlos respected Cubans for what they perceived as steadfast ideological commitment to socialism, the joke made plain their desire not to replicate the Cubans' lack of access to luxuries like steak. Carlos venerated Cubans in ways that reminded me of how the leftist middle class often idolized the urban poor of Caracas. Carlos's idolatry was dependent on overlooking the complexity of Cuban experience and was mixed with a kind of pity. Like many other committed chavistas, Carlos wanted *éxito*, success, in the form of consumer goods and packaged foods. They coveted the commodities of which they had long been deprived. This was part of their struggle for social justice. No one at Catia TVe openly talked about this. Carlos and others publicly denounced capitalist consumerism even while it was an important part of their daily life.

The uneven access to material privilege and prestige that different barrio-based Catia TVe producers gained as a result of their involvement in the community media movement drove a wedge between Carlos and some of the other Catia TVe staff and volunteers. These inequalities compromised their unity. Margarita was bitter and jealous that she continued to dedicate her time to Catia TVe while her colleagues pursued moneymaking ventures on the side. Jesica occasionally shared her suspicions with me that some staff members were unfairly gaining access to Catia TVe's resources. Carlos shielded his colleagues from certain aspects of his life that made evident his upward mobility. As some Catia TVe producers achieved far greater material gains that others, some long-term participants openly wondered whether their community television station reproduced rather than challenged historic patterns of inequality.

Conclusion

The struggles over class authority, identity, and culture which I describe in this chapter were part of an ongoing process of class formation and reformation that characterized the Bolivarian revolutionary state. The redistribution of resources, both symbolic and material, created openings for Catia TVe producers to challenge long-standing patterns of class injury and injustice. Cross-class efforts to produce revolutionary television created opportunities to challenge entrenched class privilege and to recognize popular culture as an unfolding way of being and knowing that drew creatively on the past, as well as other sources. Yet I have also charted how limiting notions of popular culture and knowledge threatened to undermine positive gains toward equality.

Middle-class allies often reduced Catia TVe producers to caricatures, as either brainwashed mimics or virtuous idols with an unchanging cultural tradition. Catia TVe producers also contributed to this limited analysis as part of a project to resist entrenched racism, classism, and capitalist co-optation. Such fixed understandings of popular culture were ill-suited to account for the multidimensional lives of the urban poor and the complexity of their entanglements with capitalism. Without an assessment of people's multidimensional pleasures, aspirations, desires, and identification with commercial media and their dialogic engagement with global cultural productions—in short, without consideration of the contest over hegemony taking place in and through the terrain of popular culture—I found that celebrations of popular knowledge and culture reinforced class hierarchies. Reductive approaches to popular culture, moreover, leaned on the oppressive logic of nationalism that cut off global solidarities.

The cross-class collaborations and struggles that I observed were processes not only of class formation and reformation but also of state formation. Through these struggles, participants in the Bolivarian Revolution determined who would lead and on what premises this leadership would be based. The effort of Catia TVe producers to assert their leadership and perspectives shaped the kind of state that was being produced, even as they struggled, often unsuccessfully, to upend historic class inequalities. In the next chapter, I continue to explore how Catia TVe producers attempted to assert barrio-based leadership over the revolutionary state building process. I focus on their identification as "the people" and their efforts to use the figure of Chávez to bolster their authority.

FOUR

CHANNELING CHÁVEZ

Multiple times a week, people from the barrios surrounding Catia TVe arrived at the television station asking for media coverage of their denuncias. A denuncia is a well-recognized mode of expression in Venezuela that people use to make complaints, demands, and denunciations.[1] Since the early 1960s, the production and dissemination of denuncia reports has been a cornerstone of the Venezuelan media world and a key process in the production of political movements (Samet 2017; Samet and Schiller 2015). People from the barrios around Catia TVe looked to the community television station to broadcast their demands for desperately needed resources, such as housing, or to denounce mismanagement of official state programs and institutions. Catia TVe producers were adamant that their station disseminate criticism of the shortcomings of the Bolivarian Revolution and expose the ongoing hardship that barrio inhabitants faced. The practice of broadcasting denuncias over Catia TVe airwaves, however, was never straightforward. Reporting and disseminating denuncias involved tense deliberation among Catia TVe producers and their various interlocutors about the meaning of the ubiquitous "key symbols" (Ortner 1973) of the Bolivarian Revolution: "the people" and the figure of Hugo Chávez.

When I began my fieldwork I anticipated that, given Catia TVe's state funding and alliance with Chávez government, fears of state censorship or other threats of recrimination would interfere with community producers' ability to broadcast criticism of the government and state institutions. During the period of my research, domestic opposition groups, international human rights organizations, and global media outlets focused an enormous amount of attention on the threat that they claimed the Chávez government posed to press freedom. I was surprised to find, given this context, that the threat of censorship was not a primary concern of Catia TVe producers. Production staff occasionally expressed unease that denuncias critical of the government could "one day," as they said, jeopardize their funding from state institutions. Nevertheless, during my research, Catia TVe producers did not, to my knowledge, face direct pressure from any government official or state institution to curb their criticisms. Of course, it was possible that Catia TVe producers concealed instances when state officials censored their work. However, discussions and interviews with my informants, as well as my long-term ethnographic observation of the station, convinced me that this was not the case.[2]

Over the course of my fieldwork, I discovered that rather than censorship, the most pressing problem Catia TVe producers faced in their coverage of denuncias was how people from poor neighborhoods understood their own roles in the Bolivarian Revolution and characterized their relationship to President Chávez. Denuncia makers regularly approached Catia TVe as if its airwaves could serve as a conduit to the president, who, they imagined, could resolve their problems directly. Although the president had been successful in encouraging massive participation in barrio-based organizations, involving the population in local problem solving, decision-making, and social change, Catia TVe producers nevertheless regularly encountered inhabitants of barrios who identified Chávez as the primary agent of change and the lifeblood of the revolution. Denuncia makers often characterized themselves first and foremost as supporters and petitioners of Chávez. Many of Catia TVe's interlocutors in poor neighborhoods emphasized Chávez's power at the expense of their own.

In this chapter, I explore how Catia TVe producers negotiated the central contradiction in the political process at the time of my research: Chávez's leadership and his use of the concept of "the people" encouraged massive political participation among the popular sectors, while at the same time he was the central force that undermined the transformative impacts of popular participation through his centralization of power. The opposing and intertwined forces of popular empowerment and domineering centralized rule were present in every Catia TVe event, film shoot, live studio program, and video production workshop that I observed. In every instance, the underlying question was who controlled and benefited from the process of state formation and to what end. During the period of my fieldwork, it was far from certain how the contradictions of Chávez's leadership would be resolved.

In contrast to their interlocutors' efforts to cast Chávez as the main agent of change, Catia TVe producers attempted to characterize the urban poor and their communities as the righteous, self-determined "people" who participated and led revolutionary state formation. Catia TVe producers endeavored to use the process of media production of denuncias to challenge the concentration of power in Chávez's hands and to cultivate a sense of subaltern political identity beyond the stance of being a Chávez supporter, even as they rejected total independence from state institutions and Chávez. Catia TVe staff and volunteers encouraged a sense among their interlocutors in the barrios and at their television station that they could and should participate in the project of state formation in collaboration with official state institutions.

In Catia TVe's workshops for new volunteers and Catia TVe producers' practice of denuncia reporting, I found evidence of how Chávez's leadership and the concept of the people created openings as well as obstacles for Catia TVe staff's goals of encouraging activism in poor neighborhoods and ensuring that the interdependence they sought to develop with official state institutions did not devolve into a demobilizing dependency. In Catia TVe's classrooms, television studios, and in poor neighborhoods, the symbols of Hugo Chávez and the people had the potential not only to contain and silence barrio-based activists, but also to embolden and authorize their leadership. Even as they created close relationships and alliances with middle-class intellectuals and cultural producers, as I described in the previous chapter, they insisted that "the people" referred to the popular or poor class. Catia TVe producers resisted reducing the term *the people* to a fluid referent that could encompass a wide spectrum of class actors. A class-inclusive notion of the people, from their perspective, decentered the role of the poor as the leaders of the revolution. Catia TVe producers used the symbols of the people and Chávez in ways that challenged the power of those who did not cede leadership to the poor, including government officials, social movement allies, and the president himself.

Much of the scholarship that has assessed Chávez's rule draws on the concept of populism, a heavily debated and much-abused approach. This framework, I argue, overlooks the competing visions among supporters of the Bolivarian movement of Chávez's role in the revolution and the meaning of "the people." In this chapter, I bring these competing visions to the fore and examine the role of televisual communication in the struggle over the direction of the Bolivarian Revolution. I show how Catia TVe producers wrestled with the contradictions that Chávez's leadership created between centralized and popular power. In doing so, I explore some of the limits and possibilities of theories of populism to understand politics and media in Venezuela. Efforts to resolve the contradiction of Chávez's leadership in favor of popular movements faced what would prove to be insurmountable obstacles. Nevertheless, the struggles I document in this chapter reveal that the hope for other possible futures was grounded in the tenuous and uneven, but nevertheless real progress in poor people's access to rights, resources, and authority.

Chávez and the Analytic Lens of Populism

Some scholarship on populism, particularly more recent revisionary approaches, rejects the negative connotations and oversimplifying logics that undergird widespread understandings of populists as demagogues and dictators (Arditi 2005; Laclau 2005; Panizza 2005; Samet 2017; Sánchez 2016). Political scientists and anthropologists have described populism as an anti–status quo movement that (1) unites a "people" by linking together disparate grievances against an established structure of power controlled by an "other"; (2) relies on a seemingly direct relationship between a charismatic leader and his or her supporters; and (3) promises political redemption (Hawkins 2010; Laclau 1977; Roberts 2003; Weyland 2001). Given that most movements labeled as populist aim to restore mass participation and rule by and for the people—ideals that form the very basis of democracy—scholars disagree about whether populism is an obstacle or a corrective to the practice of liberal democracy.

It is easy to find evidence that Chávez used the aforementioned political strategies. Many if not most leaders of mass movements rely to a certain degree on these mechanisms to build support for their leadership. Thus, Francisco Panizza argues that populism may best be thought of as a kind of "intervention" and a "mode of identification" employed by a wide variety of actors as part of broader repertoires of political action (2013, 106). The vast literature on populism helps us to think through the dangers and possibilities of charismatic leadership and the mobilization of the concept of the people. The possibility that a strong leader will become a tyrannous leader encourages many scholars, such as Benjamin Arditi, to emphasize "the undecidability between the democratic aspects" of populist modes of identification and its more "ominous tones" (Arditi 2007, 7). Additionally, Ernesto

Laclau's approach to populism, which I draw on in this chapter, provides insight into how divergent unmet social demands can be connected in order to form broad political movements in and through the concept of the people. Laclau's focus on social demands makes his analysis particularly useful in exploring the stakes of broadcasting denuncias in Venezuela (Samet 2017).

Notwithstanding these important contributions, a weakness of much of the literature on populism is that it privileges style (how a leader relates to supporters) at the expense of content (what specific political projects a leader and a group of people seek to advance). Many scholars argue that populism is ideologically promiscuous as a mode of intervention and articulation; the political left, right, and center can all advance populist politics. This tendency makes it possible for both capitalist white supremacist movements and socialist antiracist movements to be considered populist. The populist analytic, therefore, can obfuscate the vital difference between efforts to challenge social inequalities and those that seek to deepen them. This emptying out of politics is what makes the concept of populism particularly attractive to mainstream journalists seeking to explain and contain diverse movements around the world that have formal similarities.

Populism is not, to be sure, a neutral scholarly framework removed from the conflictive political contexts it is often deployed to explain. In many cases, scholars, politicians, and journalists have invoked populism as a theoretical metonym or shorthand to decry the political backwardness of Latin America. Furthermore, much of the criticism of the Latin American political movements that scholars and pundits define as populist draws tacitly on liberal capitalist democratic norms to judge political movements. These analyses privilege procedures of checks and balances, due process, and the rule of law to protect private property and capitalist accumulation as central to democracy. The attachment and passion that Chávez supporters often expressed for the president disturbed a liberal sensibility that envisions distance and autonomy from leaders and the state as foundational traits for proper democratic engagement.[3]

Given what political theorist Francisco Panizza (2013) has labeled the "toxic" connotations of widespread understandings of populism, I was not surprised to learn early in my fieldwork that Catia TVe producers rejected the characterization of Chávez as a populist leader and the revolution as a populist movement. Catia TVe producers defined a populist in ways that overlapped with prevalent disparaging understandings; for them a populist was a charismatic politician who manipulated followers through the opportunistic distribution of resources, concealing his or her true motivations to

FIGURE 4.1. T-shirts for sale in west Caracas, January 25, 2006. Photo by the author.

concentrate power rather than foment revolutionary anticapitalist change. In the interest of decentering Chávez, many of my informants at Catia TVe generally avoided calling their movement chavismo, referring to it instead as the Bolivarian Revolution. Likewise, they did not identify as chavistas, but instead as revolutionaries or *el pueblo organizado* (the organized people). Even while Catia TVe producers rejected the characterization of their movement as populist, they struggled over a central question that many scholars of populism have raised: whether mass mobilization could precipitate a redemptive democratic practice or whether it would concentrate power in the hands of the "great leader" and a self-serving upwardly mobile bureaucratic class.

Many scholars who have drawn on a populist analytic argue that Chávez ultimately undermined the political agency of those participating in the Bolivarian movement by emphasizing first and foremost the role of the leader in determining the political terrain (see Hawkins 2010; Paramio 2006, 72). My data largely supports this perspective. I highlight the ways that Catia TVe's interlocutors emphasized Chávez's power at the expense of their own. However, while most scholars who employ a populist analytic to analyze Venezuela argue that the concentration of power was inevitable, the efforts of my informants to challenge this dynamic, in part by claiming the people for their own ends, makes clear that there were other potential outcomes. There were organizations through which to build this challenge to the concentration of power precisely because the revolution included projects like Catia TVe, which redistributed access to the tools of media production. Scholars of populism have largely overlooked the struggles among Chávez supporters over the direction of the revolution. Catia TVe producers, as I have been illustrating in previous chapters, worked to cultivate radical interdependence with Chávez and official state institutions. They resisted Chávez's (and others') efforts to mobilize the concept of the people in ways that undermined the leadership of the poor. A populist analytic is often mobilized by scholars and critics in ways that ignore the ideological project at the center of mass movements and insist that a leader is alone in creating collective identification of actors who demand social change. This perspective disregards the heterogeneity at work and overlooks the messy process and divergent stakes of political struggle.

The Chávez Contradiction

The contradictory role that Chávez played in undermining and encouraging the participation of marginalized actors in state formation became particularly clear to me one evening when I watched Chávez's live talk show *Aló Presidente* (*Hello President*) at the home of a volunteer at Catia TVe whom I call Carmen. I had spent the afternoon observing Carmen and another Catia TVe volunteer edit a program about a local artisan who made cuatros, a small string instrument. Carmen lived with her daughter in a lower middle-class apartment building along the bustling Avenida Sucre in a low-income region of west Caracas. She was a short woman with light-brown skin in her early fifties. Unlike the majority of my informants at Catia TVe who had little access to higher education in the traditional university system, Carmen held an undergraduate degree in psychology from the prestigious Central University of Venezuela. Her degree, however, had not granted her a stable foothold in the middle class. Carmen struggled to provide for her two children on her salary as a teacher.

When we entered her sparsely furnished two-bedroom apartment, Carmen switched on a small television on the kitchen counter. Chávez appeared on VTV, the principal state television channel, presiding over his weekly program, *Aló Presidente*. Like many people I knew, Carmen regularly watched *Aló Presidente*. Beginning in 1999 when Chávez first came to power, his unscripted talk show was broadcast consistently, first on radio, then on television, until 2012, a year before his death.[4] At times, *Aló Presidente* resembled an extended cabinet meeting. Chávez regularly called on his chief ministers, who formed part of the president's audience, to answer questions and discuss state programs. The show also served as a kind of tribunal. Select audience members had the opportunity to gain direct access to Chávez, air their demands, and receive an immediate response. Given the frequency and extended periods for which Chávez spoke—often as long as five or six hours—Carmen, like others I had observed, directed her attention to Chávez only intermittently.

When we sat down to eat our dinner of sweet corn pancakes filled with salty hunks of white cheese, we focused on the television. Wearing a characteristic red button-down shirt, Chávez spoke that evening from the presidential palace. He described how he had just committed large sums of money to the local governance structures called communal councils. "Power for the people [el pueblo]. I have said it a million times: 'if we want to conquer poverty, we need to give power to the poor [*los pobres*]."[5] In this moment, Chávez defined the people as the poor. But when he went on to discuss inflation, his definition of the people expanded to include all the "good" Venezuelans who were being cheated by their domestic and international capitalist enemies. The president drew stark lines between an ambiguous "people" and their opportunistic enemies. Although Chávez often emphasized that the people were the impoverished, oppressed members of the population, in this speech as in others he used the term pueblo in variable ways: to define all those aligned against capitalist speculators, all Venezuelans, the poor, and the middle class. Chávez's invocation of this ambiguous people allowed diverse groups to unite under his leadership.

"El pueblo" (the people) is a potentially totalizing category for an entire citizenry, or even all of humanity. As such, the concept can be mobilized to serve reactionary, militaristic, or anti-imperialist projects. Julie Skurski argues that the concept of el pueblo has had an ambiguous place in the history of Venezuelan nation building; it was "at once inclusionary and exclusionary, horizontal and hierarchical" (1993, 18). At the dawn of Venezuelan independence, elite nation builders asserted their legitimacy by arguing that the people, rather than gods or kings, were the source of political power. However, these elites defined themselves as the qualified "*pueblo soberano*" (the sovereign people) and excluded those whom they saw as the ignorant and racially suspect masses for not having the education or culture that the elites believed was necessary for self-rule (Hébrard 1998, 198; Skurski 1993,

30). Chávez's frequent claim that the true people of Venezuela were the poor and oppressed and that they could speak for themselves—on their own and through him—challenged this long history of elite classes claiming to act for the poor (Skurski 2015). Nevertheless, as he did that evening, President Chávez often invoked the term *the people* to signify not only the oppressed poor, but also all those who supported him and his government and who had grievances against the previous status quo.

Watching Chávez speak for hours on end on a regular basis about topics both esoteric and mundane gave many of my informants a sense that they intimately understood him and that, in turn, the president understood them. In usual form that evening, Chávez shifted between ornate rhetoric and colloquial speech to explain a series of graphs that itemized the rising costs of basic food items. Chávez made complex economic processes accessible. With amusement, Chávez recounted how when he was a child his uncle rewarded him for knowing the date of Simón Bolívar's birth—July 24, 1783—by giving him five bolivars, a laughable sum in 2007 given successive currency devaluations. Carmen laughed along with Chávez. "Ay, sí, mi presidente," she said nodding her head knowingly. On numerous occasions, I had heard Venezuelans reminisce about how far a few bolivars had stretched in their youth. Chávez referenced this widely shared memory to announce that the government would begin exploring how to introduce a new currency to counter inflation. The president described his thought process about the dangers and possibilities of such a move, creating the sense that audiences were included in his decision-making.

Chávez's declarations reached my informants on an almost daily basis via television, and to a lesser degree by radio. By some estimates, Chávez spent more time live on television than any leader, anywhere, ever (Coronil 2008). Regular exposure to Chávez via television contributed to what Arditi calls "virtual immediacy," a sense of a direct and personal relationship with a politician (2007, 68). Simulated proximity, Arditi argues, veils the distance between citizens and a leader in a way that grants the leader the legitimacy to act on his (or her) own without following the institutional procedures related to the division of powers between branches of government that are central to liberal representative democracy. Of course, most mainstream forms of democracy also rely heavily on "media-enhanced closeness" to reach supporters and bypass intermediaries (Arditi 2007, 69). Arditi asserts that what differentiates populism from other practices is that the leader achieves such intimate identification that he or she can claim the ability to act not only as a spokesperson or representative of the people, but as the people. Thus, Chávez declared, "I am a little of all of you" (cited in Panizza 2005, 18).

While Arditi's analysis of virtual immediacy is vital to understanding the importance of Chávez's use of television to sustain a close relationship with supporters like Carmen, his analysis suggests that audiences have only one register of engagement with a leader. Carmen's thoughts on Chávez's form of rule and those of my other informants at Catia TVe indicated, however, that the relationship between the president and his supporters was far more varied. As we were finishing our meal, Carmen reflected critically on Chávez's speech. "Notice," she instructed me, "the way that Chávez says, 'I passed this new law' or 'I designed this new system.' This teaches a lesson and reiterates old mistakes. It really centers things on him." Carmen suggested that Chávez's assertion that he governed alone was subtle but destructive.

Carmen, like most of my interlocutors at Catia TVe, supported the president's bypassing of liberal procedure, such as his use of presidential decree (known as the "Enabling Law") to circumvent the National Assembly in order to create laws on his own. Catia TVe staff and volunteers did not see Chávez's efforts to sidestep political parties, other elected officials, and, at times, the rule of law as a dangerous concentration of power. Rather, as Gregorio, one of Catia TVe's staff explained to me, Chávez's action was "a necessary response to the reactionary forces that seek to resist revolutionary change in this particular moment in time." Gregorio and others emphasized to me how the mediating bodies of their elitist liberal representative democracy had been historically unresponsive and inadequate to create a fair and just system. Although they did not want Chávez to rule in perpetuity, for the most part my interlocutors believed that Chávez not only acted in their interest but also responded to their will of creating a socially just state. But regardless of whether Catia TVe producers accepted Chávez's bypassing of other branches of government or rejected it, like Carmen, they analyzed potential dangers and weighed the benefits of different strategies in response. They did not grant Chávez an unconditional or boundless ability to act as the people.

What was even more striking to me than Carmen's rejection of Chávez's rhetorical efforts to centralize political agency in his own hands were comments she made a few minutes later when she appealed to Chávez as all-powerful, reinforcing the very dynamic she had critically evaluated minutes before. We were clearing the table when Chávez began to speak directly to a woman who had called in to his show to request help from him. Chávez frequently appeared live on television and radio, granting needed resources or directing a member of his government to right the wrong that had been exposed.

Chávez listened carefully as the caller explained her problems addressing teen delinquency in her neighborhood. She requested computer equipment for a project she developed with her neighbors to create programs for young people. In typical form, the president quickly conjured the appropriate bureaucrat and promised the needed computer equipment. Chávez went on to respond to the requests and complaints of about twenty additional callers, performing his ability to meet people's needs. Creating what Laclau (2005) calls an "equivalential chain" between their diverse denunciations and demands, Chávez described these varied discontented groups as the good and noble "people" and defined them against a corrupt, conspiring enemy. Chávez's live performances of his successful effort to fulfill demands encapsulated the central contradiction of his leadership. Even as he advocated for the people to advance bottom-up social change, he fostered the illusion that only he could solve the country's problems. He defined the people in a way that not only depended on his effort to articulate this group as a cohesive entity, but also diluted its working-class character.

I fully expected Carmen to condemn the president's elaborate performance of directly meeting poor people's demands. Instead, as we washed and dried the dinner dishes, Carmen launched into great detail about the denuncia she wanted to present to Chávez about the difficulties she faced at the school where she worked. Despite her criticism that Chávez overlooked the broader political movements and actors that made his actions possible, Carmen daydreamed out loud, imagining how Chávez could exercise his power on her behalf. Supporters of the president, in other words, could be both critical of and enthralled by the president's performances of his power.

A few weeks later I had another opportunity to listen to *Aló Presidente*, this time with Carlos, Catia TVe's director. We listened to Chávez on a car radio on our way to Catia TVe. At a standstill in traffic, I had begun to daydream when Carlos suddenly raised his voice, jolting me to attention. Chávez had turned to discuss the importance of popular organizing, encouraging the poor to join their neighbors in collective action. Stuck in traffic, we listened to the president reiterate for a dense twenty-five minutes that it was only through daily work in local organizations that Venezuela would be transformed. "Only the people can save the people," Chávez declared. Even as Chávez asserted himself as the embodiment of the people, capable of single-handedly meeting their demands and granting them unity, Chávez simultaneously called on his supporters to develop initiatives and assume local leadership. Carlos banged on the steering wheel in excitement, physically energized by Chávez's words. "That's right! The people have the power!!" Carlos shouted. "This is why I love you, Chávez!" Carlos belted out the car window, startling the pedestrians along Liberator Avenue.

Carlos's loyalty and affection for Chávez was intense. As with many people I knew, the emotional attachment that Carlos felt for Chávez contributed to his political commitment to the Bolivarian project. But far from representing blind devotion to Chávez as the singular savior of the people, Carlos's connection to the president was predicated on his analysis that Chávez aimed to respond to the demands of poor communities and to recognize the role they had to play in the transformation of the state. For Carlos and other longtime activists, the Chávez government represented the fruition of their social movement organizing. Many saw Chávez as their creation (Ciccariello-Maher 2013).

In the following section, I explore how Catia TVe producers sought to focus expectations for change by asserting that "the people"—who they defined as the poor—were the righteous actors bringing into being a revolutionary state through their ordinary and persistent local political activism, whether in the role of health clinic volunteer, overseer of public administration, or as community media producer.

Teaching New Catia TVe Volunteers to Be the Voice and Image of the People

Catia TVe's video production courses for new volunteers provided instruction not only in how to make television, but in how to assume a class perspective. At orientation workshops, Catia TVe producers attempted to nurture a sense among their interlocutors that they shared more than just support for Chávez; they shared a class identity and experience as well. This class experience was not based on a clear relation to the means of production, as in classic Marxist terms, nor on a sense of unification through union representation or incorporation into a political party. Instead, Catia TVe producers harnessed the experiences of marginalization and precarity that their interlocutors from poor neighborhoods shared. The central antagonism that they emphasized was not between a vague "people" and their enemy, or between the political opposition and chavismo, but rather between the poor and the economic elites. The antagonism they most often highlighted was a product of the dispossession inflicted through capitalist accumulation (Harvey

2003). Catia TVe producers attempted to decentralize the role of Chávez in producing political identities.

On the first day of one of Catia TVe's regular ten-day workshops for new volunteers at the station, Gregorio, the workshop leader and a Catia TVe staff member, was visibly nervous. The workshop marked Gregorio's first time leading a video production class on his own, and signaled his rise in the ranks of leadership at the station. The training he received at the ViVe TV workshop, recounted in the previous chapter, emboldened him to assume this new role. Slender and soft-spoken with light-brown skin and thinning curly hair, Gregorio had joined Catia TVe four years earlier when he was twenty-three years old. From a nearby poor neighborhood, Gregorio attended a technical high school and had a job installing computer software when his boss, who lived in Manicomio, introduced him to Carlos, then Catia TVe's assistant director. Although Gregorio had explained to me that he was first drawn to Catia TVe by his fascination with computers, he emphasized that what kept him involved was his growing commitment to politics and social justice. After several months of participating in the station's operations as an unpaid volunteer, Gregorio joined the staff in 2003.

Gregorio's students that afternoon were, like him, from poor backgrounds. Although Catia TVe's longtime volunteers and staff included some from middle-class families, the station's staff focused their recruitment on the surrounding barrios. New participants in workshops were required to organize themselves into production teams of four to seven people loosely oriented around a specific social issue or neighborhood. The seventeen students in Gregorio's class that morning included four groups, three of whom were heavily involved in newly created state programs that encouraged and relied on local participatory action. The first group consisted of four young men from a neighborhood almost an hour away by public transport from Catia TVe, who were studying together in the Bolivarian University of Venezuela, a new public university created in 2003 by the Chávez government. A second group, all in their early twenties, worked together in a government program dedicated to homeless outreach called Misión Negra Hipólita.[6] A third group, in their forties, was studying communications at a community college created through the state's higher educational program, Misión Sucre. The final group was made up of people in their early twenties who lived in a barrio just a short bus ride from Catia TVe. Of the seventeen people enrolled in the workshop, there were five women and twelve men. Some had very dark skin and one person had very light skin; most fell in a middle range that *caraqueños* refer to as mestizo. This variation in age, gender ratio, skin color, and ongoing involvement in official state programs in education and poverty alleviation was representative of those who regularly participated at Catia TVe.

When the workshop participants had assembled in the windowless basement classroom at Catia TVe, Gregorio kicked off the class by initiating a conversation on the dynamics of power that shaped mainstream education and television. Miguel, a workshop participant in his early forties, eagerly engaged Gregorio's discussion of the problem with mainstream traditional forms of education. Miguel focused on the social class implications of education by referencing the stratified class geography of Caracas, remarking, "Education was a way to get an apartment in the east [the affluent region of Caracas] and forget your community." Others agreed with Miguel that "getting ahead" traditionally meant the opportunity to relocate to a wealthier neighborhood with paved roads, reliable water, electricity, gas lines, and, perhaps most importantly, greater security. In contrast to this long-held goal of leaving the barrio, Marta, a woman in her early fifties, affirmed that they should use education to improve their barrios.

When Gregorio asked them to describe their motivations for joining the workshop, they spoke of a desire to "unite our community," "spread the news of what we are doing," and "rescue our values." They referenced a "we" and an "us" that indexed their immediate geographic neighborhoods or their involvement in the state-funded projects and programs to combat poverty ("our work"). Drawing on the Latin American use of the word *popular* to mean marginalized, they identified as the *pueblo popular* (the popular people)—a group whose values and lives, they asserted, had been historically maligned and dismissed by past governing elites, the national media, and the dominant global culture. The workshop participants named a shared experience of marginality but avoided specifying a class position. Gregorio pushed back.

Gregorio insisted that they recognize themselves explicitly as class actors. After half an hour of boisterous discussion of the purpose of education, Gregorio had grown more comfortable in front of the classroom. He raised his voice to regain the group's attention and direct the conversation back to Catia TVe's orientation and central aims. "Look, friends, we came here to advance a project, and it's much more than just filming and saying, 'Look how pretty my documentary is.' It's a tool for organization, to help your compañeros [comrades], to create a film club so that your community comes and sees who did things, how we are, what do we need, how we see ourselves and how are we going to see ourselves." Popular communication, Gregorio explained, required producers to involve themselves in the social dynamic of the barrios they were documenting. "Here we put down the camera to argue and discuss things. Then we'll grab the camera to start recording," Gregorio instructed. The work of instigating social change rather than simply documenting everyday life, Gregorio emphasized, required an explicit embrace of a popular class perspective.

Gregorio described himself and his students as belonging to a class and equated this collectivity with the concept of "the people" based on their common experience of economic and political subordination. Taking some of the participants by surprise, Gregorio argued that as community media producers they needed to reject a stance of neutral impartiality. He declared, "We are totally partial toward the people." Gregorio used the term people to refer not to the collective totality of the nation or Chávez's supporters, but rather the poor. Gregorio noted, "The country is divided into two and this is a class struggle. That's what we are saying. Are we really impartial? We aren't. . . . If we attempt to cover ourselves with this veil of impartiality we will only confuse ourselves." Gregorio insisted that the conflict dividing the country was rooted in the fundamentally opposed class interests of the wealthy (whom he referred to as "the elites" and "the opposition") and the poor (which he called "the people," "the popular people," "the popular class," and "the community"). Unlike the defensive stance Catia TVe producers often assumed when they worked with their middle-class allies at ViVe TV, as I highlighted in the previous chapter, Catia TVe staff was far more comfortable expressing a class analysis in the courses they led exclusively for barrio residents.

For many people working in informal sectors of the economy—particularly the younger generations—the Bolivarian Revolution's experimental programs in health care, education, housing, and media production offered the first opportunity to participate extensively in formal politics. They were incorporated into the Bolivarian state's programs. During the video production course, Gregorio attempted to forge a unified political subjectivity out of the "traditionally unorganized and unincorporated sectors" of Venezuelan society (Ellner 2013). As I explored in the previous chapter, class identity is a complex historical process. Regardless of whether or not there was a preexisting or organic link between the social condition of the lives of Gregorio's students and their understanding of their own collective political subjectivity, Gregorio encouraged new volunteers at Catia TVe to see themselves as a class and to equate "the people" with the poor. While Chávez's leadership shaped the grounds on which Gregorio cultivated this form of identification, the president was not, in this moment, the key actor forming the bonds between his supporters. Laclau's analysis of the leader's role in sustaining a chain of equivalence between individuals overlooks how actors create bonds of identification based on specific class claims. Gregorio emphasized the commonalities his students faced as inhabitants of barrios and their responsibility before their neighbors to embrace each other. Against the potential vagueness and emptiness of the term *the people*, Gregorio specified their particular shared class position.

Much of the scholarly literature on populism falls short of capturing this aspect of the Bolivarian process. Laclau, for example, argues that the people is an "empty signifier." He is adamant that the individuals or groups that call themselves "the people" are not united by a preexisting shared experience such as social class. In other words, there is no a priori immanent social antagonism that brings together demand makers. The people that is formulated through the process Laclau describes "has little to do with Marxist notions of class alliances against the economically dominant class" (Panizza 2005, 16). Laclau's "post-Marxist" perspective (echoed in much of the scholarship that embraces a populist analytic) obscures the ongoing importance of the historical and material process of class formation through which some poor people form alliances as the poor. This does not happen organically, spontaneously, or naturally. But in Gregorio's workshop, we see that it was happening.

It is also important to note how Gregorio's categories did not allow discussion of the way that the popular class was, in fact, internally differentiated. Gregorio and his students faced different forms of discrimination based on color, sexuality, nation of origin, and gender, for example. As I highlight in the following chapter, Catia Tve's efforts to invoke the people had significant gendered dimensions that privileged the role of men. Additionally, Catia Tve producers at times excluded recent and historically rooted immigrant populations in Venezuela from the category of the people. Although my discussion of the concept of the people points to the possibility for this concept to extend to an international dispossessed popular class, rather than stopping at the boundaries of the nation, I found that my interlocutors' nationalist discourse often included a xenophobic and racialized criminalization of poor migrants to Venezuela, especially from neighboring Colombia. The Bolivarian Revolution's nationalist discourse provided a central unifying motif that was, at times, connected to an internationalist vision. However, anti-immigrant sentiment furthered an essentialist ethnonationalist view of difference and superiority that undermined Catia Tve producers' ability to effectively organize around a concept of working-class or popular identity.

With these complexities in mind, the key point I want to make here is that Catia TVe producers encouraged their interlocutors—a traditionally unincorporated informal sector of workers—to embrace a collective political identity in order to bypass dependency on Chávez for political cohesion.

Documenting Denuncias and Constructing the People in a Poor Neighborhood

Catia TVe producers focused on shaping social action and mobilizing collective identification during the process of media production, rather than through the impact of their television programs on potential audiences. Catia TVe's coverage of denuncias expressed support for the revolution and Chávez not by emphasizing Chávez's centrality and indispensability, but rather by advocating for popular or poor people's ability to resolve local problems together with allies in particular official state institutions.

The history of mass mediated denuncias in Venezuela provides important clues about the stakes of Catia TVe's coverage of shortcomings of the revolution and their efforts to avoid a form of populist politics that centered political alliance around support for a great leader and nothing more. With the crisis of political parties and leadership in the early 1990s, print reporters and television newscasters turned to a "journalism of denunciation" to expose government corruption and hasten the collapse of the failing two-party system (Botía 2007; Samet 2012; Yi Ng 1993). The commercial media exposed and catalyzed broad discontent by highlighting varied grievances with the existing political systems. As I have noted, business elites used this mobilization of popular discontent against the failure of the state to adequately deliver services to argue for privatization of these services. Yet this same mobilization of discontent against the status quo served what would become the anticapitalist political project of Bolivarianism.

After Chávez came to power in 1998, denuncias continued to be a central aspect of media content and an important component in producing competing meanings of the people. By the mid-2000s, denuncias that appeared in the Venezuelan media tended to be explicitly anti- or pro-Chávez, making their alignment clear by either exonerating or implicating Chávez in the problems that the denuncia highlighted. Denuncias that suggested that the only solution to the inefficiencies of the mission programs, insecurity, or corruption was to oust Chávez and topple the Bolivarian Revolution were found exclusively in opposition-aligned commercial media outlets. Commercial media highlighted people's demands and criticisms against the

Chávez-led state, which they portrayed as unresponsive and inept. Private media outlets claimed that their independence from government alliances and state funding made them uniquely able to launch sober, objective analysis of the Chávez government. During the Chávez years, commercial outlets attempted to contribute to building a wide consensus for regime change in much the way the commercial media had in the 1990s. This time, however, owners of the private media not only emphasized denunciations, but also used their considerable powers to catalyze regime change directly by participating in the 2002 coup attempt and supporting the 2003 lockout by the managers of the national oil industry.

In contrast to the private media's effort to mobilize denuncias against the government, official state-run media outlets used denuncias to strengthen support for the government. As I detailed in the description of *Aló Presidente*, denuncia makers who were given airtime on state television had their problems resolved quickly and easily, often by the president himself. In demonstrating his ability to meet poor people's demands for equal access to resources, Chávez at times cast the historically oppressed as his personal beneficiaries, rather than as state makers or citizens. At the same time, by facilitating and legitimating neighborhood-based organizations and media such as Catia TVe, Chávez also strengthened the class politics of the poor.

Departing from both commercial and official state media's approach to denuncia coverage, Catia TVe producers broadcast reports of unfulfilled demands that emphasized the role of barrio-based actors as participants, organizers, and leaders of revolutionary state projects. They attempted to avoid characterizing people from poor neighborhoods as either discontented actors against the state or as allied petitioners before the state. Catia TVe included coverage of denuncias in their live talk shows held in their studio, in edited programs that followed denuncia makers in the surrounding poor neighborhoods of Caracas, and, occasionally, through short reports that featured visitors to the station who stated their demands. The station's staff, in line with the vision that Gregorio had outlined for community producers, did not simply document people's demands and complaints about corruption or bureaucratic failings. Instead, they used the opportunity of media production to cultivate local political leadership and engage in community organizing.

These dynamics became apparent to me one afternoon in 2007 when Ana, one of Catia TVe's assistant directors, invited me to join her on a trip to a nearby neighborhood "to investigate," as she put it, a complaint at a health clinic. A woman in her late thirties, Ana had been one of the first volunteers trained

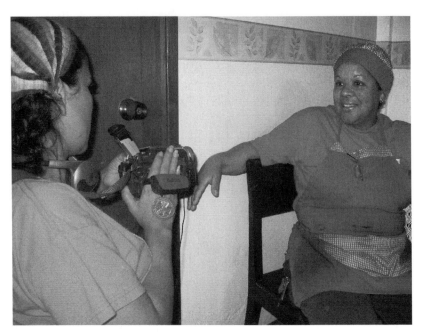

FIGURE 4.2. Catia TVe producer filming a denuncia, October 24, 2006. Photo by the author.

by Catia TVe's founders in 1998. Ana spent most of her time as a member of Catia TVe's Community Outreach Department, where she planned the station's video production classes and organized local events to advocate for community media. She also regularly met with people from the surrounding poor neighborhoods who showed up at Catia TVe to solicit help in broadcasting their denuncias. After I had accompanied Ana on several trips to the field to document various complaints and demands, she discovered that my video production skills, camera, and flexible schedule could be useful to her. Delegating the filming to me, Ana focused on political organizing, which I had begun to understand was her primary concern.

The health clinic that Ana and I visited was located in a neighborhood that inhabitants had built on squatted public land around a busy two-lane highway. Marisol, the coordinator of the health clinic, wanted Catia TVe to broadcast her denuncia about problems at her clinic. The clinic was part of a broader network of clinics called Misión Barrio Adentro (Inside the Neighborhood Mission), a program first implemented in 2003 to place direct primary health clinics in poor neighborhoods.[7] Local volunteers who formed health committees worked with Cuban doctors to staff the clinics. (The Cuban doctors replaced their Venezuelan counterparts who, from the very outset of the program, had refused to participate.)[8] Like many of the government's newly designed social welfare programs, Barrio Adentro depended on the participation of the citizens of the affected community for its implementation and operation. Apart from the Cuban doctors, Barrio Adentro did not provide salaries for the members of the committees who staffed the health clinics. Marisol was attempting to remunerate the health committee workers through a different new program known as Misión Madres del Barrio (Mothers of the Neighborhood Mission), which promised stipends for housewives.[9] A series of bureaucratic errors left the women waiting for more than six months for their promised stipends, which equaled roughly two-thirds of the minimum wage.

Marisol met us along the side of the bustling highway. We followed her up a narrow flight of stairs and down a series of paths that connected densely stacked homes, until we reached a small cement block structure that housed the clinic. The chipping plaster walls were covered with cheerful photographs of community events and several bright-red posters that officials had distributed during the presidential elections. One showed Chávez, his arms extended, with a caption that read "Con Chávez, manda el pueblo" (With Chávez, the People Rule).

Ana sat down in a chair across from Marisol and pulled out a small notebook and pen from her canvas bag. I began filming. Ana invited Marisol to describe the reasons she had invited us: "Why don't you tell us your story of what the problem is, what your proposals are, and we'll take a walk through the community to investigate, okay?" Ana's suggestion that Marisol include in her denuncia not only a description of the problem but also her proposals for how the community could remedy the situation was unusual. Denuncias aired on state and commercial television typically did not include denuncia makers' proposals to resolve the problem they described. Ana's primary concern was to encourage Marisol and her colleagues not only to demand change from formal state institutions but also to work to build stronger community organizations.

Marisol described how she and her neighbors had formed their health committee in 2003. In addition to coordinating appointments for the Cuban doctor and the Venezuelan nurse (a medical student in a state educational program called Misión Sucre), she described how they had organized vaccination brigades, delivered vitamins, and visited very sick neighbors. In her mid-fifties, Marisol had light skin, a thin frame, and thick stick-straight gray hair that reached her shoulders. She explained that she was the only one at the clinic who had an income. Marisol collected a pension after retiring from years working as a secretary in the Ministry of Education. Marisol claimed that she devoted most of her income to maintaining the clinic and organizing community events.

"How many people are involved with you in this social work?" Ana prodded. Marisol thought for a moment. "Thirteen women," she answered. Ana jotted down the figure in her notebook. Arranging the stack of newspapers on her desk, Marisol began to describe their problems with security. Plastic chairs and light bulbs had been stolen from the clinic. Marisol's demand that health clinic volunteers receive the promised stipends proved to be the tip of the iceberg. As was often the case with denuncias, Marisol's testimony expanded to include the many problems her community faced and demands that the government deliver on multiple promises.

In response to Marisol's long list of complaints and demands for accountability from official state institutions, Ana redirected the focus of the conversation to the work of local organizing. "So, for how many people does the health clinic provide services?" Ana asked.

"We are 1,500 people," Marisol responded.

"Uh huh," Ana said, resting her pen in the crease of her notebook. "Apart from the small group of people who act as the pilot and move the whole community—because this happens in practically all neighborhoods—what about your friends, the people who sometimes come by asking for favors, can't they help you? Maybe you could form a security committee?" Rather than scrutinizing and documenting Marisol's complaint about the missing stipends or the other unfulfilled government promises, Ana proposed a local approach to address the problem of security that Marisol had raised. Drawing on her own considerable experience as a community organizer and founder of Catia TVe, Ana acknowledged that many community organizations rely on a dedicated core of activists who assume much of the responsibility. She suggested strategies for how to incorporate and mobilize the health committee's social networks to expand their force. Although Ana condemned the institutional failures that Marisol and her colleagues faced, at every opportunity she insisted that in addition to making demands of official institutions they needed to assume local control and leadership. Ana behaved more as a community organizer than an investigative journalist, devoting her energy to shaping the way Marisol understood her own potential as a community leader.

Marisol responded to Ana's insistence that they focus on local organizing by noting, "Well, it has been very difficult to get the community involved. I think there's still a lack of consciousness. The community is like, if you give me love, I'll give you back love . . . they say, 'No, I need this or that. Why should I help?'" Marisol explained that her neighbors resisted volunteering their labor without the promise of something in exchange. She described how they had waited nine months for the Ministry of Nutrition to deliver bags of food (*bolsas de alimentación*) that the health committee had solicited for those in the community who qualified as living in extreme poverty. "Wouldn't you call this negligence?" she asked pointedly.

At the mention of the distribution of bags of food, Ana hastily snapped, "I'm against the 'Bag of Food' program. We don't need people coming around here to be patrons [*patrocinar*]. We need to provide workshops so that people can learn skills and improve their lives. That's why the state has all these social programs in education and health." Ana marked a difference, here, between what she considered sporadic handouts, used by politicians to win political support, and social programs that relied on local initiative and direction to distribute food and to provide education and health care. Ana had no patience with politicians who, she thought, were seeking to exchange resources for political favor. From previous conversations, I knew that Ana associated these practices, which scholars refer to as clientelism, with previous governments that distributed goods as a way to control the poor and win votes without fundamentally challenging the distribution of power.[10]

As she listened to and documented her neighbor's complaints and demands, Ana confronted how redistributive policies to transfer oil wealth to the poor and include them in local governance threatened to create a vertical relation between the government and the beneficiaries of social welfare programs in poor neighborhoods. Most projects that were created through the Bolivarian Revolution to address the needs of poor sectors, like Barrio Adentro, were facilitated, funded, and organized by state institutions under the direct oversight of Chávez. These projects were hugely successful in incorporating large sectors of poor communities into local activism. Yet even as these programs expanded possibilities for local leadership, they threatened to subordinate grassroots actors to the centralized decision-making of Chávez and other state officials, reproducing the very dynamics of patronage that many activists argued the Bolivarian Revolution was meant to overturn.

Despite Ana's efforts to discuss what could be done at the local level to alleviate some of their problems, Marisol was determined to redirect the conversation back to the unfulfilled promises of the government and to emphasize the need for Chávez's direct attention to her health clinic. Marisol noted, "If this is going to come out [be broadcast] on Catia TVe, then the president needs to find out."

Although during the previous half hour of filming, Marisol and Ana had pretended to ignore my presence filming their exchange, suddenly Marisol directed her gaze directly at my camera and said:

Presidente, I was one of the people that believed that you needed to get ten million votes or more [in the 2006 presidential election] because we are a lot, we are the majority. What happens is that there are a lot of government officials who help people that claim to support the revolution in order to fill their empty pockets. But it was us women working, we work together in this Barrio Adentro, so that you could be in Miraflores [the presidential home and workplace]. . . . And Barrio Adentro has changed my human sensibility. Before, I never knew much under that other democracy; we used to be like monkeys: blind, deaf, and dumb. Who had hypertension in the community? Who needed an identification card? Was there a child that wasn't going to school? But now we know. And this is thanks to *this* revolution, this socialism. For me socialism is what I'm advancing every day in my community. These people in the ministries have to attend to us and know who is really doing the work in the community. *We* are the ones who know how many sick people there are. Oh, but it's just great that we do the work, the doctors hand in their reports, and then they tell the president something different. No, President, not all Barrio Adentros [clinics] are working properly. No, President, not all Barrio Adentros have doctors. Enough with the runaround [*rosca*], the bureaucracy, and all those people who are negligent and do things just to do them. Because there are many people who do want to work with the president for socialism. It can't be any other way. One has to work for socialism, fight for it. . . . What happened with the bags of food [the ministry promised]? Aren't these women in extreme poverty? Nine months we had to wait, President! Is this the socialism you want to see? . . . But from here, my comrade Chávez, *comandante* [commander] Chávez, we say, we are going to support you, count on *this* Barrio Adentro and its fighting women.

At first glance, Marisol's testimony appears to exhibit a traditional clientelist relationship between populist leader and follower, one in which votes are exchanged for resources. She reminds Chávez that he owes his election to her vote and those of the women who work in the clinic ("you needed to get ten million votes . . . so that you could be in Miraflores.") Yet her claim did not simply demand goods in exchange for her political support. Marisol attempts to hold Chávez accountable for problems ("enough with the run-around,") even while she excused him from primary responsibility for short-comings by claiming he had been kept ignorant (officials "tell the president something different.") Establishing her commitment to Chávez allowed her the rhetorical space to criticize the president, his government, and state in-stitutions for not supporting the socialism and revolution she was working to create. She asserted her own moral status and revolutionary credentials while complaining about unfulfilled promises, negligence, and bureaucracy. Echoing narratives of religious deliverance, Marisol explained that once—under previous governments—she was blind, but the revolution had al-lowed her to see.

While I had previously observed people addressing Catia TVe's camera as if they were speaking directly to Chávez, my participation in this instance as videographer drew my attention to the intensity of the direct address. I looked at Marisol through the camera's viewfinder; she looked back and addressed Chávez. While the president's effort to sustain "virtual immediacy" (Arditi 2005, 85) with supporters via radio and television was obvious, Marisol's address points to an overlooked aspect of the role of media pro-duction in constituting the people and sustaining the relationship between leader and supporters. Marisol approached the camera as a direct conduit to the president. She behaved as if television was a two-way portal. She is not only a subject interpellated or called into being as part of the people by Chávez through his use of the airwaves, she also summoned his presence via the camera.

Regardless of whether Marisol actually believed that Chávez was igno-rant of the shortcomings of government programs and would one day see the footage of her testimony, by claiming Chávez as her audience, she spoke on the authority of having a direct relationship with him. The supposed di-rect relationship that Marisol assumed between herself and Chávez allowed her momentarily to claim his influence for herself. When she angrily ad-monishes Chávez, "Nine months we had to wait, President!" and asks him, "Is this the socialism you want to see?" Marisol draws on the moral authority of Chávez's will to demand a more just system. She uses her relationship with Chávez to bolster the legitimacy of her own view of how things should be. Nevertheless, even though Marisol highlighted her own agency in creat-ing socialism on a day-to-day basis in her community and used the figure of Chávez to reinforce her authority, at the same time her testimony positioned herself and her community as dependent on Chávez and his ministers to remedy their problems.

During Marisol's direct address to Chávez, Ana appeared frustrated. She stayed unusually silent, denying Marisol verbal cues that would encourage her testimony, and she avoided eye contact. Marisol was interested in using the television camera primarily as a means to effect change elsewhere, by influencing her potential televisual audience of Chávez and other government officials. In contrast, Ana focused on the importance of local direct action. She approached media making as a process that ideally mobilized community engagement in collective problem solving. When Marisol eventually directed her attention back to Ana and away from "Chávez," Ana insisted that the solutions to the problems that Marisol faced could not be found only in Chávez or in state institutions. She told Marisol, "One has to keep fighting. We have to keep building the missions. Because who is going to resolve this mess? Us, the people, well organized." Ana attempted to redirect Marisol's focus away from el comandante Chávez as a messianic arbiter of justice to mobilizing participation in everyday state formation—building the social welfare organizations—in her community. Ana claimed that she, Marisol, and the women who volunteered in the health clinic were "the people," and suggested that only they had the capacity to advance the revolution.

At the end of our visit, we visited a volunteer in the clinic who had been waiting six months for her stipend. Marisol asked, "Do you think that if the president knew about this situation, he would stay quiet?" Looking at Ana, she quickly followed this question with the claim, "There are failures in the missions, okay, fine, let's correct them." Ana nodded vigorously, affirming Marisol's assertion that barrio-based organizations needed to assert leadership and to work not outside, against, or as dependent on state institutions, but rather through a relationship of radical interdependency. While Marisol and her colleagues were seemingly held hostage to the monumental inefficiencies of state institutions, Ana suggested that they needed to approach the challenge of improving life in their community on multiple fronts. Unless they mobilized widespread participation and generated innovative strategies to assert local authority, the missions had the potential to re-create the paternalistic distribution of resources that Ana so adamantly rejected. She encouraged Marisol to view the success of the health clinic and the Madres del Barrio mission as contingent not only on efficient state institutions but also on neighborhood action, thereby urging Marisol to embrace the state as a collective work in progress.

Like other Catia TVe producers, Ana sought to convince her interlocutors that the Chávez-led state could fulfill its promise of a better world if, and only if, the people from poor neighborhoods assumed local leadership. They advocated that their interlocutors embrace Chávez and the state, not in the position of patron, but from the stance of activists working to build emerging state institutions. As with Gregorio's video production workshop, which I described above, we see Catia TVe producers working to produce a form of popular political action and identification that was not dependent on Chávez's centralized power.

Ana's effort to deflect attention away from state institutions left little room to address the question of what to do about the failing structures of a revolutionary state. While greater participation from the community might lighten the load of these volunteers and could potentially solve the problem of security, local participation could do little to resolve bureaucratic failures and the lack of accountability of official institutions. Expanded participation, in this case, seemed incapable of speeding up or guaranteeing their access to promised resources. Members of Marisol's community had previously participated in street protests organized by chavistas against the Chávez government. However, one of Marisol's coworkers in the health clinic noted that they had suspended such action until after the upcoming presidential election out of fear that their demands would undermine Chávez's reelection. In order for Marisol's demands not to coalesce into an antigovernment stance, Marisol and her colleagues had little choice but to appeal to the leader and invoke Chávez's moral authority to legitimize their demands. Laclau's formulation—which speaks only to the inception of a populist mobilization and does not account for its maintenance—overlooks the ongoing importance of the leader in making vital space for criticism and grievance.

I wondered, too, about the extent to which Ana's effort to shape Marisol's testimony was an effort to improve the performance of her demand so that Marisol had the best chance of successfully appealing to official state actors. Their interaction had semblances of the practice of "speaking bitterness" under Mao Zedong, through which communists tutored peasant populations in how to frame their laments (Rofel 1999). After all, Ana's insistence that the people of organized communities were the protagonists of change did not challenge official discourse. In fact, Ana provided Marisol with cues on how to present her denuncia in terms that reproduced official government discourse that the people led the Bolivarian Revolution from the bottom up.[11] The impossibility of separating social movement and official state discourse presented Marisol and Ana both the opportunity to hold Chávez and other officials accountable for their words and the risk that proclamations of the importance of "the people's power" would ultimately legitimize top-down control. Marisol's savvy performance for my camera, however, indicated that she could employ her own strategies for harnessing Chávez's authority.

Over the next week, I reduced the ninety minutes of footage to a twenty-minute segment edited in a documentary realist style, which included Marisol's address to Chávez, her description of the labyrinthine state bureaucracy she faced, and her interactions with Ana. Before the segment was broadcast, I screened a rough cut for various Catia TVe staff members. Ana seemed pleased that her work as a community organizer had been showcased; the male leadership tended to dominate the public face of Catia TVe, as I highlight in the next chapter. I asked Ana what she thought of broadcasting Marisol's criticism of the government. She noted, "The government should know." Catia TVe broadcast the segment over their airwaves multiple times over the following weeks.

In the months after our visit, Marisol occasionally visited Ana at the station to discuss new problems she faced and to vent frustrations. When I bumped into her several months later, she told me that the women in her health committee still had not received their stipend from the Misión Madres del Barrio program. Catia TVe's broadcast of her denuncia had not produced the results that she had hoped for. Nevertheless, she was optimistic, describing a vaccination brigade her health committee was planning. "If you don't have health, you can't even make a denuncia!" she told me, laughing.

With or without Chávez? Denuncias Live on Catia TVe

At the start of Chávez's second presidential term in 2006, the president was seemingly everywhere. Not only did he have a constant presence on live television and radio broadcasts, his image also appeared on billboards, graffiti, murals, bedroom walls, hats, bags of state-subsidized rice, T-shirts, and bandannas. Scholars assert that Chávez's constant presence on the airwaves and throughout the visual landscape of the city on billboards and graffiti contributed to his exercise of "top-down direct democracy" (López Maya and Panzarelli 2013, 254). Indeed, Catia TVe producers and their allies regularly faced government officials who used the symbol of Chávez in an attempt to silence dissent. Catia TVe producers, in turn, invoked Chávez and the people to deflect top-down impositions of authority. Careful attention to the immediate contexts in which various actors invoked Chávez and the people permit us to understand the struggle to manage internal class and status inequalities while at the same time maintaining solidarity in the face of a formidable opposition. Catia TVe producers regularly faced situations in which their efforts to advance their vision for the revolutionary state involved contentious debates in which all sides linked their perspective to Chávez's. As I have been arguing thus far in this chapter, Catia TVe producers attempted to mobilize both the symbol of Chávez and the concept of the people to encourage barrio-based leadership and local problem solving. The ubiquity of Chávez's image created opportunities for Catia TVe activists to channel the meaning of the president in ways that undercut not only top-down leadership, but also existential dependency on the great leader.

I observed a telling example of competing efforts to invoke Chávez and the people one evening at Catia TVe when a large crowd gathered at the station to debate a denuncia against the then mayor of the metropolitan district of Caracas, Juan Barreto, a distant Chávez ally. Mayor Barreto's supporters and detractors had converged at Catia TVe to appear on a live studio talk show hosted by Luis, one of Catia TVe's founders. Over the course of the three-hour program, the participants consistently invoked Chávez in an effort to position themselves as the truly righteous and revolutionary people capable of knowing and fulfilling Chávez's will.

I had never before seen so many people at Catia TVe. In addition to the seventy-five people who rallied in support of the mayor in the street outside the station, there were about a hundred more people inside. Some were there to support the mayor. Others were aligned with his critics. Everyone present that evening openly embraced the Bolivarian movement and declared their support for Chávez. Catia TVe—the physical space of the station as well as the ephemeral broadcast over their VHF airwaves—served in this moment and in others as a vital site for reckoning with internal dissent within the Bolivarian movement. Those crammed inside the station sat and stood in the passageways around Catia TVe's central atrium and crowded in front of the small television set in the cafeteria area watching Luis's talk show, which was being filmed in the adjacent studio.

Those launching the accusation of corruption against the mayor were former participants in an anticorruption program known as "social oversight" (*contraloría social*). Social oversight committees were designed to allow citizen involvement in the administration of public institutions in order to improve transparency and efficiency (Wilpert 2007, 61). After receiving a brief training session from the mayor's office, local groups formed committees to monitor hospitals around Caracas. They kept track of the medicines and supplies entering and leaving the hospital and advocated for patients' rights. Early in the development of this program, participants agreed with the mayor's office that their work should be done on a volunteer unpaid basis to ensure their independence. Volunteers were nevertheless granted a monthly stipend for travel expenses and food, which the mayor's office called an "incentive." The incentive or stipend equaled about two-thirds of the official minimum wage at the time. Although the group of social overseers asserted that the primary reason for their denuncia against the mayor was that he had intentionally covered up theft at the hospital, it quickly became clear that what had brought the conflict to a head was that this group had not received their incentive pay for several months.

This group of now former social overseers had invited Luis to document their testimony and film a rally they had organized the day before. Luis decided to continue to explore the story by inviting officials from the mayor's office and some of the former social overseers to present their cases on his weekly evening talk show, filmed live in Catia TVe's studio. Under the bright studio lights, six people from the pro-mayor faction sat on Luis's left, and six people from the former social overseer group sat on his right. In contrast to the electric tension in the station, Luis's voice remained calm and upbeat as he welcomed his viewers.

Luis's opening comments provided important cues to understanding the stakes of that evening's program and the role of mediation in the power struggle within chavismo. Luis began by sending salutations to a long list of community media organizations around the city. In doing so, Luis aligned Catia TVe with a host of other barrio-based groups, creating a sense of an abstract collectivity of popular barrio-based activists. Luis had, in fact, acknowledged to me on several occasions that few people watched Catia TVe's programming on a regular basis but did tune in during politically significant moments. Luis was well known among activists and government officials not because they saw him on television, but because he had been involved in neighborhood organizations for more than twenty-five years. His association with the television station, however, elevated his status among fellow activists and acquaintances. The possibility of a broader viewing audience was critical to his ability to convene his immediate face-to-face audience that evening. He communicated to all those present that "the people"—the politically organized poor—existed out there somewhere and were paying attention. This assertion made it clear that Chávez was not alone in using television to constitute the people as the subject of politics. Whether or not there were large audiences who would respond to his call, this absent presence of the "popular people" helped grant Luis the political influence to challenge the government officials who were guests on his show that evening. The contentious debate that unfolded during Luis's talk show made clear how the political unity of variously positioned actors within the revolution depended on the symbols of Chávez and the people.

Luis introduced his guests and invited Pablo, the former coordinator of the social oversight committee, to explain his group's denuncia. Pablo wore red, the color associated with the Bolivarian Revolution, and a red baseball hat with the slogan, "With Chávez, the people rule" (Con Chávez, manda el pueblo). First used during the 2000 presidential elections, the slogan declared Chávez as a vehicle for the fulfillment of democracy's promise of the population's sovereignty or self-rule. Pablo was not alone in wearing a piece of clothing that referenced Chávez. Five other people in the circle wore a hat or T-shirt that invoked the president's image or name.

Pablo described how he and his colleagues had discovered medications and supplies hidden in an unused area of the hospital, which they suspected were going to be diverted for illicit sale elsewhere. He suggested that the mayor was complicit in pilfering the hospital supplies. Pablo asserted that the social overseers were doing what Chávez had asked of them. He claimed to know Chávez's will and argued that it was being transgressed by the mayor's office, which was not granting him or members of his committee the respect they deserved. Before he relinquished the microphone, he complained about their missing pay.

In contrast with the T-shirts and jeans worn by almost all Luis's guests, Francisco Ochoa, the next guest to join the debate, sported a finely tailored gray suit and white button-down shirt, which typically signaled professional middle-class status. Ochoa worked in the mayor's office and was responsible for coordinating the social oversight committees in the region. He defended the mayor by claiming he acted to fulfill Chávez's vision and was following through on Chávez's proposal to create oversight committees. He denied the charge of corruption and reminded the participants that social overseers were not contracted workers or employees, but had agreed to lend their services voluntarily. This formulation implied that the mayor's office owed no explanation for the missing incentives.

The next speaker, Samira, who also worked in the mayor's office, corroborated Ochoa's assertions. She was dressed more informally than her colleague, in a jean jacket and a tight red tank top. She grew heated as she spoke. "When the president said that the functionaries needed to go out to the street, Licenciado Ochoa was the first one out there." She declared that Ochoa was united with those who inhabited "the street," a euphemism for the poor. Yet by calling him "licenciado," which referred to his official status as a university graduate, Samira highlighted his elevated class position. Samira admitted that she did not know why the social overseers had not been paid. She belittled their demand to be remunerated for their labor, scolding the ex-overseers: "I ask that you reflect for a moment; the revolutionary desire to do social oversight should come from inside, from the passion of wanting to fight for our communities, for our hospitals." She dismissed the overseers' focus on their financial incentive, noting, "You are parents that have to maintain families, you can't rely on 600,000 bolivares in any case. I'm sure with all the talent you all have you could find good jobs, if you look for them."

Samira's statements reflected a socioeconomic position and perspective that differed from that of the people I knew who lived in barrios. She derided the former social overseers' focus on what she suggested was an insignificant sum of money, and she cast the job market in a way that little resembled the experience of most people from poor neighborhoods, who struggled to find stable formal employment.

On the other side of the semicircle, an older man named Tómas gestured for the microphone and adjusted his posture. Tómas's red baseball cap was embroidered with white thread that read "El Bravo Pueblo Con Chávez" (The brave people with Chávez). Tómas identified himself as an activist from El 23 de Enero, the massive poor neighborhood of west Caracas that boasted a history of revolutionary commitment. He declared:

> One doesn't learn to be a revolutionary by taking workshops; this is proven in the struggle, in years of struggle. My witnesses that I'm a revolutionary aren't in the government. No, my witness is the people. I agree with the licenciado and the licenciada [referring to Ochoa and Samira] that we should unite ourselves. . . . We need to know the origins of each one of us to see who we really are. And yes, I think that being guided by the pocketbook or your stomach is a weakness. But when there is inequality, the issue is different. It's easy to say what you're saying when you have a job and monthly salary. I call on

officials to put their salaries on the line, make your salaries available! What we need is social oversight of the social oversight program!

Tómas argued that the notion that the poor should contribute volunteer labor based on their revolutionary commitment was absurdly hypocritical coming from those safely ensconced in salaried government positions. He suggested that Ochoa's university education and position of official power rendered his claims to being part of the people suspect. Tómas asserted that a person's "origins," which simultaneously referenced political, geographical, and class background, provided a key to deciphering one's true commitments. As he finished, a tremendous round of applause could be heard from the adjacent cafeteria where dozens were watching the program.

When the cheers finally died down, Ochoa reclaimed the microphone to respond to Tómas. "When you say that it seems to you that we are from the outer sphere, or some height, look, my friend, I'm from the 23 de Enero [barrio]. I graduated from Central University of Venezuela and it was a struggle." Ochoa rejected the divide Tómas had asserted between himself and "the people" by revealing his own origins in the same poor and famously revolutionary neighborhood that Tómas was from.

Debates like this one reveal how in everyday life in Caracas the concept of the people was endowed with what Thomas Hansen calls "ideological knots" (1999, 25). In the face of middle-class professionals who claim to be part of the people, Catia TVe and their allies worked hard to tighten the knot that binds the people to the oppressed and disenfranchised poor. Despite Ochoa's counterclaim that he too was part of the people and shared roots with Tómas, Ochoa's access to a university education and a position of power in the mayor's office made this assertion tenuous. The claims and counterclaims around who belonged to the people and who could declare their belonging as part of the popular class were made more complex by the fact that the Bolivarian Revolution aimed to allow the poor access to higher education and leadership in state institutions. Ochoa's upwardly mobile status ostensibly represented what the revolution could accomplish. Nevertheless, for Tómas the class-tinged condescension that Ochoa and his colleague Samira had expressed about the volunteers' demand for their promised stipend rendered suspect their claims of belonging to the people.

With his claim that he was part of the people falling flat, Ochoa redirected everyone's focus to a statement that Tómas had made about Chávez on camera at a rally the day before. Ochoa argued that video evidence from the rally made clear Tómas's disloyalty to the president. Luis, the Catia TVe host, interrupted to suggest that we all watch the video Ochoa referenced alongside footage he himself had shot of the same rally.

The audience turned their attention to the flat-screen television at the back of the studio. First we watched eight minutes of haphazard, unedited footage that Luis had filmed of interviews with both the ex-volunteers and the mayor's representatives. Next we watched the mayor's video of the same rally. The video had been selectively edited by someone in the mayor's office to cast Tómas and his allies as traitors to the revolution. In the video, Tómas accused the cameraperson of being an elite functionary who had no knowledge of revolutionary struggle. The word "threat" suddenly appeared on the screen above Tómas's image. The editors slowed down the footage, distorting Tómas's movements and giving his voice a menacing quality. The video concluded with Tómas's strident assertion, "We continue to be revolutionaries, with or without Chávez." The video's editor looped this final clip so that we heard Tómas repeat the phrase "with or without Chávez" five times in rapid succession. Tómas's comment suggested that while he and his allies supported Chávez, the president was not an essential aspect of their revolutionary struggle.

Up until this point in the evening, Luis, the program's host, had stayed almost expressionless, betraying little sympathy with any of his guests' interventions. But watching the video, Luis fidgeted uncomfortably in his seat. Evidently, the mayor's video edged him out of a stance of neutrality. Before letting his guests respond, Luis noted, looking straight into one of the massive studio cameras, "I just have to say here, and I hope all the producers at Catia TVe are listening, never ever try to make a film like the one we have just watched made by the mayor's office. Such a horrendous display." Ignoring Tómas's assertion, which provocatively concluded the video, that revolutionaries could persist "with or without Chávez," Luis condemned the mayor's office for deliberatively misrepresenting events, his voice trembling in anger. He directed his attention to his guests from mayor's office: "In truth, this seems to me a grave manipulation."

A member of the mayor's staff named Edward tried to redirect the conversation back to the question of Tómas and his allies' loyalty to Chávez, which he seemed to assume would make clear that the denuncia makers were traitors with unjustified claims. "To the comrade who says that he is a revolutionary with or without Chávez, look at me, my friend," he said addressing Tómas from across the circle. "With Chávez everything, without Chávez nothing!" The mayor's faction asserted complete devotion and connection to Chávez as a litmus test of revolutionary commitment. Cheers erupted from supporters of the mayor inside the studio and in the adjacent room.

The effort of the mayor's representatives to push the dissident group out of the category of the people into the category of the enemy fell flat. Luis's strident accusation that the mayor's film manipulated the truth, together with his uncut footage of the same event, made it impossible for those siding with the mayor to gain control of the narrative. Luis defended the ability of the denuncia makers to challenge Chávez's indispensability and question the righteousness of government actors.

Luis's program made abundantly clear that the Bolivarian movement was rife with dissent and disagreement and that it was far from clear whether the poor were gaining meaningful access to power. Catia TVe had proven to be an arena to expose and discuss this question. The debate exposed the shifting lines of identification with the concept of "the people." Tómas argued that the people's enemy was not only an elite oligarchy, but all those who stood in the way of meaningful challenge to class inequality. Yet despite the efforts of Tómas and his group to pitch themselves as the authentic people against a rising new middle class of government officials, the lines were not in fact so clear. Officials working in the mayor's office, like Ochoa, occupied ambiguous positions. Some were from and continued to live in poor neighborhoods and built on experiences of popular organizing. Moreover, as I explored in the previous chapter, Catia TVe's leadership itself included not only people who were from solidly middle-class backgrounds, but also people from poor neighborhoods but who had managed to become upwardly mobile. Who counted as the people was an ongoing struggle. The challenge Catia TVe producers and their allies like Tómas faced was to keep the struggle for social justice central so that the voice and outlook of the oppressed were not excluded from emerging state institutions, even if at times the category of the oppressed was ambiguous and shifting.

During Luis's program, the figure of Chávez was open to appropriation in ways that challenged official state actors; their lack of transparency and dismissal of class inequalities within the Bolivarian movement were exposed. Denuncia makers invoked Chávez to challenge calls for unity that concealed corruption and inequity. Even as Chávez and many of his supporters drew on the Manichaean distinction between friend and enemy, Catia TVe producers and some of their interlocutors resisted this simplifying logic to open up debate among supporters of the revolution. They did so by claiming to know Chávez's will and by suggesting that they could build the revolution without him.

Conclusion

Catia TVe producers often confronted practices of devotion to Chávez in their interactions with people in poor neighborhoods that undermined local problem solving and concentrated power in the figure of the president. Moreover, in their dealings with some officials in state institutions they confronted bureaucracy and its class privileges and opacities. In the face of both these challenges, Catia TVe producers continually worked to unify people from poor neighborhoods and to assert them as agents of change, preventing "the people" from being an interpelletive move performed only by the president. Catia TVe producers' denuncia coverage allows us to understand how they attempted to channel faith in Chávez's superhuman capacities into popular power. During the period of my fieldwork, the outcome of these efforts was still unclear. Ten years later, it is apparent that Catia TVe producers and their allies were not able to sustain the contradiction that Chávez's centralized leadership presented between demobilizing and emboldening popular activism.

My ethnographic accounts in this chapter have illustrated how under Chávez's leadership the concept of the people was thrown asunder. Neither Chávez nor other state officials controlled the meaning of the people. We have seen how community media producers and their interlocutors used the process of television production to constitute the people and call for accountability from Chávez and his government. I have illustrated how Chávez's ubiquity created opportunities for social actors, like Catia TVe activists, to challenge those who invoked Chávez in order to quell dissent. What the president represented and what his wishes were proved to be elastic, and so Catia TVe producers and denuncia makers could reference Chávez in ways that undermined efforts to silence criticism. Catia TVe producers and their allies invoked the president not simply to extend his power but to bolster the standing and legitimacy of the poor as a class. Catia TVe's organizing approach challenged both liberal norms, which assert politics as a practice of autonomous individuals, and demagogic strategies, which aim to produce the people as a fluid category existentially reliant on a leader.

Contradictions, as David Harvey reminds us, are rarely resolved once and for all. Instead, problems are shifted around, leaving "marks and sometimes scars from their passage" (2014, 3). Even while toward the end of the president's life and in the post-Chávez era, efforts to centralize power overwhelmed the attempts to assert popular leadership, my interlocutors from Catia TVe continue to struggle and strategize about how to challenge systemic inequalities given the changed political circumstances. It will be some time before we know if or how the marks left by efforts to develop class consciousness and popular political identities during the period I documented come to shape future movements.

FIVE

MEDIATING WOMEN

A central aim of Catia TVe's staff, as I have noted in previous chapters, has been to encourage participation in state formation through the process of media production. I have explored how Catia TVe staff attempted to situate the marginalized poor as revolutionary actors and leaders never wholly separate from nor determined by official state actors and institutions, but rather in a relationship of radical interdependency. In this chapter I continue this exploration of the interdependency between official state actors and barrio-based organizations by demonstrating how Catia TVe producers, together with their allies from the state-run ViVe TV, produced a gendered dynamic of power that prioritized male leadership and authority.

Gendered oppression persisted despite the fact that activists inside and outside official institutions worked to make considerable gains for women's rights during the Chávez era. Building on a groundwork of activism in the 1940s and legislation in the 1990s, the new 1999 constitution included considerable advances for gender equality, including rights to pensions for women who work at home and protections for women who are breastfeeding (Espina and Rakowski 2010, 181). For the first time, the constitution used nonsexist language. New women's rights legislation included laws against domestic violence and for women's equal employment opportunities. Although they were still vastly outnumbered by men, women from multiple racial, ethnic, and, to a limited degree, class backgrounds were appointed or elected to positions of leadership in the upper echelons of the Chávez government. With the development of the Bolivarian Revolution's social welfare programs, women from poor communities

FIGURE 5.1. The 1999 constitution for sale on Caracas street, January 25, 2006.
Photo by the author.

in Venezuela became increasingly active in local politics through their participation in community health initiatives, community governance councils, soup kitchens, educational programs, and community media organizations.

Nevertheless, stark gender inequalities and traditional gender norms continued to shape Venezuelan society and marked the Bolivarian Revolution. Although legal changes under Chávez represented steps forward for women's rights, many of the principles and rights expressed in the constitution were not implemented or have been "so general and poorly written as to be un-implementable without significant reform" (Rakowski and Espina 2011, 163).[1] The 1999 constitution omitted the right to safe and legal abortion (as had the previous constitution).[2] Venezuela continues to trail behind other Latin American countries in gains for women's and lesbian, gay, bisexual, queer, and trans rights (Buxton 2015).[3] The revolution's social welfare programs in health, nutrition, and housing invoked and enacted a maternalist discourse that naturalized women as caregivers of families and communities.

Many proponents of the Bolivarian movement, including my informants at Catia TVe, focused almost exclusively on class inequality as the central form of discrimination around which to unite, overlooking the ways, for example, that class is always a gendered and racialized process. Catia TVe leaders and staff, for the most part, did not prioritize a critique of gendered relations of power as vital to advancing Bolivarian socialism. Women who participated at Catia TVe made remarkable gains in the field of media production, an arena long dominated by men. Nevertheless, men at Catia TVe enjoyed greater opportunities than women to develop their technical knowledge, as well as their skills in public speaking and leadership. Men and women participants at Catia TVe most often explained these inequities as individual deficits and the result of capitalist culture rather than as a product of the Bolivarian Revolution. They saw attention to gender oppression as separate from their struggle against the class domination of capitalism.

The persistence of traditional gender hierarchies and inattention to intersectionality that I observed at Catia TVe were not unusual.[4] The sidelining of gender hierarchies and the lack of analysis of the interrelations of class, race, and gender by progressive social movements has numerous historical antecedents in Latin America and elsewhere. Feminist scholars of Latin America noted in the early 1990s how in many male-dominated progressive and revolutionary movements in the region, "women and 'their issues' were invariably relegated to secondary positions" (Sternbach et al. 1992, 209). Unlike other revolutionary contexts where mass organizations of women emerged to politicize sexist oppression, such as the Federation of Cuban Women, the All-China Women's Federation, and the Isabel Amanda Espinoza Association of Nicaraguan Women, women in revolutionary Venezuela were not participating in large numbers in either officially state-led or self-proclaimed "autonomous" women's organizations (Rakowski and Espina 2011).

Prominent explanations for why there was no cogent women's movement within the Bolivarian Revolution have largely missed the mark. Central in much scholarly analysis of the ability for feminist movements to make inroads during the Bolivarian Revolution are the concepts of *state* and *nonstate*. Scholars often explain the absence of a mass women's movement by highlighting the lack of autonomy of women's groups from centralized state management. According to many feminist scholars and critics, the Chávez government's top-down state management of social movements inhibited the development of a strong women's movement in Venezuela (Blanco 2007; Espina 2007; Rakowski and Espina 2006).

These scholars' contributions to understanding the failures and successes of struggles for women's rights in Venezuela have been enormous. However, their categories of analysis—nonstate (sometimes referred to as nongovernmental or popular) and state—make it difficult to recognize the dynamism and interrelation between spheres. While scholars were justified in their concerns about the vertical decision-making that characterized many of the new social programs, the distinction between democratic community and a domineering masculinist state apparatus prevents us, methodologically as well as theoretically, from tracing the way that gender oppression was coproduced in the overlapping and mutually constituting fields of state and society.

Building on the analysis I have advanced in previous chapters of the insufficiencies of a binary approach to state and society, this chapter extends the argument to the domain of gendered power. Rather than seeing the state as a separate and coherent site in which power is concentrated and legitimated, I redirect focus to the perpetuation of gender inequalities through the radical interdependencies that emerged between and among community and official state institutions such as, in this case, Catia TVe and ViVe TV. As I have explored, state institutions were created and re-created during interactions between multiple differently situated actors. I highlight that what happens in these interactions—that is, the construction of state power and the construction of gendered power—not only rehearses previously given relations, but also generates emergent relationships of power. It was not only or even principally male dominance from within the ranks of official state institutions that threatened women's political participation in barrio-based organizations like Catia TVe or prevented the development of a revolutionary women's movement. Catia TVe producers negotiated and produced gendered dynamics of power in the mutually constituting fields of community and official state media production. I document and analyze how efforts to sidestep gender oppression within and beyond the Bolivarian movement were joint productions of community activists and official state actors who together were involved in a process of state formation. From this perspective, we can better understand that the problem barrio women faced in gaining access to leadership and decision-making was not the state as a separate monolith apart from community organizers, but rather the coconstitutive patriarchy, classism, racism, heterosexism, and capitalist logics that ordered local and global relations and were internal to the revolutionary movement itself, not imposed upon it from without.

In order to make recognizable how male supremacy and sexist oppression—what is locally referred to as machismo—was produced and reinforced in the media world of Caracas, in part through men's dominant presence on television, I closely examine discursive practices (Gal 1995; Kulick 1993) and television production choices during one talk show that proved exemplary of the relations I documented throughout my fieldwork. Linguistic anthropologists and gender theorists have long explored the interplay between interpersonal interaction and large-scale structures of power (Butler 1990; Cameron 1997; Gal 1991). I build on this theory to understand speech and gender as kinds of social performances that create relations of power and ways of being. The talk show I analyze provided useful data for me to examine how gendered inequalities were produced and enacted through the social practices of speaking and media production in a setting unambiguously shaped by both community and state media makers. I uncover how media production decisions shape speech events and can create and reproduce gender inequalities in access to public speaking. Finally, I consider some of the reasons why my informants at Catia TVe avoided analyzing and challenging the traditional gender order.

Gender Oppression and Maternalist Discourse at Catia TVe

In both official state arenas and neighborhood settings, women Catia TVe producers embodied a break from the traditional gendered division of media labor. Through their filmmaking, women at Catia TVe regularly challenged the notion that only elite male professionals could be journalists. Unlike the professional environments of official state and commercial television production, where women were sidelined from certain jobs such as studio camera operator, Catia TVe's leadership embraced the notion that staff and volunteers should learn to be what they called "integral producers," equipped to perform all the tasks involved in television production. Often, as I have noted in previous chapters, staff and volunteers from Catia TVe were the only female camera operators and only nonprofessional media producers present at an event. In their work at Catia TVe and elsewhere, women faced gender bias and discrimination.

Although, as I highlighted in the introduction, Catia TVe's earliest incarnation was as a male-dominated film club, under Blanca Eekhout's leadership this dynamic shifted; by the late 1990s, 75 percent of the people who participated in the community television station were women (Eekhout 2004). Reflecting on Catia TVe's history, Blanca noted, "traditionally audio-visual production has been an elite and masculine activity . . . nevertheless, our experience in the community media has been extraordinary. The interest of women of the barrio to learn and create is so enormous that now we have to worry about attracting men to be producers" (2004, 42). Blanca's concern proved unwarranted. The numbers of female staff and volunteers at Catia TVe declined from the 75 percent that Blanca documented in the late 1990s to 36 percent by the time of my research in 2007. Given the disproportionate burden that poor women shoulder in caring for their families and the intense time commitment that television production requires, the difficulty of sustaining widespread participation among women was not surprising. Catia TVe's leadership—Blanca and the men who succeeded her as director—did not direct explicit attention to the gendered dynamics of power at Catia TVe, thus creating little possibility for challenging male privilege or developing strategies to support women's participation.

When I interviewed Ana and Margarita, who helped found Catia TVe, both women described how dominant gender norms shaped their ability to participate. Ana's and Margarita's commitment to their political work at Catia TVe caused considerable conflict in their households. Ana often mentioned that her husband was not supportive of the long hours she dedicated to Catia TVe. Margarita's partner was far more intolerant, and their relationship ended. She noted, "He didn't believe in Catia TVe and he didn't want me here. But I did believe in it and I am still here." Burdened with most if not all of the labor of childcare, Ana and Margarita frequently had their young children in tow. In contrast, the men at Catia TVe who had children only occasionally brought them to the station.

Ana explained to me that when she began devoting more energy to community activism in the late 1990s, she and her women friends explicitly recognized the need to address what they called "family dynamics" as an arena of politics that required transformation. Ana noted,

> We began to meet in the communities and something that we said was, "the Revolution has to begin inside the family." Because it can't be that we participate in meetings, but then I have to do everything in the house. If your partner is also there, then he has to understand the situation and collaborate. In my case, this more or less happened. But for other compañeras [female comrades], this didn't happen. Instead, they were running around trembling because their husbands were calling and they couldn't go to the workshops. . . . These are gigantic steps that women are taking to be apart from men and be able to

complete goals like studying and participating in assemblies, in politics, decisions, and work.

Ana explains that her and her compañeras' participation in politics challenged central aspects of the dominant ideology of machismo in Venezuela, including the belief that women "should stay in man's shadow and in the private realm" (Acosta-Alzuru 2003, 275). Machismo is often understood as virulent sexism and a particular performance of tyrannical masculinity in Latin America and Spain that promotes and legitimizes gender stratification (Gutmann 1986).[5] For decades women in Venezuela have headed 25 percent of households; in poor neighborhoods, this proportion rises to half (Friedman 2000). There are, nevertheless, widely held assumptions that a man works to provide for the family and in return should exercise total authority and command respect (Smilde 2007; Zubillaga and Briceño-León 2001).

Even as Ana and Margarita highlighted the injustice of the gendered division of labor in the domestic sphere, the idealization of women as caretakers of family and community was, in fact, a central trope that many activists mobilized to celebrate women's contributions to the Bolivarian Revolution. This discourse, which scholars call maternalism, held that women had a particular kind of moral and political authority based on their traditional roles as mothers caring for their families and their broader communities (Chase 2015). In an interview, I asked Hector about the role of women at Catia TVe and in state-supported community organizations more broadly. He responded:

> The strength of the Bolivarian Revolution is in the communities. With other revolutions it has been the workers, the peasants. Here in Venezuela, one sees that it is the community. And the community is the women, fundamentally. When we are working in the neighborhood, every time we do social work, we always encounter women; they are the ones working in the neighborhood, concerned for their children, the family. I think this has also given strength to the [political] process. On the political level of direction, there's a lot of political concern for including women. Since the revolution started, women have been the protagonists. They have been the most concerned about feeding their families and began to take to the streets.

Hector's assertion that women's labor represents the central force propelling the Bolivarian Revolution is an important recognition of women's contributions. Yet the classification of women as "most concerned" about the well-being of their families naturalized women as caretakers without drawing attention to both the economic conditions and gender ideologies that sustain such a division of labor and responsibility. Hector frames community organizing as "women's work" (see also Fernandes 2007). He characterizes women as the protagonists of the revolution insofar as they labor as mothers and caretakers.

Although Ana and Margarita drew overt attention in our interviews and conversations to the need for a revolution in both gender and class relations, neither Ana nor Margarita explicitly incorporated questions of gender-based oppression into their efforts to organize around the democratization of access to media in poor neighborhoods. Moreover, neither woman regularly spoke about the need to address gender oppression and its relationship to class oppression at Catia TVe.

An exchange between Ana and Hector, coassistant directors at Catia TVe, revealed some of the barriers Catia TVe women producers faced in drawing attention to gendered dynamics of power and assuming roles as public speakers. I joined Ana in Catia TVe's production office one afternoon watching ViVe TV's live broadcast of a meeting of the Women's International Democratic Federation (WIDF), an international organization holding its conference that week in Caracas. WIDF is an explicitly socialist, antiwar, antifascist women's rights organization founded by communist women in Paris in 1945. On the opening day of the five-day conference, hundreds of women from more than one hundred countries sat in a large assembly hall in downtown Caracas listening to a Brazilian woman give a speech about the importance of fighting for gender equality. The Chávez government's effort to host the WIDF in Venezuela signaled an official affirmation of the importance of fighting for gender equality as part of the process of building socialism. Yet discussion between Ana and Hector made clear the lack of consensus at Catia TVe about the need to examine gender oppression. Passing through the office, Hector paused to watch the broadcast with us. After a few minutes, Hector dismissed the conference as "opportunistic." He suggested that these women were deflecting attention from the more important issue of class in order to advance their individual careers. Hector reproduced a widely held belief at Catia TVe, expressed most prominently by the male leadership, that liberation for everyone—including women—would be achieved once socialism was firmly established. In this view, countering the sexist, racist, and heteronormative oppression that is part and parcel of capitalism was not central to the process of constructing socialism.

Ana exhaled loudly. "It's because of people like you," she said to Hector, "that working-class women haven't developed a consciousness about gender and aren't participating!" Jabbing her index finger heatedly into the air, Ana continued, "It's our job to educate working-class women and teach them a different ideology than what they know, what they've learned from the crap on television." While many supporters of the Bolivarian Revolution frequently blamed commercial television for exploiting women and propagating oppressive gender norms to sell products, Ana went further, suggesting that her longtime colleague Hector, a strident socialist, was implicated in the perpetuation of gender oppression. Hector dismissed Ana's assertion by laughing and walking away. His stigmatization of women's efforts to highlight gender-based subordination as opportunistic and divisive contributed to an environment at Catia TVe that discouraged open attention to gendered power and male supremacy.

A traditional gendered division of labor informed by maternalist ideology shaped Catia TVe. For example, men did all the driving. The cleaning staff was made up exclusively of women. All the security guards were men. Despite a stated commitment among the leadership to training media makers capable of undertaking every aspect of production, the gendered division of labor among the staff extended to the arena of television production. Margarita, who was among the first cadre of Catia TVe volunteers, taught video production to many of the men at Catia TVe who later became her colleagues. Over time, however, her former male students surpassed her in their knowledge of the technical aspects of filmmaking. Margarita often looked to Gregorio, her former pupil, for help in resolving problems with a computer or a camera. Unlike Margarita, Gregorio did not hesitate to dissect electronics, unplug and reconnect cables until he found a solution or concluded that there was a problem he could not fix. Overall, men at Catia TVe were much more comfortable than women in experimenting when they encountered a technical problem. Margarita's lack of confidence with electronics undermined her status at the station. While this division of labor is not surprising and certainly reflects broader societal and global patterns, given the social upheaval in other areas of everyday life during this period in Caracas, the lack of reflection and critique of the gendered order was a noteworthy blind spot.

Male dominance was particularly stark in the area of public speaking and leadership of community media organizations. My observations of larger gatherings that brought together community media organizations from across Venezuela—both radio and television—revealed that men led the

FIGURE 5.2. Catia TVe volunteers learning to edit, January 14, 2007. Photo by the author.

majority of these media groups. These findings corroborate what other scholars have documented about male-dominated leadership of community media (Fernandes 2011; Tanner Hawkins 2006). After Blanca Eekhout left Catia TVe to lead ViVe TV in 2003, only men have filled the position of Catia TVe's director. Ana, who held the position of coassistant director at the time of my research, exerted considerable influence at the station through her organization of the station's community outreach initiatives. Often, however, she was left out of decision-making by the male director and her male coassistant director. Ana's authority, like that of her women colleagues, was often undermined by her male colleagues' domination of competitive public speaking arenas and the lack of support for her development of technical skills.

As the following ethnographic examples illustrate, gendered inequality was not a top-down practice but was instead created in the mutually constitutive and interdependent fields of state institutions and barrio-based organizations. First, I show how ViVe TV and Catia TVe producers created conditions that did not encourage Darnelis, a woman Catia TVe producer, to develop her skills as a cinematographer. Next I consider how staff from the two stations used the tools of media production to shape the speaking floor of a televised talk show in ways that buttressed men's leadership and silenced Ana, the only woman guest on the show.

Gendered Power On and Off Screen

The filming of a live studio talk show coproduced by Catia TVe and ViVe TV, which I observed one morning in April 2007, nicely illustrates the discursive and media production dynamics that shaped the gendered struggle for power at Catia TVe, and to some extent the Bolivarian Revolution more broadly during the time of my research. To commemorate the fifth anniversary of the failed 2002 coup, when major commercial television networks aligned with leaders of the political opposition to orchestrate Chávez's removal and create a media blackout of the popular resistance, ViVe TV filled its broadcast schedule with programs that focused on community media producers' memories of the dramatic events. For Chávez supporters, the coup had come to represent the manipulative power of the commercial media and the capacity for popular organization to shape history. The fifth anniversary of the coup was an opportunity for the government and its supporters to highlight the antidemocratic practices of Chávez's opposition, to celebrate popular social movements, and to highlight the government's expansion of press freedom to the poor. What had been an unplanned outpouring of support for Chávez and the Bolivarian Revolution in 2002 was carefully recreated and restaged by barrio activists and official state institutions in 2007.

The producers of one of ViVe TV's morning talk shows asked Carlos, Catia TVe's director, if ViVe TV could film their program on the morning of the coup's anniversary at Catia TVe. Carlos readily granted ViVe TV's request. The decision to stage ViVe TV's show at Catia TVe was a way to enact the message that ViVe TV, an official state television station, was supported by and connected to popular sectors. As I have recounted in previous chapters, the two stations frequently collaborated. Hosting this program at Catia TVe was one of the many ways that the government and official state actors depended on Catia TVe for legitimacy and ongoing support. Given the symbolic weight of the day's commemoration of the 2002 coup, this program held rich potential to assert the role of the poor in determining the meaning and direction of the Bolivarian Revolution. While Catia TVe and ViVe TV carefully staged the program in ways that emphasized the expansion of popular power in order to legitimize the revolutionary project, these performances always had the possibility of moving beyond empty gestures to produce meaningful analyses and advance popular demands. Yet even as these allied media producers advanced popular empowerment, they did so in ways that re-created and reproduced gender oppression.

ViVe TV's crew arrived at Catia TVe at 6 A.M. that April morning, just as the sun began to blaze across the valley. Of the nine-person ViVe TV production crew, which included a producer, a director, three camera operators, two hosts, and one assistant, only the assistant and one of the hosts were women. As in many ViVe TV productions, women were assigned the tasks of helpers and hosts. The director and camera operators arranged a bare-bones set of eight plastic chairs in a semicircle on the roof of Catia TVe's headquarters. Visible from the roof were several nearby barrios, the presidential palace, and the Caracas metro. Intermittent car horns and alarms from the street below placed the program almost directly in the street, substantiating the message about ViVe TV's connection to the barrio and the barrio's centrality to the revolution. The two hosts, a young man and woman from ViVe TV, settled into chairs in the middle of a semicircle, flanked by six guests. The ViVe TV hosts had grown up in middle-class neighborhoods. The guests on the program that morning included Ana and Luis from Catia TVe, representatives from a pro-Chávez website, the director of a community radio station, a Catia TVe volunteer, and a singer-songwriter well known among government supporters in Caracas. Carlos, Catia TVe's director, arrived midway through the program. Of the six guests on the program, Ana was the only woman.

Missed Lessons

Although the ViVe TV crew included three camera people, in the spirit of collaboration, the director of the show invited Catia TVe staff to operate the studio cameras for the program. Werner and Nestor, two male Catia TVe staff members, and Darnelis, a female staff member, volunteered to do the camera work. Werner, Nestor, and Darnelis regularly filmed live talk shows in Catia TVe's studio using similar equipment. Nestor, eighteen years old, and Darnelis, twenty-eight years old, joined Catia TVe's staff at the same time the year before and had equal experience in filmmaking. Werner, in his late thirties, had worked at Catia TVe for several years and had far more experience as a camera operator. Darnelis's participation as a cameraperson on a ViVe TV studio show was unusual. During my research, I never observed a woman operating a large studio camera at ViVe TV, although this was common practice in Catia TVe's studio.

Darnelis's identification as a lesbian was widely known at Catia TVe, although I had never observed her openly discussing her sexuality with her coworkers. Her gender performance was overtly masculine in certain ways. Darnelis wore her hair short and always dressed in baggy T-shirts, jeans, and hiking boots, a style popular among the men at Catia TVe. Darnelis faced regular harassment from several of her Catia TVe colleagues, mostly couched in derogatory jokes about her attraction to women and her taste in hairstyle and clothing. The sexism she faced was compounded by homophobia and heterosexism.

As the crew continued to set up, I took the narrow stairs down from the roof to the first floor of the station where the ViVe TV crew had set up their mobile transmitting unit. The show's director sat behind a series of monitors; three screens displayed the three different camera angles being filmed on the roof above. The director looked to be in his fifties. He impatiently barked commands over his headset at the camera operators, Werner, Nestor, and Darnelis.

I returned to the roof just before the program began to observe the beginning of the show. Just before they were set to go live on the air, Darnelis shook her head and removed the enormous headphones she was wearing. Looking around, she asked the male ViVe TV cameraperson to take over the camera she had been operating. Darnelis excused herself, explaining that she had forgotten that she had an appointment and would have to leave before the program was over. Despite this claim, Darnelis not only stayed to observe the entire program, but remained long afterward to help clean up.

During prior months of fieldwork with Darnelis, I had observed her negotiate discrimination at Catia TVe and in the various venues in which she filmed events on behalf of Catia TVe, including poor neighborhoods and the presidential palace. These observations along with interview data encouraged me to understand Darnelis's decision to observe rather than participate as shaped by her anxiety about her competence as a studio camera operator and the lack of support at Catia TVe in developing both knowledge and confidence. In an interview a few months before this incident, Darnelis had explained to me her uneasiness at filming in certain venues: "I think in the community [in poor neighborhoods] it's more normal to see anyone with a camera. But at a press conference for example, there are only trained journalists. At a press conference when one goes to film Chávez, it's only men doing camera, only men, and one feels, 'Ahhh, what am I doing here? Why? What's happening? [laughter]. Oh God!' But they [the male camera operators] are usually really friendly because you're a woman and they act all gentlemanly. They help you with the cables." Darnelis's comments reveal a level of discomfort in production arenas dominated by professionally trained middle-class male camera operators. She questions whether she belongs ("What am I doing here?"). This anxiety seemed to be shaped by Darnelis's experience of intersecting gender, sexuality, and class hierarchies. As with other women, Darnelis was subjected to the practice of "gentlemanly" behavior, which superficially was a sign of respect, but rendered her incapable of certain crucial aspects of camera work, such as moving cables. At the same time, Catia TVe and ViVe TV were environments often marked by heteronormative expectations and homophobic humor, making many arenas of production hostile places for Darnelis to negotiate. In addition, the ViVe TV producer, a man with considerable professional experience in the television industry, exerted middle-class authority over Darnelis. These multiple and intersecting expectations of her limited competence worked to undermine Darnelis's participation.

Throughout the recording of the show that morning, one of the unoccupied members of ViVe TV's crew took Nestor, Darnelis's colleague, under his wing, providing Nestor with pointers on how to manage the brightness and focus in the difficult outdoor filming conditions. For Nestor, the program became an opportunity to sharpen his camera skills and gain familiarity with ViVe TV's production style and expectations. Darnelis missed these valuable lessons.

"Taking the Word"

Television talk shows in Caracas were "locally meaningful speech events" (Hymes 1972) through which social actors competed to assert themselves as leaders. As in many places, talk shows were usually loosely structured conversations, during which hosts often dominated what scholars of language call the "speaking floor" (Edelsky 1981) at the beginning and end of each segment between breaks for promotional information. Before they went on the air that morning, ViVe TV's cohosts distributed two handheld microphones to the show's guests. Javier, a heavyset man in his fifties who directed a community radio station, reached out for one of the handheld microphones, and Luis, a founding member of Catia TVe, gestured for the other. Gazing steadily into one of the cameras, the female host opened the show. Dabbing the beads of sweat from her upper lip, the woman cohost noted, "We are broadcasting live from the headquarters of Catia TVe, where five years ago on a day just like today, Catia TVe was fighting the good fight." By 7 A.M. the sunshine on the open roof was fierce. Piercing horns grew louder as the traffic below intensified.

Before inviting the program's guests to speak, the cohosts read a brief news summary. "Yesterday, Chávez affirmed that the socialist woman of the twenty-first century is anti-machista. He affirmed that twenty-first century socialism should differentiate itself from capitalism in its fight against machismo." They described Chávez's speech the previous day to the Women's International Democratic Federation, the international organization holding its conference that week in Caracas. This was the same conference that Hector had dismissed as "opportunistic" in the exchange with Ana I described above. Reading from a paper he held in his lap, the male cohost noted that Chávez stated, "Women have been so mistreated throughout time. Socialist society should be one of equals, without any type of exclusion, where all kinds of people fit and gain access without any kind of discrimination."

Although initially Chávez did not appoint any women to cabinet positions and did not address gender inequality explicitly in his speeches, under the pressure and influence of activists long involved in the struggle to advance women's rights in government and in social movements, Chávez began to back efforts to elevate gender equality (Rakowski 2003). Chávez began to incorporate some aspects of a feminist analysis into his speeches to argue that the socialism under construction in Venezuela needed to be antisexist. Chávez's insistence on gender equality as the basis for Bolivarian socialism was always at odds with his own patriarchal style and strains of his discourse, particularly the masculine model of heroism he celebrated (Valdivieso Ide 2004). That morning's events made clear that the president's words alone were far from sufficiently powerful to compel his supporters to enact his stated vision. The disjuncture between Chávez's declaration of the Bolivarian movement's commitment to gender equality and the discriminatory practices of committed revolutionaries involved in producing that morning's program would prove enormous.

Moving on from the opening segment, the show's hosts asked their guests to reflect on the role of the commercial media on the day of coup. "I don't know who wants to speak," the woman cohost began. "Here, we are completely democratic." The cohosts had small wireless microphones pinned to their clothing, enabling them to interject in the conversation and assume the speaking floor at any time. The guests on the show, however, had to negotiate control over the two handheld microphones, which they passed between them. The host's claim that the show was organized democratically belied the power-laden struggle between participants on the program who exerted different kinds of gendered and class authority in their effort to gain and hold the speaking floor.

Javier, the community radio producer who had already claimed one of the mobile microphones, discussed how, during the coup, people used cell phones, megaphones, and fliers to counter the commercial media's claim that Chávez had resigned. When Javier finished his turn, he settled the microphone on his lap and looked at the hosts. The woman host then directed her attention to Ana and Luis, asking them to explain Catia TVe's activities during the coup. Having secured possession of the microphone before the program began, Luis immediately responded, describing how Catia TVe producers took to the streets with camcorders to document popular resistance and to spread the news that Chávez had been kidnapped. He spoke for five minutes without interruption. There was no light on the top of the cameras to indicate which of the three cameras the program's producer was choosing to broadcast in each moment. However, a television monitor tuned to the broadcast was set up facing the guests so that they could see which camera the producer was transmitting over ViVe TV's airwaves. Luis periodically glanced down at this monitor to see himself on screen. Being on screen seemed to provide him encouragement to continue.

Five minutes into Luis's speaking turn, he paused to take a particularly long breath. Ana seized the opportunity to reach for the microphone, which Luis readily relinquished. Ana began, "Also on that day, the twelfth [of April 2002], we didn't have much equipment, but with the little equipment we did have we supported Channel Eight [Venezolana de Televisión, the state channel]. And with this equipment, Channel Eight came back on the air. . . ."

"Hold on one second Ana," the female host broke in. "Excuse me for interrupting you but they are giving me the signal that we have to take a quick pause."

Ana immediately respected the request and stopped talking, ceding authority to the host. She held the microphone with the expectation that she would continue her turn. During the seven-minute break, ViVe TV broadcast material that promoted the channel's programming and celebrated the accomplishments of various state institutions. Ana nervously fiddled with the microphone, passing it back and forth between her hands. When the programming break ended, the male host welcomed viewers back to the program. Ana was poised to speak. But rather than returning to Ana, the male cohost shifted the focus of the conversation. Ana readily complied. She relinquished the microphone and folded her arms across her chest. In contrast, Carlos, Catia TVe's director—who had arrived during the program break—gestured for the microphone, demanding that one of Catia TVe's volunteers, who was poised to speak next, hand it over. Carlos decided when to speak and disregarded others' claims to the speaking floor. Ana did not successfully regain the speaking floor for the remainder of the hour-long show.

Context shapes the meaning of speech and silence. Linguistic anthropologists have revealed how verbal skills are not universally requisite for political power, and silence can generate authority in certain contexts (Gal 1991). However, at Catia TVe, producers and volunteers explicitly invoked the act of expressing one's "voice" and "taking the word" (*tomando la palabra*) as a metaphor for asserting oneself as a politically significant actor. One of the television station's prominent slogans claimed that Catia TVe represented "the voice and the image of the people." Speaking and having a "voice" was equated with asserting one's political rights and abilities.[6] In this context, for Ana to be interrupted and passed over by the talk show's hosts signaled a denial of rights and political influence. Dominant gender norms and expectations shaped access to "voice" and, thus, to authority in ways that neither the leadership of Catia TVe nor their ViVe TV colleagues acknowledged.

Catia TVe's male leadership regularly spoke at great length to audiences about the need for "el pueblo" to assert their voices, while the women at Catia TVe, who did most of the work organizing meetings, often watched from the sidelines or from the audience, far from the spotlight. Almost all Ana's women colleagues at Catia TVe during the time of my research assiduously avoided speaking in front of large groups. I found that men at Catia TVe dominated both formal and informal conversations where they competed with other men to display rhetorical fluidity—their ability to tell a story or joke quickly, with compelling detail and confident delivery. This fluidity granted male speakers considerable respect from their peers.

In the media world of Caracas, authoritative leadership was constituted and depended on the ability to gain the speaking floor and to hold it by expressing oneself with ease and confidence in front of large groups and often in the face of multiple television cameras.[7] Ana did not flourish in this context of competitive public talk, an arena in which her male working-class colleagues practiced regularly and were learning to thrive in, although their ability to do so was always shaped by particular contexts and relations of power. A longer in-depth analysis of gender, class, and language in Caracas would be necessary to do justice to the patterns I observed. For my purposes here, it is crucial to note that in exploring the gendered dimensions of public speaking, I follow Deborah Cameron (1997) in understanding that the way men and women talk is not the result of hardwired innate differences, but rather that speech is accomplished jointly by men and women in particular contexts. People speak and are verbally fluid in particular ways because of power relations of dominance and subordination, not because of their nature as men or as women (Gal 2001).

In this context, Ana's input was neither encouraged nor respected. She complied with the hosts' interruptions and instructions; her male colleagues defied their efforts to control the floor. Ana's subordination—during this program and in other moments—denied her an opportunity to develop fluidity and confidence as a public speaker and undermined her status as a leader. The host's redirection away from Ana may have been an effort to ensure that representatives from each of the various media outlets present had an opportunity to participate. Nevertheless, it suggested not only a lack of respect for Ana as a leader, but also a disregard for the imbalance of men and women participants on the show.

In an interview I conducted with Margarita weeks later, I asked why women from Catia TVe did not speak on behalf of the station as much as men. Margarita noted:

> If we examine the past, they taught us [women] to be unable to involve ourselves or speak. . . . Look, I feel sometimes inhibited to say a lot of things because I think I'm going to say something wrong, or mix something up and not make sense or that it's not the right moment to say something. . . . It's a barrier I create for myself because I'm nervous. . . . I have to dominate the camera, not let the camera dominate me. I dominate the camera when I film a documentary, but I don't dominate it when I see it and it sees me. This is what I need to do and there are a lot of women at Catia TVe just like me. I know they are really good. They are triumphant [*triunfadoras*]; they are powerful. My compañeras have a lot to give, like I do. But still, we haven't become accustomed to speaking in front of a camera and saying what we really feel.

Margarita acknowledges that she has been taught patriarchal gender norms that undermine her familiarity with speaking on camera. Here she also attributes her heightened anxiety around public speaking to her own particular insecurities.

Margarita was painfully aware of how the ability to be a persuasive public speaker was linked to social recognition and authority. Although I observed

Margarita assume central speaking and leadership roles in small groups, such as the ViVe TV workshop I described in chapter 3, she never spoke in front of the large gatherings of community members and new volunteers that she organized in poor neighborhoods or at Catia TVe. Margarita worked on her own at home, she told me, to develop her ability to speak comfortably in front of groups and on television. She explained, "When I am angry, I speak with myself in front of a mirror and say, 'If I can talk with myself in front of a mirror, why am I still like this?'"

Margarita often expressed to me that she felt that her work at the station was underappreciated. Indeed, I observed on several occasions how male producers cut footage of Margarita out of television programs they were editing about Catia TVe's work because they found her manner of speaking indirect and unpersuasive. One colleague described her speech as "watery." Despite her frustration, Margarita avoided an exploration, at least with me, of the gendered hierarchies at Catia TVe that shaped her confidence in the social world around the camera. Without a collective effort to examine and challenge male supremacy at Catia TVe, Margarita's only recourse was to practice in front of her bedroom mirror, away from the social relations that contributed to her lack of confidence.

Gregorio, who led the workshop that I detailed in the previous chapter, also acknowledged to me that public speaking made him nervous. Like Margarita, he explained that he forced himself to practice. When I asked him about the gendered inequalities in public speaking at the station and his own path to becoming more comfortable speaking in front of groups, he noted,

> I decided to learn and in one way or another I learned to insert myself into discussions with fear or without fear. So, why can't women do this? . . . There are examples, right? Blanca Eekhout is an example. Blanca speaks and she has a discourse and Blanca didn't just come up with it from nothing. She wasn't born with this discourse. She trained herself for this, see? . . . And you could say, perhaps, that men have more opportunities than women. Maybe. That could be one of the problems. But I believe that part of it is also that women need to demand the opportunity.

Gregorio, like most men and women at Catia TVe, acknowledged that fluidity with public speaking was a learned skill, rather than an innate capacity. Yet, despite Gregorio's usual attentiveness to class power, his analysis of Blanca's ability to learn to be an effective, well-respected public speaker did not take into account her middle-class education or her very fair skin, which granted her privileges in the barrios where she developed her public speaking skills. Gregorio, like many of his colleagues (both men and women), characterized the barriers that women face as individual rather than structural. He did not assess the role that both men and women play in creating environments that undermined women's public speech. He, like many of his male colleagues, exhorted women to "be more stubborn" about their speaking capacities, placing the burden on women to fix the problem rather than embracing it as a collective challenge necessary for all to assume in the struggle for Bolivarian socialism.

Calling the Shots

During the next break between segments in the joint ViVe TV—Catia TVe talk show, I revisited the control room two floors below, where the show's director brusquely issued a command over his headset. He instructed Nestor to focus his camera on the metro, which passed directly in front of Catia TVe. The ViVe TV director had three possible camera angles to choose from in order to stitch together or edit in real time the visual text of the program. In addition to broadcasting images of the program's hosts and guests, he directed the three camera operators (the two Catia TVe men, Nestor and Werner, and one ViVe TV operator) to compose shots of the surrounding environment. The director cut between images of guests on the show speaking and listening to shots of the cityscape.

It was commonplace on ViVe TV talk shows for directors to include not only shots of the surrounding landscape but "behind-the-scenes" images of the production of the show itself. The show's producer included several shots of Nestor, Werner, and the ViVe TV cameraperson—all mestizo men—operating the cameras. While the inclusion of behind-the-scenes shots compromised the realist construction of the text, these images crucially drew attention to the participatory process of media production and the entrance of young brown men from the barrio into state institutions. The attention that ViVe TV regularly drew to the technology of mediation worked to bolster not only the feeling that their station's practice included the total reality but also that this reality was democratic and egalitarian; the station seemed to hide nothing and to exclude no one. In one striking instance, the ViVe TV cameraperson panned from images of the surrounding poor neighborhood to Nestor operating the massive studio camera. Nestor was connected to and placed within the landscape of the barrio. These images served to support the program's explicit message that "the people" had seized the tools of media. And yet, although the program emphasized specific racial and class traits of the people, a move that bolstered claims for the leadership of the poor (as I argued in the previous chapter), as in many moments, the people represented during this ViVe TV show, with the exception of Ana, were all male.

The female host introduced the final section of the program by framing Catia TVe as the emblematic case of the people's empowerment under Chávez. "We are coming to you from Catia TVe," she said, "because Catia TVe is a magnificent example of community media that symbolizes that communications are for, by, and made by the people and the control and management of the people." The male host invited each guest to reflect on the importance of community media. Carlos gestured with an outstretched hand to the female host that he wanted to speak. She turned the speaking floor over to him. Carlos, however, changed his mind. "Actually," he said, "come back to me, I'd like to speak in closing." Instead, Harlan, the Catia TVe volunteer, spoke at length for a second time, followed by the website producer.

Just as the hour-long program was coming to an end, the woman host turned toward Ana and asked her, "How do you think that we can continue to consolidate our media, made by the people and for the people?" The image of the female host appeared on the screen but Ana did not. Rather than cut to a shot of Ana, the program's director switched to a shot of the surrounding scenery that Nestor had been composing and practicing with great care over the previous few minutes with the assistance of the ViVe TV cameraperson. Nestor carefully panned the camera from the cityscape in the distance to a wide shot of Carlos and several of the other guests, sitting on the other side of the semicircle from Ana.

Ana held the microphone and was about to respond when Carlos spoke up, noting, "There's something I'd like to say about this. . . ." Rather than cut to the camera that was focused on Ana, the program's director kept broadcasting the wide image that included Carlos. The visual text broadcast over ViVe TV's airwaves excluded any trace of Ana's second attempt to speak and Carlos's interruption. Her effort to speak went unsupported. While the ability of men to dominate conversation is often buoyed by what sociolinguist Judith Baxter (2006) calls "sidekicks," peers who help male speakers take and keep the speaking floor, in this instance, the camera, operated by a male cameraperson, served as Carlos's sidekick, encouraging his monopoly of the airtime. Speaking strategies combined with the process of visual production to undermine Ana's ability to win a turn in the competitive speaking arena. With the support of his coparticipants and the program's producers, Carlos once again took and held the floor.

The program's director, who literally called the shots, could have followed closely Ana's thwarted attempts to speak. He had the power to choose what aspects of the social field to highlight. Viewers of the broadcast were privy only to the camera angles he chose to include, not the surrounding world beyond the frame of the image. Together with the camera operators, the director omitted from the broadcast Ana's unsuccessful struggle to speak, making it appear as if it was a fluid and seamless conversation without miscues, inequalities, competitive clashes, or struggles for power.

"Long Live Women"

The minute details of this struggle provide clues to understand how different participants constitute power relationally. The gendered inequalities I am highlighting cannot be explained by pointing to how a masculinist hierarchical state was dominating the democratic grassroots. Autonomy from official state institutions could not contribute to greater gender equality given that the production and reproduction of these inequalities took place in the relations between and among actors who inhabited multiple positions in and outside official state institutions.

The seemingly spontaneous and unconstrained conversation during this studio talk show was, in fact, produced through struggle, shaped by and productive of social hierarchies, and influenced by the production choices of camera operators and producers. Kulick notes that conversations do not simply "reproduce already existing relations of [gender] dominance" (1993, 534). In the space of the program, men constituted themselves and were privileged as representative of popular empowerment. Subtle and overt interactions between those in front of and those behind the cameras undermined Ana's participation. In the moments when Ana attempted to speak, she was not "on camera" and therefore did not have the visual attention of either the director of the program or the potential television audience.

After Carlos interrupted her, Ana dropped the microphone to her lap. In a barely audible voice, she murmured, "They don't let me speak."

"We're inviting all . . . ," Carlos continued. As he spoke, Ana smiled uncomfortably and handed the microphone to Luis, sitting at her side. Ana shook her head and Luis patted her on the back. Ana muttered, "They are machistas." As she was no longer holding the microphone, her comment was inaudible over ViVe TV's airwaves but had attracted the attention of the female host, Luis, and a community radio volunteer. Carlos raised his voice in an effort to regain everyone's attention. "We're inviting all the community committees to come to Catia TVe for a meeting next week," he belted out. Carlos spoke for another four minutes, giving special thanks to all the "anonymous heroes" of the day of the coup. In the moment when Carlos "stole" the speaking floor, talking out of turn despite the fact that he had thoroughly dominated the time of the program, Ana was off screen.

When Carlos finished, the female cohost announced that they needed to wrap the program up. The ViVe TV director instructed her that they were out of time. Immediately, the Catia TVe volunteer and the community radio director pointed at Ana, indicating that she wanted to speak. Luis encouraged Ana, handing her the microphone. Unlike Carlos, some of Ana's colleagues grasped how Ana had been repeatedly excluded from the conversation.

"Well," Ana began, "what I wanted to say is that we have a country full of machistas [sexists]." She paused as the train rumbled by the building, making it more difficult to hear. Luis laughed uneasily.

"What?" asked the male cohost, confused about what Ana was referencing, seemingly unaware that Ana had been interrupted the two times that she had attempted to speak.

"We should borrow the slogan of the women who spoke last night," Ana said and paused.

"Last night . . . ," the community radio producer repeated, in an attempt to encourage Ana to go on. Traffic noise from the street below made it increasingly difficult for the program's participants to hear one another.

"What?" Ana asked.

"Last night," the female host repeated, also encouraging Ana to finish her thought.

"That we shouldn't be machista," said the radio producer, speaking for Ana. Ana could not hear him. She looked confused and did not continue her thought. After an awkward pause, Luis began chanting and clapping, "¡Qué viva la mujer! Long live women!" Another guest began to clap. "¡Qué viva la mujer!" In an effort to recognize Ana and the exclusion she experienced on the show, Luis interjected this celebration of women. Even as the chant drew attention to the dynamic of gendered oppression that had unfolded during the program, without discussion of what had taken place, his celebration of women's lives further concealed rather than opened up the workings of patriarchy. Ana passed the microphone back to one of the hosts. Luis stopped chanting and laughed uncomfortably. Disregarding the female host's effort to end the show, the radio director insisted on speaking for another minute about an upcoming event at his station. He seemed entirely unshaken by the urgent time pressure to close the show.

On national state television, Ana had denounced her community and state media colleagues as sexist and accused them of impeding her right to express herself. She clearly identified her experience of marginalization as a product of machismo. Given what was broadcast, viewing audiences would not have been able to follow what transpired or why Ana had labeled her colleagues as sexist. When the program ended, there was no discussion of what had happened. Ana's effort to participate in the discussion was unsuccessful. She made speaking on television neither look nor sound easy, traits that were crucial to managing the social authority on and off television. Although Gregorio and others tried to explain women's absence as public speakers at Catia TVe as a result of their lack of persistence, it was clear in this instance that men from Catia TVe and ViVe TV repeatedly blocked Ana's efforts to speak.

Although the program was intended as a display and reaffirmation of the unity and progress of "the people," the difficulty Ana faced in asserting herself into the speaking field directly contradicted the notion that this process of empowerment had been universal for the poor and working classes. Despite the hyperconscious valorization of popular expression and Chávez's condemnation of machismo, there was no attention among the male participants and female host to the structure of hierarchy they created, either during that program or within the revolution more generally. The men on the program—to varying degrees—were able to successfully "break and enter" into the speaking floor, control the microphone, gain the hosts' consideration, and attract the cameraperson and director's attention. They communicated the message that the people had assumed the reins of history, while denying the only woman guest on the program the opportunity to participate. Chávez's assertion, cited at the outset of the program, that "socialist society should be one of equals, without any type of exclusion," gained little traction in the space of this program.

A few days later, a different ViVe TV program came to film another live talk show at Catia TVe. This time there were no women included among the speakers or producers. I asked Hector, Ana's coassistant director, about the exclusion of women from the program. He assured me that women had been invited but none had shown up. Just then, Ana and Gregorio walked over to us and joined the conversation. Hector pointed out that Ana had been on the ViVe TV program the week before, described above, and noted that she had not spoken.

"Ana tried to speak several times and each time someone interrupted her," I noted.

"Well, she has to be more forceful," Hector responded.

Gregorio added laughing, "Yeah, when Ana really wants to talk, she screams!"

"It's true," Ana said smiling. She seemed reluctant to continue the conversation and avoided the opportunity to address the issue of machismo, which she had highlighted at the end of the talk show.

During the program, Ana explicitly named gender bias as the force impeding her access to the speaking floor. Scholars note that when gendered inequalities of public speaking are addressed, it is often not "the 'floor' that is judged as inauspicious, rather women are seen as timid or unable to express themselves" (Gal 1991, 188). Gregorio and Hector blamed Ana for her own exclusion. Significantly, she was either not forceful enough, or when she did speak, Gregorio marked Ana's speech as "screaming," a classification that rehearsed a common disparaging association between women and unreasonable emotion. Gendered relations of power, produced and reproduced in this arena of state and community collaboration and interrelation, shaped Ana's supposed "lack of forcefulness" and her unwillingness to disobey the hosts' directions.

The hierarchies exercised and constituted during the program undermined the inclusion and ongoing empowerment of poor communities that the ViVe TV talk show intended to promote and celebrate. For brief moments, as with her analysis of Hector's sexism and the machismo of her colleagues on live television, Ana challenged the notion that there was a unified people supporting the revolution and men's claim to represent it.

However, there was neither support nor incentive for Ana to launch a sustained critique of the exclusion she faced during the joint Catia TVe–ViVe TV show. Ana had multiple bonds and affiliations not only at Catia TVe but also with ViVe TV. She regularly championed ViVe TV as a model of inclusion when she spoke in poor neighborhoods about Chávez's transformation of the field of communications. Many close relations (including her sound-technician husband), political allies, and acquaintances worked at ViVe TV. Later, when we were alone, I asked Ana about her experience on the talk show. She downplayed the issue of machismo, attributing the men's domination of the speaking field to their passion and excitement at participating. As I see it, Ana's refusal to address the entrenched sexism that she faced was not as a sign of passivity or false consciousness. Instead, I interpret Ana's silence with me and in the interactions I observed with her colleagues as a "strategic response" (Gal 1991) that indicated her view that highlighting gendered inequalities could have potentially divisive consequences for the Bolivarian Revolution. Nevertheless, by calling attention to machismo during the talk show, Ana revealed a fault line, a constitutive flaw in the celebratory discourse of popular empowerment.

An analysis that concludes that ViVe TV's sexism was a result of a top-down authoritative state structure ignores how gender inequalities are constituted relationally, in language and through the social practice of media making in the collaboration between Catia TVe and ViVe TV. As I have argued in previous chapters, we require a dialectical approach to state formation that can capture the unfolding and unbounded character of the social fields that Catia TVe producers created and negotiated. Just as talk and gender relations on this talk show were joint accomplishments, that is, the product of collective interaction, so too was the process of state making. During this collaboratively produced talk show, there were several opportunities to address gender inequities and craft a more equitable state project. From Chávez's assertion that socialism entailed the destruction of machismo, cited at the start of the program, to Ana's interventions about the sexism she experienced during the program, there were openings to enact a state that acknowledged and rejected gender bias. What they coconstructed during the program, instead, was a flawed performance of popular empowerment that rested on the subordination of a barrio woman activist. Male supremacy did not emanate from above—from the masculinist vertical structures of the state—but was instead created through practices and interactions between differentially situated actors involved in state making.

The Struggle for Gender Equality in Venezuela under Chávez

Since the "second wave" of global feminism in the 1970s, debates about gender inequality have constituted a vital aspect of political struggle in Venezuela among left-leaning political parties and organizations. In many arenas, the social policies, legal protections, and welfare programs put in place by the Chávez government, building on decades of previous organizing, improved the lives of poor women. Despite a context seemingly ripe for challenging individual and institutional sexism, several dynamics were at work that encouraged Catia TVe producers and their allies at ViVe TV to avoid extending revolutionary change to the domain of gender relations. These factors include the Bolivarian Revolution's embrace of a maternalist discourse and practice, the history of liberal feminism in Venezuela, and the resistance to an intersectional analysis of the relationships between class and gender (as well as other social dimensions of inequality).

Bolivarian Maternalism

Women were the majority of those who not only benefited from but also staffed the Bolivarian Revolution's largest programs (called "missions") in health care and education (Cooper 2015; Espina and Rakowski 2010, 187). New social welfare programs attempted to alleviate class inequalities that were particularly burdensome for poor women. These programs collectivized and formalized domestic tasks as labor rather than placing these burdens on individual women. Efforts to pay women for the social reproduction of families and communities—the labor of feeding, cleaning, and caretaking—made visible that women were part of the relations of production and that they produced value through their work. Yet aspects of the revolution's legislative and welfare initiatives confirmed rather than contested institutionalized gender oppression, in part because they were guided by maternalist ideology that legitimized women's place in the domestic sphere (Fernandes 2010a).[8] The Mothers of the Barrio mission, for example, recognized and respected women's work in the home, but reaffirmed an ideology that framed women's burden of responsibility for family and community as a natural outcome of women's innate qualities.[9] The initiative to create soup kitchens to feed the hungry in poor neighborhoods was organized around the assumption that women would do the work of food preparation. Venezuelan feminist scholar Giaconda Espina suggests that paying women to do the domestic work for which they have historically been held responsible signaled a retreat rather than progress in challenging gender hierarchies (2007).

Nevertheless, for many poor women the revolution's social programs extended vital, immediate support that improved their quality of life. Dismissing these gains as a retreat from the movement to end sexist oppression overlooks how practical issues around which women organize—such as food, education, infrastructure, and media democratization—can create political space for the strategic advancement of campaigns for social justice, not only by increasing women's access to needed resources but also by granting them visibility and leadership experience.[10]

Liberal Feminism

Since the 1970s, the struggle against women's oppression in Venezuela has been divided largely between those who embraced the term *feminism* and prioritized a notion of individual autonomy, and activists from poor neighborhoods, who did not organize under the banner of feminism (Friedman 2000). Groups of poor women advocated for easing the day-to-day burdens of poverty, while middle-class and more elite women most often sought to raise consciousness about the kinds of gender oppression that formally educated women faced (Friedman 2000, 165). Affluent middle-class women in Venezuela built on liberal commitments to the importance of individual self-determination for producing freedom. Poor and middle-class women managed to collaborate successfully in the early 1980s to mobilize for the reform of Venezuela's Civil Code. The revised Civil Code ended married women's legal subjection to their husbands and advanced the equal legal status of all children. Much of the reform, however, did not speak to the reality facing poor women, because it prioritized the rights of women who were formally married, a practice common only to the middle and upper classes (Friedman 2000, 186).

For many feminist activists working in Latin America, the question of autonomy gained greater importance as women across the region increasingly began working to advance feminist agendas within state institutions (Alvarez et al. 2003). Elizabeth Friedman argues that as Venezuelan women's organizations began in the 1990s to rely on state funding and close collaboration with state institutions, they saw a rise of internal hierarchy and clientelism (2000, 234). Nevertheless, even women's movements that sought to distance themselves from the official state apparatuses were in vital ways entrenched in social relations and institutional arrangements in Venezuela and abroad, arrangements that belie their claims to act independently. The ability to claim autonomy from state institutions is a class-based capacity that affluent women have been far better positioned to invoke than poor women who, regardless of their political views, rely on official state resources.

Long-standing divisions between more affluent women and poor women became more pronounced and difficult to bridge during the Chávez era. Partly informed by the divisions that emerged in the 1990s as women's organizations began to work with state institutions, middle-class feminist intellectuals and the traditional leaders of the formal women's movement in Venezuela were distant, critical, and deeply suspicious of Chávez and his government. Chávez's patriarchal and hierarchical leadership style, as well as his military background, further alienated them. They viewed the tendency of Chávez's supporters in the highest echelons of government and the poorest barrios to characterize him as the sole agent capable of improving women's lives as a sign of the maintenance of patriarchal power and the lack of necessary autonomy. Venezuelan feminist scholar and activist Jessie Blanco argues, "to make a god of Father Chávez is once again to render invisible the role of women" (Blanco 2007). Attributing women's political participation and leadership to Chávez, according to Blanco, undercuts the accomplishments and authority of women leaders. Middle-class and elite women's emphasis on the need for autonomy from the state rendered feminism anathema to women and men at Catia TVe who embraced the possibility of revolutionary liberation through the process of collaborative statecraft.

Prominent feminist scholars attempted to overcome divisions between women aligned with the Bolivarian government and those aligned with the political opposition by arguing that Venezuelan women needed to put aside their political, ideological, and class differences and unite in the interest of women. Some advocated for an autonomous "Broad Movement of Women" that was not directed by Chávez or his government (Huggins 2005; Rakowski and Espina 2006, 326).[11] This impetus to downplay differences recycles many of the pitfalls of second-wave feminisms (Moraga and Anzaldúa 1983). The notion that either impoverished or elite women could "put aside" the experience of class and race to unite as women does not sufficiently acknowledge that gender, class, and race are not isolatable vectors of experience. Women at Catia TVe were not eager to affirm a specific political identity around their experiences as women or even as barrio-based, government-aligned women activists. Although Catia TVe producers including Ana were concerned about the capacity for grassroots groups to challenge official state discourse and gain meaningful access to decision-making, the view that women should assert their autonomy from the state to align with middle-class and elite women in the interest of "women" had little strategic appeal.

While my informants at Catia TVe generally supported the idea of women's equality in the abstract, most Catia TVe staff identified feminism as a middle-class women's movement that sought to privilege women's rights over men's. Blanca Eekhout expressed contempt for her academic colleagues who she asserted organized in the name of "women's rights" but only defended the interests of affluent women (Eekhout 2004, 41). My informants at Catia TVe viewed separate and autonomous movements for women's empowerment as being against the interests of the poor. Indeed, the notion that they needed to fight for "women's equality" with "men" overlooked how class and race intertwine with gender to create hierarchies; working-class men—particularly those of color—did not enjoy equality with wealthy light-skinned men in Venezuela's racist, capitalist, patriarchal class structure, a structure that continued to exist within the emergent institutions of Bolivarian socialism.[12]

FIGURE 5.3. Catia TVe producer filming an interview, July 21, 2008. Photo by the author.

My informants at Catia TVe largely understood feminism as the counterpart of machismo or male dominance. For example, Gregorio noted,

> The woman committed an error; when she had the opportunity to destroy machismo, what she did was to create feminism. This [feminism] was a force to counter it [machismo] but it continued to have the same posture. There isn't another option, an option to really destroy machismo. Now one puts feminism out there and now feminism is going to be equal to machismo, but for women. So in order for us to think about being equals we have to destroy both feminism *and* machismo. I think we have to have the same conditions and the same opportunities for everyone. There should be equality for everyone.

I found that Gregorio's perspective—that feminism represents a movement to assert women's domination of men—was common among Catia TVe producers. They expressed that women's oppression was typically blamed on men, when it ought to be blamed on capitalism. Missing from the discussion was how gender oppression and racism are fundamental to capitalist exploitation. When the general assumption was that feminism was divisive and concerned with middle-class women's supremacy, it was not surprising that most producers at Catia TVe did not embrace the strategic expression of the need for women's advancement through the term *feminism*.

Conclusion

This chapter has demonstrated how community and official state producers of the Bolivarian revolutionary media undermined women's public speech and leadership through their collaborative work of statecraft and media production. I have detailed how women at Catia TVe encountered their male colleagues' resistance to thinking through gender oppression, as well as impediments to developing their technical filmmaking and public speaking skills. On screen, in the national televisual sphere, women at Catia TVe faced steep barriers in advancing themselves as representatives and leaders of organized popular communities. Off screen and on screen, male leaders at Catia TVe publicly represented, spoke for, and asserted themselves as ideal embodiments of the unified popular class; popular power and voice were often implicitly equated with men's voices and experiences. I also noted a crosscurrent of women's efforts to contest the reinforcement of male supremacy and the rare incidents when Catia TVe leaders highlighted gender inequality and the ideas and actions that framed and followed these occasions.

In many ways, this is a familiar story. Gendered inequities in technical knowledge and public speaking are far from unique to Catia TVe or to Venezuela. Media production in most contexts worldwide is male-dominated. Moreover, the move to privilege class inequalities over gender or race inequalities and other experiences of exclusion has numerous precedents in the 1960s and 1970s Latin American male-dominated leftist movements. What is critical to understand about the dynamics I have described in this chapter is that a conceptual divide between state and community only obscures an understanding of how and why people perpetuate gendered inequalities. Gendered inequality was produced in and across the mutually constitutive realms of official state and community media. This sidelining of explicit struggles against women's oppression was not only a top-down practice, emanating from official state actors, but was produced relationally across multiple social fields. "Community" or "the people" and "the state" were interrelated at every point. Catia TVe producers and their allies perpetuated gender hierarchies while simultaneously challenging class hierarchies in their work to craft representations, discourses, and institutions of the state.

More of this kind of ground-up analysis is necessary at a range of sites in order to understand how the Bolivarian Revolution (re)produced gendered norms.

My observations of ongoing inequalities do not discount the ways that Catia TVe's efforts to organize people in poor neighborhoods changed how women were viewed by expanding their visibility as media makers. Nevertheless, despite important practical improvements in women's lives that did go some distance to challenge gendered inequalities, without an explicit politics that articulated how injustice of gender subordination was intimately connected with, rather than distracting from, inequalities of class, race, and sexuality, there was little ground to critique hierarchies and demand that women have equal access to public speaking and social authority. What was missing was a locally viable discourse that characterized critiques of gender-based inequalities within the Bolivarian Revolution as absolutely central to advancing, rather than undermining, the process of building socialism.

SIX

RECKONING WITH PRESS FREEDOM

"Who pays you?" asked the tourist from Massachusetts. He tapped his sandal against the mildewing carpet of Catia TVe's basement auditorium. During the previous hour, Luis had described the origins and goals of Catia TVe to twenty-seven U.S. and British tourists, who were visiting as part of a "reality tour" of Venezuela coordinated by a San Francisco–based human rights organization. They arrived in Caracas in January 2007, hoping to learn about the polarizing changes taking place in Venezuela almost ten years into Chávez's presidency. Luis often fielded similar probing questions from groups of foreign visitors to the station. They expressed solidarity with the Bolivarian Revolution's stated aims of redistributing power and resources in Venezuela, but they also voiced concern over Catia TVe's ability to exercise press freedom, given the station's close alliance with and financial dependence on the Chávez-led state.

Luis calmly reflected, "We are different from state television stations. It's obvious that the Chávez government pays them. What the state gives us is permission to broadcast." Before Luis could continue, another visitor asked, "Does the state give you the money?" Luis emphasized Catia TVe's editorial independence from the Chávez government before disclosing that state institutions had provided around $25,000 to purchase Catia TVe's equipment in 2000. He avoided discussion of the station's ongoing agreements with state institutions to broadcast state publicity spots in exchange for the resources to maintain the station. Luis struggled to describe the implications of Catia TVe's financial dependence on and political alliance with the leftist government in a way that would not confirm the visitors' suspicions that the station operated as a mouthpiece for the Chávez government. Grounded in selective

FIGURE 6.1. Street banner celebrating the new television station TVes, reading "People, how good you look. Chávez guarantees freedom of expression," May 26, 2007. Photo by the author.

tenets of liberalism that have held particular sway in public discourse about the press in both the United States and Venezuela, the visitors assumed that financial and political autonomy from the state was necessary for Catia TVe producers to maintain their freedom and act as a critical "watchdog." As I have argued in the previous chapters, Catia TVe producers' shifting relationship with state officials and institutions encouraged them to question the bedrock assumption that the state was a threat to their freedom.

Some liberal press traditions maintain that an interventionist state is a necessary apparatus to sustain liberty; the United Kingdom's BBC is testament to this idea (Born 2005). Nevertheless, the common idea that shaped much of the international criticism of Venezuela's changing media world held that state involvement was a danger to free expression. Luis's encounter with the U.S. and European visitors raises two key issues I address in this chapter. The first concerns how a dominant contemporary strain of liberalism—one that maintains that state and society are separate spheres and that connections between the two threaten freedom—shaped the conditions of possibility for the Bolivarian Revolution and critical analysis of media in

Venezuela. This version of liberalism prioritizes attention to political and civil liberties and largely ignores economic and social rights. This particular understanding of liberal rights decisively shaped debates about press freedom in Venezuela.[1]

Catia TVe's producers' political practice and aspirations for the meaning of press freedom were created in a context in which this liberal episteme was simultaneously reaffirmed and rejected, both by the producers themselves and by officials in state institutions. Although Catia TVe producers formulated a strident critique of the limits of such a liberal approach to press freedom, they intermittently reasserted expectations that a media outlet's autonomy was necessary for liberty as they struggled to protect dissent and difference.

My second concern in this chapter is to uncover how the efforts of Venezuelan community media activists to reckon with liberal ideals of press freedom were shaped first and foremost by how they understood the state and participated in statecraft.[2] Using ethnographic accounts, I extend the argument of previous chapters to illustrate that media producers at Catia TVe embraced the state as processual, by which I mean as an unfolding and uncertain process. The disproportionate focus in scholarly and journalistic work on the threat that Chávez posed to liberal ideals diverted attention from consideration of everyday processes of state making and of how Bolivarian activists engaged liberal norms. I chart the conflicts that emerged for Catia TVe producers who were firmly allied with the Bolivarian Revolution but who nevertheless had misgivings about the Chávez government's changes to the media world. Their concerns differed from those expressed by globally dominant governments, politicians, and other observers about the Chávez government's transgression of the autonomy of civil society and the liberal commitment to equality of opportunity; indeed, my interlocutors viewed this liberal commitment as sustaining a capitalist ruling-class hegemony. Catia TVe producers struggled instead to advance a meaningful redistribution of media resources.

My analysis of the liberal episteme at work in this context and of Catia TVe producers' view of the state as processual lays vital groundwork toward the development of a critical anthropology of press freedom, a neglected subject within the anthropological literature on the state and, more broadly, within liberalism. We face abundant and conflicting claims about press freedom. Although in the first decade of the twenty-first century many journalists around the world risk their lives to do their jobs in the face of arrest and assassination, newspapers, human rights organizations, and governments in

Europe and the United States have devoted disproportionate attention to threats to press freedom in places such as Venezuela, Bolivia, and Argentina, where the ruling parties challenged commercial media conglomerates and expanded public, state, and community media outlets.

With a few exceptions, however, anthropologists have been reluctant to take up press freedom as a subject of ethnographic inquiry, even though press freedom is part and parcel of a liberal political vocabulary that has been amply critiqued in the discipline for its assumption that individual autonomy and choice are central to human freedom (Mahmood 2004; Povinelli 2006).[3] Although distinct approaches to the state are central to how producers make media and how press freedom is understood, few anthropological analyses of media producers have thoroughly engaged analyses of the state or of liberalism.[4] We need greater attention to what "the state" means in various sites of media production and how the legacy of liberalism and its disciplining dichotomy of freedom and constraint shapes "media worlds" (Ginsburg, Abu-Lughod, and Larkin 2002).[5] Establishing an anthropological approach to press freedom requires assessing ethnographically the local meanings, experiences, and limits of liberal norms as well as critically analyzing the kinds of freedom media producers aspire to and practice.

In this chapter, I explore ethnographically how Catia TVe producers negotiated liberal expectations about media autonomy from the state in the context of the Chávez government's controversial December 2006 decision not to renew the broadcast license for Radio Caracas Television (RCTV).[6] One of four major commercial television stations in Venezuela, RCTV formed a cornerstone of Venezuela's corporate-dominated media landscape for over fifty years and was stridently critical of Chávez and the Bolivarian Revolution. The government's decision not to extend RCTV's broadcast license dominated political discussion in Venezuela for much of 2007. National groups in opposition to Chávez, prominent international governance and human rights organizations, and many foreign governments characterized privately owned corporate media in Venezuela as vital "independent" voices and depicted the move as a brutal attack on press freedom. Chávez government officials, in contrast, argued that the decision was a legal decision of a sovereign state and insisted that they were replacing the private monopoly on communications with genuine pluralism by opening up the broadcast space occupied by RCTV to vaguely defined "public service" programming. The government noted that RCTV had broken content laws designed to protect children and had instigated violent insurrections of the population during the 2002 coup and the three-month anti-Chávez strike.

The government's renewal of the licenses of other commercial stations that were responsible for similar transgressions in 2002 and 2003 but had since toned down their critique and outright deceptive reporting suggested that RCTV's nonrenewal was meant, at least in part, to counter the opposition's efforts to weaken Chávez and his government.

For their part, Catia TVe producers celebrated the decision to not renew RCTV's broadcast license as a step toward creating widespread access to the means of media production. Many long-term members of Catia TVe first started advocating for the government to exercise greater regulatory control to counter the power of commercial media in the wake of the 2002 coup, in which the commercial media had played such a prominent supportive role. They saw the government's decision about RCTV as the fruition of their efforts to work toward radical change of the media world.

In my analysis of Catia TVe producers' uphill battle to generate popular support for nonrenewal of the license and to shape the direction of the new state-managed television channel that would replace RCTV, I uncover how Catia TVe producers approached statecraft as an uncertain process and attempted to forge a radical interdependency with official state institutions and actors. I track their unsuccessful bid to challenge middle-class control over the new station that replaced RCTV. In certain moments, my informants and their allies advanced a critique of commercial and mass media that emphasized the importance of *venezolanidad* (venezuelanness), downplayed the centrality of class conflict over media resources, and overlooked how people struggle over the meaning of media's messages. The efforts of Catia TVe producers to reckon with liberal expectations about press freedom exemplified their struggle to establish terms of engagement with official state institutions and middle-class allies that would allow for both their embrace of the Bolivarian Revolution as a necessary path to construct social and economic justice and their ongoing constructive critique of the shortcomings of the political process.

Catia TVe's Approach to Press Freedom

When journalists asked Argentinean workers in 1945 whether they were concerned about the possibility of losing their freedom of speech if Juan Perón were elected, the workers replied, "Freedom of Speech is to do with you people. We never had it" (James 1988, 17). I heard versions of this refrain repeatedly from community media producers as they were peppered with questions, including my own, about the possibility that RCTV's "shutdown" would stifle press freedom. In the period leading up to and following RCTV's license expiration, journalists at private domestic commercial newspapers and television and radio stations asserted openly and persistently that Chávez was undermining freedom of expression. The terms of this account, which characterized massive private media outlets as "independent" and state-aligned media outlets as always already "unfree," allowed little opening to consider alternate conceptions of freedom or, for that matter, of the state. As the conflict over the future of RCTV's airwaves gained steam in 2006, Catia TVe producers voiced an increasingly explicit critique of dominant liberal norms of press freedom.

Julio, a Catia TVe producer in his mid-twenties, who was from a nearby poor neighborhood, echoed many of his colleagues when he told me, "The people who complain about freedom of expression have always had their stomachs full." (Julio, like most people I encountered in Caracas, freely interchanged the concept of "freedom of expression" with "press freedom.") Julio argued that the basic preconditions necessary for the exercise of press freedom, which include rights to food, health care, housing, and education as well as access to the means of media production, were usually overlooked in the chorus of concern about the Chávez government's threats to press freedom. International attention to the violation of press freedom in Venezuela overwhelmingly privileged the middle-class and elite sectors of society, which historically had their perspectives, lives, and creative production well represented in the mass media.

Carlos explained, "Freedom of expression has become a kind of cliché." For him, the corporate media rendered the concept of press freedom meaningless. Within the media world of Caracas, the phrase "press freedom" immediately worked to legitimize the commercial media's rights and projects while undermining state-sponsored and state-aligned projects. For Julio, Carlos, and many of their colleagues, the campaign by the owners of private media companies to defend free expression was, in actuality, an effort to protect the privileges of the wealthy by monopolizing the airwaves, while ignoring the inequalities that worked to stifle the expression of the majority. In the name of free expression, private owners of media and their allies defended the accumulation of private capital.

As I prepared to do formal interviews with Catia TVe producers, I felt that no matter how I tried to phrase the question, asking about freedom of expression or press freedom seemed unavoidably to reassert the dominant view of private business as the terrain of freedom and the state as a coherent headquarters of power that menaced liberty. One afternoon, I awkwardly asked Gregorio, "Do you think there's a way to think about freedom of expression that doesn't repeat the approach to freedom that seems to dominate this discussion?"

We sat in Catia TVe's frigid, windowless editing office. Two staff members were at work at the computers beside us, editing footage of a communal council election that they had filmed that morning. Gregorio fiddled with the USB flash drive that hung around his neck and told me,

> I don't use the notion of freedom of expression exactly. I don't use these words because it doesn't really exist. We aren't free. We are tied to norms, borders, concepts, ideologies. And perhaps some of these make you more or less free. It depends on how you use them. I believe that freedom has to do with understanding the possibility of mutual respect, collective construction, and a series of things that capitalism itself doesn't allow. It [capitalism] makes you become an individual. You become individualistic so that you can be free. But free from what? From people? So ultimately, you can enter a shopping mall where they tell you where to walk, how to walk, how to speak, how to dress. This isn't freedom.

Here Gregorio points to the illusory character of individual social autonomy and the self-authorizing subject. Perhaps what is most interesting about his statement is that he does not address media at all. For him, my question about press freedom was an invitation to criticize the way that human freedom is defined under capitalism. Gregorio dismisses the idea that freedom means being unfettered or independent of norms, of an ideology, of politics, or of other people. Dependence on or adherence to political projects, he suggests, may make you more or less free, but this depends on "how you use them." Gregorio points to the pitfalls of liberal capitalist notions of freedom, insisting instead that people are interdependent and shaped by their environment.

Catia TVe producers like Gregorio, Julio, and Carlos viewed explicit invocations of the right to press freedom with skepticism and disdain. Rather than experiencing this liberal discourse as an empowering and accessible framework of rights, they argued that claims to press freedom were part of an underhanded attack on their efforts to channel—or, in Gregorio's terms, "use"—statecraft to dismantle systemic inequalities. They explained that while the commercial media characterized the Chávez government's efforts to challenge the power of private for-profit media corporations as "intolerance" to difference, in fact what was unfolding was a revolutionary campaign to democratize access to media production and make television programming attuned to the life experiences of the majority of the population.

At the same time, Catia TVe producers were aware of the possibility that their efforts to make media production accessible to the poor majority might be co-opted by professional managerial middle-class people who claimed revolutionary commitments but resisted radical change to systems of media production and challenges to their own influence. Despite their rejection of the dominant global perspective that the Chávez government was stifling freedom of expression by silencing RCTV, Catia TVe producers and their interlocutors in poor neighborhoods did express concerns about the commitment of official media outlets to cover what they sometimes referred to as "the revolution inside the Revolution," meaning internal criticism.

Community media producers debated how to protect dissent and differences of opinion within a shared goal of radical social change while being suspicious of those that aimed to maintain class inequality. Julio, for example, was strident in stating that discussions among community media producers were characterized by "contradictions and criticisms of the process." But he quickly added, "One assumes that if you are being critical it's because you are part of this mess [esta vaina]. If someone is outside it, then one would be more than critical, one would be directly part of the opposition. But we are inside this process. We criticize it in order to improve it, in order to make it a process that's *more* from below." Julio expressed that community media producers wanted television programs to disseminate critique, but from a perspective that sought to redress and advance the revolution in the interest of popular power and leadership. Yet as I highlighted in the previous chapter, committed participants in the Bolivarian process often faced steep barriers when they attempted to articulate criticism of power inequalities within the movement. There was often disagreement about whether criticism was in the interest of popular power.

During the period leading to the nonrenewal of RCTV's license, I observed Catia TVe producers manage their interdependencies with allies in official state institutions in multiple sites. Catia TVe producers attempted to hold the leadership of official state institutions, specifically the Ministry of Communication and Information and ViVe TV, accountable to their own commitments to remake media outlets by and for the poor. To this end, Catia TVe producers emphasized the interdependency between state institutions and popular participation. As I recount in the following sections, Catia TVe producers expressed conflicting ideas about the importance of autonomy from and relatedness to the state as they worked with diverse allies, mourned the loss of RCTV's telenovelas, and challenged and reasserted liberal notions of press freedom.

Experiencing the Processual State at ViVe TV

Catia TVe engaged in countless meetings, rallies, conferences, and discussions—many of which they broadcast on their airwaves—in an effort to support the nonrenewal of RCTV's license and discuss the kind of channel that should replace it. Many of these meetings were organized together with state institutions; others included only community media producers. I attended a meeting convened by ViVe TV's leadership to discuss proposals for a new station and to strategize with community media producers and local barrio activists about how to generate popular support for the decision not to renew RCTV's license. Thierry Deronne, the vice president of ViVe TV, who had a long career promoting popular education in media production, invited community media producers to gather at ViVe TV's headquarters in Caracas. I joined forty people, including Ana and Carlos, sitting in a circle in ViVe TV's glass-walled conference room. In addition to many familiar faces of community television producers from stations across the country, there were also participants who identified themselves as members of nearby community organizations. Through the glass, we could watch the buzz of the station's staff working on computers and setting up studio lights to record an upcoming program.

A young man from a community station in Maracaibo, a city eight hours away from Caracas by bus, told the group, "We have been trying to organize discussions in our community . . . but it's difficult. People are really misinformed about what's going on with RCTV." Carlos responded that the struggle over RCTV's future was vital to deepening the Bolivarian revolutionary process.

Thierry nodded enthusiastically and asserted, "Our challenge is to make the new channel [that would replace RCTV] a space for the people [el pueblo] to produce media." He continued, "The best way to respond to commercial media is to make your own media because then you really understand how lies are produced. You can take video production classes at Catia TVe and here at ViVe TV. And ViVe TV is always available to go to your communities and transmit your debates." Echoing the treatise on "imperfect cinema" advanced by Cuban film theorist Julio García Espinosa in the 1970s, Thierry concluded, "The division of labor between people who make media and people who make other things is a form of censorship." Thierry recast the standard liberal definition of censorship as the constraint of ideas, highlighting instead how censorship could be embedded in the broader class-based organizational structure of media production. From this perspective, press freedom did not rest on the unconstrained expression of ideas or autonomy from the state but on the organization of access to the means of media production.

Others also endorsed this nuanced idea of freedom as access. A woman who identified herself as a member of a community organization in a nearby low-income neighborhood embraced Thierry's invitation. "Sometimes it's difficult to get the confidence to speak. But we need to appropriate this space of ViVe TV, which is so close to where we live, in order to strengthen this political process." The participants decided to hold more meetings for community organizers aligned with the Chávez government in different parts of Caracas to discuss RCTV's impending loss of its license and generate proposals for the profile and content of its replacement. For Thierry and his interlocutors, greater access to the means of media production was achievable by embracing the Bolivarian movement and participating in the official state project to reclaim the broadcast airwaves of RCTV.

Scholars and observers of Venezuela during the Chávez era often wondered whether these kinds of interactions between community organizations and state officials were anything more than an empty orchestration of popular empowerment meant to bolster the power of those in charge of state institutions (García-Guadilla 2011). Undoubtedly, in addition to the stated goal of encouraging widespread participation in media production, the meeting I attended met a pressing need for state officials to create visible evidence of "grassroots" action in support of the RCTV decision. Nevertheless, reducing Catia TVe and other community organizers to pawns of state actors overlooks both the significance of these experiences for participants and their own savvy understanding of the dynamics of interdependency between the organized activist poor and official state actors and institutions.

For many participants, this meeting was an important opportunity to see behind the scenes of the production of state institutions and media. Their involvement inside official halls of power was a way for them to gain confidence in their capacity to contribute to political outcomes. Moreover, collaborating with ViVe TV by showing up at meetings like this one allowed many producers from community television stations to develop the necessary contacts and knowledge to advocate for support for their projects in towns and cities far from the power center of Caracas.

Despite ViVe TV's goal of "giving voice" to marginalized Venezuelans, community media producers and activists often criticized the station's programming for sidestepping urgent problems plaguing new social welfare programs. Together with many supporters of the revolution, community media activists recognized the shortcomings of the programming and internal structure of existing state-run media outlets—particularly the older state channel, VTV, but also of their allied station, ViVe TV. My interlocutors were not interested in seeing these inadequacies replicated by newly created television outlets. Much of the programming on existing state-run media outlets mimicked the format and aesthetics of for-profit commercial television but replaced advertisements for consumer goods with messages that attempted to promote socialist values. Even while Catia TVe producers understood the dilemma that their colleagues who worked in these official outlets faced in trying to counter the constant onslaught of commercial media's manipulative reporting, which framed the revolution as a total failure, Catia TVe producers were nevertheless adamant that the official state media needed to provide space for internal criticism and substantial debate. They were acutely aware of the frequent disjuncture between ViVe TV's goals and its practice. Yet, significantly, these attendees also saw ViVe TV as a space of potential to participate in media production and fight for the inclusion of meaningful debate.

From the perspective of these community media producers, the commercial media's claims that Chávez was the chief threat to press freedom seemed ludicrous. The dominant liberal ideals of press freedom so avidly espoused by commercial media owners, which assert autonomy from state institutions as a necessary condition for freedom, did not account for how state institutions might expand poor communities' access to rights and resources to participate in media production. This example makes clear how community media producers embraced ViVe TV as a space of possibility. As I have traced in previous chapters, in Catia TVe's effort to collaborate with ViVe TV, many community media producers saw official state employees as allies and state institutions as within their reach. As I have also illustrated, however, this collaboration was compromised by the reproduction of power hierarchies.

The Artist's House

As I accompanied Catia TVe producers to the varied spaces where they engaged in debate about the future channel to replace RCTV, the class divisions regarding what should be done with the new channel became clearer. The Independent National Producers Association, a state-managed organization led by professionally trained television producers and artists, held a well-publicized meeting in central Caracas at a state-operated foundation known as the Artist's House to discuss the future channel. "Independent national producers" were media producers who were officially licensed by the state but were deemed independent or autonomous because they were unaffiliated with any established state-run or commercial media network. Independent national producers were an outgrowth of the 2004 Law of Social Responsibility of Radio and Television, which required television stations to increase domestic independent production. In order to become certified, these producers were required to use 70 percent Venezuelan capital, locations, and labor, and, by law, also had to have the "experience and capacity to produce *quality* national productions." The quality requirement proved to be a major barrier for those who were not professionally trained media producers. According to my informants, and as confirmed by my own observations, most independent national producers were from middle-class backgrounds and had prior professional training in private schools and corporate media. Many state officials celebrated the so-called independence of these producers as a symbol of the government's commitment to deepening media democratization, overlooking the dependence of these media producers on the unequal opportunities afforded to them by their class power. The growing prominence of these media producers was testament to the inconsistent politics of the Chávez government regarding the concept of liberal autonomy.

Despite their misgivings about the class character of this association, many volunteer producers at Catia TVe registered as independent national producers, hoping to be able one day to support themselves financially by selling their video productions to television outlets. Given their inexpensive video equipment and minimal experience, most community television producers did not meet the established quality standards. Almost every volunteer group from Catia TVe that had attempted to sell programming to a state channel had been rejected on the grounds that their video production did not meet sound and image criteria. Despite the appearance of an equal playing field, their low-priced equipment and nonprofessional training did not allow them to compete. In this context, as in most, the ability to assert oneself as autonomous was contingent on unequal, class-based access to resources.

The daylong conference at the Artist's House focused primarily on cultivating middle-class cultural producers' support for the government's decision on RCTV by emphasizing the employment possibilities the new station might afford them. Community media producers had a minimal presence at the meeting. Carlos, Catia TVe's director, and Carmela, a Catia TVe staff member who worked as Catia TVe's accountant and rarely participated in events outside of the station, were invited to speak about the future of Venezuelan television alongside ten professionally trained male media producers, artists, intellectuals, and politicians. Carlos expressed to me intense skepticism about the opportunism of the Organization of Independent National Producers, but nevertheless recognized that it was important to be present and advocate for the poor to control the future channel.

At the outset of the conference, the middle-class cultural producers who spoke touched on familiar themes including the negative influence of foreign commercial media on the masses. One after another, the professional media producers on stage argued that RCTV sold "anti-values" of violence, promiscuity, and individualism and seduced Venezuelans to want things and behave in ways that were foreign. Several speakers emphasized the importance of promoting venezuelanness on television. One screenwriter noted, "In Venezuela we have so much talent. Are we going to watch Argentinean or Brazilian television or are we going to show our own culture, histories, heroes, and faults?"

Although these largely middle-class intellectuals and artists echoed debates I had heard among community media producers about the importance of developing national talent and creativity through television production, the notion of "the artist" that they referenced did not resemble Catia TVe's discourse—expressed by Carlos and Carmela—about media production as a tool of popular collective empowerment. Carlos and Carmela's effort to argue for radical reorientation of the media world was largely drowned out by the other speakers, who avoided any discussion of the possibility of remaking Venezuela's media world as part and parcel of a broader project of radical redistribution of class power. As one of the speakers, a light-skinned screenwriter, emphasized, "This process is about including the excluded without excluding the included." According to this man, in other words, the middle class should have nothing to fear from Chávez. For their part, Catia TVe producers' own dismissal of "popular tastes" together with their anti-

imperialist, nationalist discourse made them bedfellows with upwardly mobile and elite media producers and intellectuals with whom they competed
to shape the new space for media production. In this venue, nationalist
sentiment momentarily smoothed over the class divisions between barrio-
based and more affluent media producers.

An Uphill Battle to Generate Popular Support

Catia TVe producers devoted enormous energy to building support for the
government's decision and advocating for their vision of a new station that
would replace RCTV. In promotional audio-visual segments repeated many
times daily on state and community media, the government and community media producers described RCTV's exile as a move to allow the state to
control national resources in ways that benefited Venezuela's poor majority.
At the same time, RCTV broadcast constant appeals from famous telenovela
actors and writers who protested what they termed the government's clamp-
down on freedom, particularly the freedom to choose what programming
they wanted to see. Hosts of RCTV's talk shows regularly appeared on air
with tape over their mouths. Groups of predominantly middle-class university students, many linked to opposition parties, attracted worldwide media
attention when they closed down major arteries in Venezuela's largest cities
to protest RCTV's shutdown.

Catia TVe producers faced resistance to the decision to replace RCTV not
only from a diffuse group of political parties, private media outlets, business
groups, and "civil society" organizations that made up the opposition, but
also from barrio-based supporters of the Chávez government. The battle
over RCTV's future divided the more militant politically engaged activists
involved in the Bolivarian Revolution, such as Catia TVe producers, from
those who supported Chávez and his government but did not regularly participate in organized political activism or discussions.

In my conversations with people from this latter group in the poor
neighborhood where I lived and in visits to other poor neighborhoods
where Catia TVe organized, I noted that many people believed that much of
RCTV's programming was manipulative and untruthful. Even while critical
of the station's owners, however, they expressed attachment to some RCTV
programs. In response, Catia TVe producers argued that corporate media
were not independent but reflected the outlook and politics of the rich and
powerful classes. They argued that ViVe TV, in contrast, reflected the concerns of the poor. Catia TVe's arguments, however, gained little traction and

were ultimately unconvincing to many of their interlocutors in poor neighborhoods. In the first place, the corporate media did sometimes address issues pertinent to the poor that the official state media avoided. People in poor neighborhoods were frustrated by the limited space for criticism of the government on state-run media. Moreover, in unexpected and sometimes contradictory ways, it was on the private commercial media's telenovelas that people in these neighborhoods sometimes found their lives, contradictions, hopes, and fears reflected. In interviews I conducted at Catia TVe and in the barrios where the station ran workshops, many people expressed frustration about the impending loss of their favorite entertainment programs on RCTV, particularly the telenovela that they were watching at the time. This concern for the loss of their soap operas was not apolitical, nor was it a sign of their false consciousness, as many ardent revolutionaries claimed. Catia TVe's leadership's contention that popular audiences were totally encapsulated, overdetermined, and controlled by the dominant elite ideologies via telenovelas, as I discussed in chapter 3, reproduced a patronizing logic that mistrusted the ability of the poor to judge and make decisions for themselves.

A Revolutionary Mourns the Loss of Her Telenovela

While most Catia TVe producers disparaged telenovelas, there was a small cohort that were both militantly committed to the revolution and avid fans of telenovelas. One afternoon Darnelis invited me to her house to have lunch. With a smirk, she whispered that we had to leave Catia TVe *immediately* so that we would not miss a moment of her favorite telenovela. In the ten-minute walk to the house where Darnelis, her younger brother, and their mother shared a single rented room, Darnelis exchanged greetings with almost every person we passed. Darnelis was active in local politics, trying to form a communal council in her neighborhood. As she waved to a group sitting in front of the corner bodega, Darnelis laughed, "All these people think you're my girlfriend!" Darnelis's identification as a lesbian was public knowledge in her neighborhood. (In chapter 5, I observed the subtle effects of sexism, homophobia, and heterosexism on Darnelis from within the ranks of Catia TVe and ViVe TV.)

When we arrived at her house, we found Darnelis's brother, in his early twenties, sprawled out on one of the two full-size beds in a square, dimly lit room, watching the telenovela, which had already begun. He worked at an American-owned fast-food chain in the food court of a shopping mall in central Caracas. Their mother was at work in a wealthy neighborhood on the other side of the city, where for many years she had spent half the week as a live-in maid. One wall of the small room was crowded with images and memorabilia, which represented Darnelis's many interests. A poster from the 2006 World Social Forum held in Caracas hung between a collage of Krishna iconography that Darnelis had made on a spiritual retreat and an election placard of Chávez smiling widely. A black-and-white photo of Madonna, the American pop idol, was tacked between colorful posters that advocated recycling. Piles of clothes, books, DVDs, and CDs were stacked haphazardly in every available inch of space. A refrigerator hummed between the two beds.

During the first commercial break of the telenovela, *The Kings* (*Los Reyes*), Darnelis stepped onto an outdoor balcony where there was a single hot plate and a dish rack. As Darnelis doled out portions of chicken and pasta for each of us, she quickly tried to fill me in on the plot of *The Kings*, a Colombian-produced show broadcast on RCTV. She explained that the central protagonists were a poor family called the Kings, who suddenly became fabulously wealthy. But an evil rich family was attempting to thwart their happiness. In an added twist, the head of the evil family had fallen in love with one of the daughters from the King family. Darnelis noted that the daughter was what she called a *transformista*, both in the telenovela and in real life. A transformista is a term used in Venezuela for individuals who are labeled male at birth but who live their lives as women (Ochoa 2008, 150). In the U.S. taxonomy, transformistas fit into the category of transgender.

My lesson was interrupted when *The Kings* resumed after the commercial break. Darnelis laughed heartily as a humorous scene unfolded over the King family breakfast table. The transformista character was certainly the main comedic foil, and her depiction could be interpreted as demeaning. Yet the program provided ambiguous cues for sympathy, not just humor. Darnelis adored this character.

"She is who she is," Darnelis remarked, "and the rest of them can go to hell." Darnelis expressed empathy and identification with a character who, like her, transcended and challenged gender and sexuality norms. At the next commercial break, Darnelis flopped herself back against the mattress. She moaned dramatically, laughing at herself, "Why, Chávez? Why do you have to take this channel away?"

Darnelis's grief over the loss of her beloved television show and her own laughter at this predicament signaled her conflicting thoughts and experiences both about the telenovela and the state-building project of which she was a part. On many occasions, I had heard Darnelis vehemently defend the Chávez government's effort to challenge the power of the commercial media. For example, in an interview, she explained,

> They [the commercial media] aren't interested in the beautiful things that happen in your community. On the contrary, they are interested in harming you. Harming your consciousness and selling you models that are impossible to copy. . . . The novela, the commercials—they had us blind. . . . Everyone [on a telenovela] who lives in a barrio has to be a thief and the woman has to be a whore. Why do they sell us these images? It's always the maid who comes from a barrio that goes to live in a wealthy house and aspires to marry the owner of the business, which is never going to happen. They paint poor people in really grotesque ways. . . . The commercial media will remain grotesque forever while we remain quiet. I think the people [el pueblo] have to have this debate of what we really want to see on television. We have to go out into the street and ask the people [el pueblo], "What do you really want to see? What do you hope to have? How should the perfect society be?"

The complex pleasure and identification that Darnelis experienced with *The Kings* was nowhere reflected in her critique of the way commercial media denigrated poor men and women. Her disgust at the trope of the maid character was particularly piercing given the many years she had watched her own mother labor as a live-in maid in Caracas's wealthy east side without experiencing the life-transforming benevolence of her employers. Darnelis, however, did not seem "blinded," as she put it, by telenovelas. *The Kings* contained certain elements, such as the rags-to-riches story, that Darnelis dismissed as harmful fantasy. Yet Darnelis identified and felt clearly emboldened by aspects of this show. Her focus on the commercial media's class bias did not account for how *The Kings'* inclusion of a character who challenged conventional norms of gender and sexuality provided her with something rarely found on the open broadcast airwaves, whether on state, commercial, or community channels.

Commercial media in Venezuela have largely excluded positive depictions of gay, lesbian, and transgender characters, although the increased activism of gay and lesbian groups attracted some mainstream press attention (Muñoz 2003; Ochoa 2008). While community media afforded some possibility for transgressive depictions of gays and lesbians, these openings on Catia TVe were extremely narrow. The only images of openly gay, lesbian, or transgender people broadcast on Catia TVe during the period of my research were produced by Darnelis and a former staff member who also identified as gay. Together they documented a gay, lesbian, bisexual, and transgender pride parade a year earlier. This was the one program from a list of hundreds of Catia TVe productions that the station's leadership designated as "inappropriate" for prime time viewing hours and was instead broadcast on Catia TVe during evening hours. Even while Darnelis celebrated how *The Kings'* transformista character lived her life as she chose, confidently dismissing any who would get in her way, the reality for transformistas in Caracas was far more violent. The official security apparatuses run by state institutions—such as the Metropolitan Police—regularly perpetrated deadly force against the transformistas who worked as sex workers along one of Caracas's main avenues.

Darnelis connected with the pursuit of social justice and the indictment of capitalism, which she believed was at the core of the Bolivarian movement. For her, independence from the revolutionary state project was not the answer to the discrimination and injustice she faced. Nonetheless, she connected with *The Kings* in ways that she could not connect with much of the programming produced by community and state outlets. Consequently, even while she rejected other aspects of the telenovela's politics of representation and scorned RCTV's owners' claims to be defending press freedom, Darnelis wanted to continue seeing this transgendered character from *The Kings*. In fact, what seemed to constitute a "perfect society" for Darnelis included television's regular depiction of diverse gender identities and sexualities. Darnelis's enjoyment of commercial television involved a battle for meaning, one that was often overlooked or misunderstood by other Catia TVe producers and their allies, who dismissed people's pleasure in commercial media as a symptom of their ideological domination. Darnelis's political analysis excluded consideration of her own contradictory experience of commercial media as bringing both pleasure and multiple forms of injustice. The complex issues of pleasure, power, and struggle that characterized everyday engagement with popular culture were entangled with, though not identical to, the battle over the meaning of press freedom.

Rejecting the Ministry of Communication and Information's Approach to Quality and Press Freedom

A month before the expiration of RCTV's broadcast license, the Ministry of Communication and Information, together with the Ministry of Participation and Social Development, called a meeting with community television stations from across the country. The meeting further highlighted state officials' inconsistent approaches to liberal ideals of freedom. While some state officials, such as those at the ViVe TV meeting highlighted at the outset of this chapter, challenged liberal norms of autonomy, in this meeting the Ministry of Communication and Information representatives lauded liberal principles of equal opportunity and media producers' autonomy from the state.

The explicit aim of the meeting organized by the ministries was to solicit proposals for the content of the new station to replace RCTV. Twenty-six community television producers gathered in a circle in a squat room with harsh fluorescent lights. At the meeting, Catia TVe staff and volunteers proposed that RCTV be replaced with a nationally broadcast channel of content created by nonprofessional community media producers from around the country. During a mini–press conference at the start of the meeting, reporters from state television and radio outlets asked Carlos, who dominated the spotlight, to share his thoughts on the future shape of the new channel. Dressed in his bright-orange Catia TVe T-shirt, Carlos noted, with a clever play on words, "I believe that it's important to remind the minister and all the people that are responsible for this that we make the *parrilla* for the new channel with the people." The Spanish word *parrilla* means both barbeque and, in the television industry, a lineup of television programs. Carlos continued, with a glimmer in his eye, "Because one makes a parrilla [barbeque] in the street, nothing would be better than trying to set up the new parrilla [lineup] of the new channel in the street with all the sectors: the farmers, the fishermen, the workers, and everyone else." With this pun, Carlos emphasized the necessity of the channel's being in the hands of those on "the street," a euphemism for the common or poor people. He argued that a channel dedicated to broadcasting community media would allow for the consolidation of the power of the people (*poder popular*), making clear that the people were the historically disenfranchised and poor. A persuasive public speaker, Carlos pressured the state officials to be accountable for the claim that the government was dedicated to shifting the dynamics of power to the historically disenfranchised poor.

A woman from the Ministry of Communication and Information was careful to emphasize in response that she and her colleagues were consulting not only with community and alternative media producers, but also with groups of independent national producers about what shape the new station should take. She explained that she hoped to learn from "the accumulated experiences of our community television stations." She paused awkwardly, quickly clarifying, "I say 'our' because I feel reflected in them, not 'our' because the government imposes an editorial line. This has to be very clear. If any collective is critical of the actions of the government and incisively, with good judgment, shows how state institutions are not acting correctly, well, it is the community media." Her effort to emphasize the independence of community media outlets from state institutions, in fact, drew attention to how the relationship was under constant contestation.

By the middle of the meeting, ministry representatives made it obvious that their central and most urgent concern was to fill the programming schedule for the new station with a steady stream of what they called "quality" content. Ministry representatives suggested that they should replace RCTV with a public service television station that would purchase programming from independent national producers, the licensed media producers who were officially unaffiliated with any television outlet and drew on Venezuelan talent, capital, and labor. Exasperated, Hector, Catia TVe's assistant director, explained to ministry representatives that independent national producers served what he called "private interests" because they depended on private capital for finance and development. The celebrated independence of these producers, he maintained, was illusory. Hector pointedly warned that while opening a new channel dedicated to the work of independent national producers might appear to be a step toward democratization of access to the broadcast airwaves, this model would instead perpetuate class inequalities if "quality" was evaluated largely according to standards of market-oriented programming, meaning high production values in sound and lighting and a particular editing aesthetic. Although the idea of the independent national producer fulfilled liberal tenets of equal opportunity and the autonomy of producers from existing television networks, this model did not recognize the inequality of conditions, the conflation of private capital with autonomy, or the dominance of a commercial media aesthetic.

Together with other community media producers at the meeting, Hector argued that state institutions needed to reorganize the political economy of communications to prioritize newly trained nonprofessionals from poor communities. In their attempt to assert this radically reconstituted media world, Catia TVe producers argued that state institutions needed to more equally redistribute media resources and increase integration between state and community media outlets.

At this meeting, Catia TVe producers openly criticized the proposals put forth by state officials. Here they experienced firsthand how a state institution that leaned on liberal tenets to legitimize its projects was creating impediments to gaining access to the rights and resources of communication. The community media producers suggested that a truly free and democratic press required state management of resources and the joining of official and community efforts to ensure access to the materials necessary to enable broad participation. They cast state support and integration with community media not as a threat to their autonomy or freedom but as a path toward challenging class inequalities that have barred them from access to the means of media production.

In their work with various state institutions, Catia TVe producers encountered a range of priorities and approaches to liberal ideals. This variability further cultivated their awareness that the state was an inconsistent collection of institutions and individuals subject to contestation and rife with conflict, rather than a mysterious force or a monolith removed from the populace. Their experience of the state as an ongoing and uneven process of deliberation was incomprehensible according to a liberal framework of press freedom in which the state is an intractable external force and freedom and constraint are assumed to be binary practices.

Catia TVe Producers Reassert Liberal Arguments
for Autonomy from the State

At a gathering at Catia TVe just a few days after the tense meeting with the representatives of Ministry of Communication and Information, the inconsistency and struggle that characterized Catia TVe producers' approach to the state came to the fore. In the interactions described above, producers had argued that close integration of official state and community media projects was necessary to expand broad and meaningful access to the means of media production and decision-making. At a meeting held for staff and volunteers at Catia TVe to discuss the status and future of their station, however, some participants advocated greater financial independence from official state institutions.

Fifty people gathered in Catia TVe's musty basement auditorium. Carlos asserted, "It's true that right now we have Chávez, but he won't always be here. Catia TVe, however, has to stick around." Carlos introduced a proposal to limit the station's dependence on state funding. He framed station leaders' reluctance to rely on state funding not as concern about Chávez's concentration of power or the threat of imminent intervention by official state actors, but as a way to ensure Catia TVe's longevity, even without the support of Chávez or of state institutions. His statement signaled an awareness of the instability of the state project and the possibility of a growing over-reliance on the figure of Chávez, a prescient concern given the president's unexpected death six years later.

Hector, who had pressed for greater state management of media resources in the ministry meeting described above, took the microphone and advocated that Catia TVe decrease reliance on state resources by raising money from people who lived in the producers' own neighborhoods. Hector commented that reliance on resources from state institutions produced complacency and overdependence of community media producers on state institutions to resolve problems. Hector's comments made clear the uncertainty and fears that many Catia TVe producers felt about their efforts to embrace official state institutions as a collective project and foster radical interdependency. Hector explained that his proposal drew on the model of audience-funded media developed in the United States by KPFA, a radio station that forms part of the listener-funded Pacifica Radio network. Hector and Carlos had first learned about this model when they presented the work of Catia TVe in an exhibition at the Berkeley Art Museum in California in 2006. Hector described how KPFA relies exclusively on funds generated through donations and memberships.

Several Catia TVe volunteers expressed immediate outrage at Hector's proposal. With palpable tension in his voice, Elario, a longtime volunteer, exclaimed, "The state's resources are *our* resources. We've been fighting tooth and nail to get the priorities straight here and build Bolivarian socialism. Why should we reject what belongs to all of us?" Elario had been producing short videos about his neighborhood to air on Catia TVe since the station first began broadcasting. A former taxi driver in his early forties who had recently secured a position on the local mayor's commission for alternative media, Elario often expressed frustration to me about the difficulty he faced recruiting his barrio neighbors to become involved at Catia TVe without any financial compensation in the time-consuming task of making television. A listener-supported model struck Elario and many others at the meeting as wildly impractical given the poverty of their neighbors. More important than this pragmatic concern, however, was the volunteers' sense that demanding a share of state resources was not a stance of dependence but a claim of rights, an important aspect of a participatory and democratic socialism. Elario and several others argued that they used funds from state institutions to fight for a state that serves the interests of the poor. Catia TVe members roundly rejected the suggestion that the station rethink its reliance on state funds.

Hector's suggestion that they embrace the model of the listener-funded Pacifica Radio network, which emerged in the liberal capitalist context of the United States, where autonomy from both commercial and state institutions is seen by many as a guarantee of editorial independence, exemplifies the struggle of Catia TVe's leadership to find a conceptual rubric to legitimize and defend freedom of communication.

The urge to assert financial autonomy suggests that producers had fears about two things: their ability to voice criticisms without endangering their funding and, second, more broadly, to maintain a radical long-run interdependency in which they could exercise control over the official state support they received so they could meet their objectives in their own ways. The most prominent perspective to emerge from the debate that afternoon at Catia TVe was the view that popular activists needed to approach state institutions and resources as weapons of the poor in their struggle to create freedom and equality. For most producers at the station, Catia TVe's freedom and control over internal decision-making required intensive interchange and interdependency with state officials, rather than atomistic decision-making and a stance of autonomy. Nevertheless, this contentious meeting underscored how tentative Catia TVe's leadership was about the station's position vis-à-vis the possible futures of state institutions. Their experience of the intransigence of state officials regarding proposals to transfer the new station to popular control encouraged such uncertainty.

Catia TVe Producers Embrace the State

In the final setting I describe in this chapter, a community meeting in a poor neighborhood in west Caracas, Catia TVe producers publicly displayed their embrace of state institutions and sought to redefine freedom as an alliance with the Bolivarian revolutionary state. Catia TVe's leadership had reservations about how to secure future local editorial control and ongoing participation, and they had faced impediments in challenging liberal norms of equal opportunity and quality at the Ministry of Communication and Information. Even so, on the eve of RCTV's license expiration, Catia TVe's leadership promoted hope among their neighbors that the new state-run station replacing RCTV would make true communicative freedom possible.

In the open-air patio of a high school located in a densely settled neighborhood near Catia TVe, staff members set up one of their many presentations about RCTV and the importance of a new model of communication. Catia

TVe's audience that evening consisted of students attending night classes as part of the Chávez government's high school and community college programs. Two young girls, around eight years old, approached Margarita, a Catia TVe staff member, eager to inquire about that evening's activity. We learned that the girls' mothers were studying law as part of the community college program. The girls registered no recognition of Catia TVe. One volunteered, "We like the shows on RCTV." Her friend added, "Plus, RCTV has been on the air for fifty-three years!" RCTV's argument against its shutdown—its duration as a fixture of Venezuelan media—easily slid off their lips, testament to the success of RCTV's advertising campaign against the government's decision. "Yes, *mami*," Margarita answered, "but this station does nothing good for you. It doesn't teach you anything. Our new channel will show you how to dance joropo [a traditional Venezuelan dance associated with rural life] and play *tambores* [drums with Afro-Venezuelan roots]. It will teach you how to read and tell you great stories." Margarita embraced the new state-administered station that would replace RCTV as "ours," indicating her hope that the new channel would be open to the participation and leadership of Venezuela's poor, would serve pedagogical needs, and strengthen dedication to popular cultural forms tied to historically disenfranchised populations. The first girl wrinkled her nose in an unpleasant grimace, seemingly unconvinced by Margarita's vision of educational programming.

Luis kicked off the group conversation, inviting the audience of about fifty people to enroll in Catia TVe's free video production classes. With his typical confidence in public speaking, Luis quickly captured the audience's attention. He explained the technical and political-economic framework of television in Venezuela, highlighting the meaning and importance of the invisible radio waves that carry television signals. Luis noted,

> This electromagnetic spectrum is ours; it is something that belongs to each one of us. Many years ago the government gave the rights to use this spectrum to [the commercial television stations] without consulting us. Now we have a different government. . . . But outside this country, including in the United States, the information that arrives there says that there is a dictatorship here in Venezuela. This is no secret. Do you think there is a dictatorship in Venezuela? [The crowd chimed together in unison, "No!"] Well, there is a dictatorship, but it's a dictatorship of the private media who lie, manipulate, and misinform.

Luis's comments reflected a heightened awareness of international criticism—particularly originating from George W. Bush's White House—of the nonrenewal of RCTV's broadcast license. His rhetorical question pinned the threat of dictatorship on the commercial media's domination of the airwaves, denaturalizing the model of advertising-supported commercial television. Echoing political-economic critiques of commercial media, Luis decoupled commercial media from notions of freedom.

Luis insisted that the station replacing RCTV would present plural opinions and representations of human experience. Invoking his regular refrain, Luis noted, "You will see people just like us, fat, ugly, missing an eye, black, whatever." He drew attention to the racism and classism of commercial television and how, in contrast, community-produced media created positive and complex portrayals of people who live in barrios. "But," he continued, "*ojo*, watch out, in these media outlets that we are going to have, we will say the good and the bad." Luis pledged that the new channel would not reproduce the content of the already existing state channels, which he argued did not broadcast enough overt criticism or denuncias of state officials and programs. In other words, he promised that the new station would not serve as a mouthpiece for the Chávez government. What was left implicit was that the kind of criticism he and his colleagues welcomed was criticism that was aligned with the Bolivarian Revolution's overall goals of resource redistribution, the transfer of power to the poor majority, and the construction of socialism. In other words, there would be freedom to critique what commercial media did not: the actions that advanced a capitalist economy and world system and the class inequalities that such a system entailed.

Luis invited audience members to voice their perspectives, noting, "We are going to have a debate. Because if you want to come up here and say 'I support RCTV,' this is valid also. We believe in the battle of ideas." Students and teachers lined up in front of the microphone. A man in his late forties asserted, "This is a historic opportunity. This is the moment of the pueblo, the moment of the excluded, a historic moment. Because the elite wants to own the spectrum and according to our constitution, this belongs to all of us. In other words, the state administers it, and decides whether to renew [the broadcast license] or not." A woman who looked to be in her late twenties gripped the microphone and passionately said, "We are going to have a station open to our collaboration that says the truth about what happens in our communities from day to day." Luis's audience eagerly extended a discourse of constitutional rights to the electromagnetic spectrum and declared RCTV's nonrenewal an act that would afford them greater opportunities for expression.

Above the din of cheers, the sound of metal on metal ricocheted around the open courtyard of the high school. Following the gaze of the audience, I looked up at the fifteen-story apartment building adjacent to the school. In the distance, I saw someone leaning out of his or her apartment window, banging together two metal pots, an act of political protest known as a *cacerolazo*, which people opposing the government had recently taken up. The commercial media had begun advocating for audiences to perform collective cacerolazos at designated times to protest the government's decision about RCTV's license. Ana, Catia TVe's assistant director, energetically grabbed the microphone from Luis. Facing the building, she began to chant, "¡No volverán! ¡No volverán!" (They will not return!). The audience in the patio joined in. The expression "they will not return" was a common rallying cry among Chávez supporters, indicating a steadfast rejection of the previous ruling elite.

After a few minutes of chanting, Ana gestured up at the building and exclaimed, her voice thick with anger: "These are the few *escualidos* [literally, squalid ones, a pejorative term for the opposition to Chávez] that remain. But we have to talk about them. Because we had a coup in 2002 and they participated in this. Although it wasn't these people, because this isn't the elite class. It was the transnationals, the owners of businesses. Not us. We're the ones who live in barrios. *We* are the owners of the petroleum and of the radio-electric spectrum. And we tell them, 'No more license!' We own the radio-electric spectrum!" Ana promptly returned the microphone to Luis. In her intervention, Ana characterized the dissenting voices in class terms, grouping them with the elite owners of the commercial media who she pledged would not be allowed to return to power. But, notably, she changed direction mid-speech, remarking "Although it wasn't these people" in recognition that those who lived in the building next to the patio where we sat, while not desperately poor, were certainly not the counterparts of the owners of much of Venezuela's wealth. Ana's framework of the people (the historically oppressed poor) against RCTV's owners (the usurpers and foreign exploiters of Venezuela's resources) could not account for those from poor and working-class backgrounds who defended the commercial television channel.

Despite Luis's claim that they would have a debate and engage in a "battle of ideas," no one from the patio audience voiced criticism or doubts about the decision not to renew RCTV's license. The inability of Catia TVe leadership to foster an open discussion about people's apprehensions was a product, in part, of the tense, polarized, and embattled context, where any opening to criticism of the decision was seen as a capitulation to the opposition. In fact, Luis, Ana, and Margarita's confident support for a new national station that would broadcast content created by nonprofessional, barrio-trained producers belied the fact that they were, in fact, quite frustrated with their efforts to collaborate with the Ministry of Communication and Information to shape the new station. As I have detailed above, Catia TVe producers had experienced firsthand how the government's participatory projects were plagued by inconsistency and contradiction. Nevertheless, in their public presentations they did not allude to their own concerns about the new channel. Luis and other Catia TVe producers claimed instead that the new channel would democratize access and socialize ownership. They did not discuss whether this democratization would follow a liberal pluralist approach that privileged atomized autonomous media producers or if it would recognize class divisions and redistribute control.

Catia TVe producers' reluctance to openly criticize state institutions at this meeting was shaped by their own concerns that they would add fuel to counterrevolutionary sentiment at a hotly contested and tense political moment. Their emphasis on the possibility that the poor would gain greater access to a television channel that operated in their interest, rather than on the problems Catia TVe producers faced in bringing this vision into being, emerged from the desire of Luis and his colleagues to encourage their interlocutors to participate in building this future. However, there was a glaring disjuncture between the "future imaginary" (Coronil 2011a, 232) that Luis and his colleagues conjured—an ideal state-managed television channel in the hands of poor communities—and their daily experiences of the uneven commitment to this vision on the part of many state officials. This disjuncture explains Luis and his colleagues' mix of skepticism, hope, commitment, and apprehension vis-à-vis state institutions.

"It's Out of Our Hands"

After months of debate and efforts to promote popular support for the impending nonrenewal of RCTV's license, the Ministry of Communication and Information finally provided concrete details about the new station that would replace RCTV. Two weeks before RCTV went off the air, officials announced that the new station, named Television Venezolana Social or TVes (a pun in Spanish that means "you see yourself" or "you look"), would be a nonprofit government foundation, overseen by the ministry with funds granted by the executive branch. TVes would broadcast programs created by the largely middle-class groups of independent national producers, imported educational programming from the United States and Europe, and the same state promotional segments that could be found on the two other state-managed television stations. Lil Rodriguez, an Afro-Venezuelan middle-class woman journalist, was designated president, a move that signaled a departure from the status quo of white male leadership but the continuation of middle-class management.

Taking up the language of liberal pluralism and equality of opportunity, the new station avoided explicit alignment with social movements and the call put forth by community media activists to radically redistribute media resources. According to official publicity, TVes's defined mission was to become "a space for the creation and re-creation of a new televisual narrative of our own, with a national and Latin American identity, through the design of inclusive, diverse, plural, equitable, quality programming." The Ministry of Communication and Information declared TVes's programming would not be "imposed by the Executive," and would not reproduce the models of the two already existing state channels. Instead, the government promised that it would offer a diversity of political opinion, philosophy, and culture.[7] The structural, strategic, and political barriers to creating such an idealized sphere of open debate and reflection were not acknowledged. Under pressure to deflect global and local criticisms, there was little latitude for community media producers and their allies to address the problems that plagued already existing official state media outlets.

The Ministry of Communication and Information made no explicit commitment to including community-produced programming in TVes's lineup. Community media activists at Catia TVe and from other stations had failed to promote their vision of a new state-run station dedicated to community media production. Catia TVe staff and volunteers complained that TVes was going to be a channel for the "petite bourgeoisie," supplying employment for independent national producers. Gregorio noted that the reality was that community media producers were in no position to be able to produce extra content for the new channel. "We don't make enough programming for our own station," he noted. One longtime volunteer was reluctant to concede defeat in the struggle for TVes, arguing that they needed to work to immediately claim the channel for the people. He asserted, "The time is now; we can't wait to make changes. No socialist government has ever lasted for very long." Others at Catia TVe were less pessimistic, taking the long view that the station would improve and that the next generation of Venezuelans would benefit from it.

For their part, Catia TVe's leadership, Carlos, Hector, and Ana, expressed to me their tremendous frustration with the Ministry of Communication and Information. "Now it's out of our hands," Hector told me. "We're not going to get more involved. There's lots of opportunism and sectarianism going on." Carlos rejected the ministry's invitation to join the group of ten prominent intellectuals, professional journalists, and university professors who had agreed to serve on TVes' board of directors. Carlos was unusually reticent when I asked why he had rejected the invitation, suggesting only that he did not feel it was worth the hassle of getting involved. Following the months of debates, meetings, and resolutions that the people needed to determine the shape and content of the new channel, Catia TVe leadership's resignation about the future of TVes was a marked reversal. Carlos's reluctance to join TVes's board of directors indicated the contingency of Catia TVe's alignment with state institutions.

Overall, it was unclear to many producers I spoke with at Catia TVe whether the slow pace of the Ministry of Communication and Information's inclusion of community groups in decision-making was part of a process of a much-embattled political project gradually heading toward greater distribution of power, or if it was an ominous portent of the formation of an unaccountable new power elite uninterested in radical changes to Venezuela's media world. At the forefront of this struggle, as I have highlighted, was how to amend, reject, or assert liberal values of pluralism, equal opportunity, and autonomy.

Neither Watchdog nor Lapdog

From the foundational moments of liberalism in Venezuela to the present, people fighting for universal equality and freedom have struggled over whether liberal principles can be mobilized to create a free and fair world or if liberalism is a discourse that serves first and foremost to legitimize and protect elite privilege. Catia TVe producers were taking up this long struggle over liberal values, particularly around what has come to be a dominant notion that press freedom—and human liberation more generally—requires autonomy from the state. Despite Catia TVe producers' challenges to the norms of liberalism—most observable in their questioning of the importance of media's independence from the practices of statecraft—my interlocutors at the station also occasionally appealed to liberal ideals. They rejected suggestions that they could or should assert autonomy from the state, given what they understood as a revolutionary context, even while exploring avenues to decrease their financial reliance on state institutions in the name of necessary independence. In managing the ongoing power asymmetries between their station and state institutions, Catia TVe producers attempted to create radical interdependency with state institutions, while also resisting the paternalism of official state actors. Producers continued to explore and draw attention to problems in poor neighborhoods. They were adamant in their belief that only by creating trust and encouraging participation in the process of producing a more just state could problems be resolved.

Many scholarly and journalistic critiques of the Bolivarian Revolution drew on a globally dominant liberal conceptual framework to describe the Chávez-led state as a unitary set of institutions under Chávez's tight control. Fieldwork with government-aligned community media producers allowed me to experience alongside my interlocutors the extent to which the state was, in fact, an incoherent and inconsistent collection of institutions and individuals. State institutions often worked at cross-purposes, at times aligned with the interests of community media producers at Catia TVe, and at times opposed. This inconsistency between ViVe TV's leadership and the Ministry of Communication and Information, for example, did not belie the potent influence of President Chávez or official state actors on state institutions; yet it made clear that official state actors and institutions followed multiple, sometimes competing agendas that were far from singular in approach.

Recurring questions about press freedom, such as those posed by reality tourists and other domestic and international observers, required community media producers at Catia TVe to negotiate the liberal discourse of media autonomy. Understanding how media producers reckon with liberal approaches to press freedom requires an understanding of how they perceived and negotiated the state, both as an idea and as a set of institutions, policies, and actors. As I have illustrated, producers' perspectives on the importance of autonomy from state institutions varied as they moved between contexts. At certain moments, Catia TVe goals aligned with those of state institutions; at other times, they demanded a far more radical departure from liberal norms than state actors were willing to advance. These contradictions were also internal to Catia TVe's own approach. What the state means and what threats or possibilities state institutions represented were under negotiation. Considering a processual approach to the state allows us to grasp the context and dilemmas that Catia TVe producers faced in reckoning with the liberal discourse of press freedom. It also points to the inadequacy of a liberal framework to evaluate or analyze their struggle to democratize access to media production and to challenge the class inequalities that structured Venezuela's media world.

While they debated the very terms through which to understand freedom, it was clear that Catia TVe producers and their allies had made little headway in generating broad support for the creation of TVes. Each evening in the weeks that followed TVes's replacement of RCTV, I heard the clanging of metal on metal in poor and famously militant neighborhoods of west Caracas. People were performing cacerolazos to protest the nonrenewal of RCTV. Official rating measurements showed that TVes captured only 5 percent of viewers, down from RCTV's 40 percent (Cañizáles 2007, 17). In poor neighborhoods, long lines of customers overwhelmed booths selling DirecTV, the satellite cable station. The decision not to renew RCTV's broadcast license was the first move the Chávez government made since coming to power in 1999 that generated widespread disapproval from his supporters. The glaring lack of consensus for the RCTV decision among the usual strongholds of Chávez supporters was an early indication of the shortcomings of the revolution's approach to mass media and popular culture. In the conclusion, I examine Catia TVe producers' assessments of why and how middle-class officials maintained control over Venezuela's media world. I analyze what went right and what went wrong in their efforts to embrace statecraft.

CONCLUSION

Nestor focused intently on a computer screen in the production office of Catia TVe. He was struggling to condense four hours of footage he had filmed at a presidential press conference into a five-minute segment for broadcast on Catia TVe. Searching for a way to trim President Chávez's sentences, Nestor played and replayed Chávez's statement: "I am an instrument of the people, a collective that was repressed, persecuted, exploited, and lived in exclusion under dictatorships disguised as democracies." In defiance of claims made by then U.S. president George W. Bush that Venezuelan democracy was in peril, Chávez denied his own considerable agency, asserting instead that he acted on the people's will to reverse the historic betrayals of democracy. Nestor replayed the president's words multiple times as he considered what to include in his abridged version of Chávez's speech. "Dictatorships disguised as democracies . . . dictatorships disguised as democracies . . . dictatorships disguised as democracies." Chávez's words bounced around the room.

Suddenly, Darnelis, who was working at a computer by Nestor's side, slammed her fist on the desk. I assumed that Nestor's noisy editing was bothering her. Instead, her frustration had another source.

"How absurd that the escualidos claim we live in a dictatorship! What the hell do they mean by that anyway?!" Darnelis asked angrily. *Escualidos* (squalid ones) was the derogatory term Chávez and many of his supporters used at the time to describe the political opposition to the Chávez government. Darnelis rose abruptly from her desk and crossed the room to a small bookshelf where she pulled down a thick dictionary.

"Let's see," she said, thumbing through the thin pages. "A, B, C . . . here we are! '*Democracia*,'" she said, reading aloud. "'A political doctrine favorable to the intervention of the people in the government.'" Darnelis paused to consider the definition. "Well, you know that the people never participated in the government before," she said to Nestor and me. "The people were never granted any importance at all. . . . So then, there wasn't democracy. So, dictatorship, that's what we had?"

She shook her head and turned her attention back to the dictionary, clearly enjoying the exercise. "D, I, C, T, A . . . '*Dictadura*. Government that under exceptional conditions rules with sole authority.'" Darnelis looked up, considering the definition. "So if we didn't live in a democracy before, then we lived in a dictatorship. So it can't be a dictatorship now. The escualidos say that there's a dictatorship because they say we have to do everything that Chávez says. But he's doing things in a socialist way, for the good of everyone; he's not dictating anything negative. Maybe we're in a socialist democracy? . . . The problem is no one likes it when someone shows up and creates rules. They like to claim they are free."

She turned back to the dictionary to look up the word *regime* when a song by R.E.M., an American rock band popular in the 1990s, emanated from the fanny pack strapped around her waist. It was her cell phone ringing. Someone from the Ministry of Communication and Information (MINCI) was calling to invite Catia TVe to film an event in Caracas's main theater the next day. Hanging up, Darnelis shot me a smirk. Laughing, she said, "We can't say no to MINCI, otherwise we won't get paid!"

Darnelis's frustrated search for clear definitions that afternoon reflects the contested nature of freedom, democracy, and dictatorship that she faced as she engaged in concrete struggles to gain access to resources and rights. As I have traced throughout this book, underlying Darnelis's pursuit of conceptual clarity was the question, what did it mean to be truly free, both as people and as media producers? Her everyday experiences of greater access to education, health care, and the means of media production did not align with the claims being advanced by the opposition to the Chávez government that freedom was under attack in Venezuela. She criticized Bush's efforts to measure Venezuela by what she believed were false standards of democracy and liberty. At the same time, Darnelis and her colleagues at Catia TVe experienced the considerable challenges and shortcomings of the Bolivarian movement. Darnelis's quick comment referencing Catia TVe's obligations to the Ministry of Communication and Information signaled her awareness of the complexities of the television station's collaboration with state institutions, a relationship that was simultaneously constraining and liberating.

Throughout this book, I have elucidated this confounding dynamic of intertwined constraint and liberation. Liberal epistemologies often lead us to imagine freedom as always the antithesis of constraint. Yet liberalism—the complex, polyvalent, and powerful political philosophy that few scholars agree how to describe—was absent from the list of concepts that Darnelis sought to define and understand. Some of the bedrock norms of the version of liberalism that were central to political discourse in Venezuela as well as the United States at the time of my research included a binary understanding of state and society, deep suspicion of the state as the enemy of freedom, and a strident commitment to individual liberty, tolerance, and the rule of law. Often implicit in this dominant version of liberalism was the notion that capitalism constituted a prerequisite for freedom. As I have argued, this version of liberalism served as the central theoretical scaffolding for the perspective that democracy and freedom were under attack in Venezuela under Chávez. This dominant version of liberalism sidelined any positive project to use the state to build social equality and justice.

Many of my informants at Catia TVe, as I have indicated in this book, relied on certain liberal ideals while rejecting others. Sometimes they explicitly invoked a liberal approach to freedom as autonomy from the state, as was the case when they debated how to produce financial independence from official state institutions in an effort to protect their ability to denounce the government. At other times, however, they dismissed the dominant norms of liberalism. This dismissal was obvious in their support for Chávez's disregard for aspects of liberal procedure and in their disdain for dominant notions of press freedom, which they saw as a de facto class-based privilege that defended the interests of the powerful. Most consistently, they rejected these dominant ideals of liberalism in their collaborative work with state institutions.

Rather than approaching "the state" in general terms, as if all states were the same in every place and time, I have paid attention to its historicity—how a specific constellation of resources, relationships, and historical circumstances shaped Catia TVe producers' practice of statecraft during the first decade of Chávez's presidency. Although in many contexts state making undoubtedly can and often does have violently oppressive and co-opting outcomes for popular politics, Catia TVe producers' statecraft challenges the basic assumption that the poor and oppressed are always clearly aligned against state power. Poor people and their allies, in certain contexts, engage in everyday state formation as part and parcel of progressive social movements. Catia TVe producers' statecraft was one piece of an extensive puzzle that needs to be understood in order to grasp the revolutionary political process during the Chávez era.

Catia TVe producers' practice of community media making and state formation suggests that we must reorient the well-worn question of how community media or so-called grassroots social movements are compromised by state support; instead, we need to parse the mutual impacts and complex constellations of power that exceed the conceptual containers of "state" and "community." I have argued throughout this book that Catia TVe producers' practice of media making and state formation demand a shift in thinking about the concepts of the state, the media, and the autonomy of popular movements. Attention to the overlapping histories and interwoven practices of community and state media projects in Venezuela during this period—most vividly observable in Catia TVe producers' roles in the formation of and participation in ViVe TV—reveals how exchanges and collaboration between community media producers and official state media employees created provisional radical interdependencies.

Catia TVe producers' efforts to sustain radical interdependencies with their allies who worked at ViVe TV and other official state institutions reaped mixed results. In every encounter, Catia TVe producers negotiated how to shape state institutions in the interest of the poor and gain the knowledge, funding, and equipment they needed to bolster their project. Through their presence and participation at official meetings, joint television production workshops, and press conferences, they demanded that middle-class administrators, popular allies, and even President Chávez himself be held accountable to barrio-based activists. Their endeavor to produce radical interdependency at times degraded into mutual instrumentality or co-optation. Catia TVe producers' frustrated attempts to shape the station that replaced RCTV into an outlet for popular expression and leadership provides one example of their lack of power to shape outcomes. Leaders of state institutions—in this case, the Ministry of Communication and Information—were inconsistent in their support for Catia TVe's radical proposal to socialize the means of media communication, a process that would entail a challenge to Venezuela's middle class, which has historically produced both private and official state media. Yet, rather than work to seal themselves off from the uncertainty and compromises of alliances, Catia TVe producers embraced official state institutions with an awareness that the ground was constantly shifting, and with a commitment to continue to fight to assert popular interests.

Analysts who describe the Bolivarian process in the first decade of the twenty-first century as a "top-down" authoritarian project overlook the daily struggle among activists to channel the process of state formation in the interest of the poor. While a description of the Bolivarian Revolution as being simultaneously constructed from "two directions," that is, "from above" and "from below," more accurately grasps the reality of the political terrain and the class struggle (Azzellini 2010), this formulation also creates roadblocks for analysis. My ethnographic data shows how interactions and relationships could rarely be cleanly or accurately characterized as from above or from below, precisely because the Bolivarian Revolution did have partial success in being a poor people's movement. Poor people were involved at various institutional levels and collaborated with middle-class allies to advance progressive social change. As I have documented, the poor continued to face entrenched middle-class and elite power and were divided by their own individual aspirations for upward class mobility and the maintenance of gender-based oppression. Nevertheless, the two-directions analysis too easily slips into the replication of a state–society binary and does not sufficiently embrace the dialectical relationship between autonomy and dependency of social actors and spheres of action.

Gains, Openings, and Mistakes

Exploring the everyday practice of politics in the first decade of the Bolivarian revolutionary process, I have uncovered how the Chávez-led revolutionary state was an ever-evolving ad hoc project. Catia TVe producers' efforts to transform official state institutions had provisional and uncertain impacts. Yet it is clear that Catia TVe producers expanded the media literacy of the thousands of people from poor communities who, over more than a decade, enrolled in the station's hands-on media production courses and exchanged knowledge with community media producers. Through the process of media production, Catia TVe provided space for debate about revolutionary strategy and the denunciation of shortcomings in the political process. In their daily interactions with communities across Caracas, Catia TVe producers provided vital mentorship and encouragement for people attempting to engage social change in their communities. At the same time, Catia TVe producers challenged class inequality inside official state media institutions like ViVe TV, demanding that media be produced by, for, and about historically oppressed communities.

We see in the Bolivarian movement an effort by the poor and their allies to reassert the language of class to describe the process of dispossession, structural hierarchy, and conflict over class interests. I observed how my interlocutors struggled with the challenge of exploring how class is always already a gendered and raced relation (for starters). And while the Bolivarian movement drew energy from the experience of dispossession and the precariousness of life in the barrio, I have highlighted how the articulation of this experience was in no way fixed. Despite Catia TVe's efforts to ground the concept of the people in a class identity, many of their fellow travelers embraced a vision that was more closely attached to the figure of Chávez. The struggle over what constituted the people—a class identity or political allegiance to the president—reflected a series of internal hierarchies and contradictions within the Bolivarian Revolution.

While making important gains, Catia TVe producers' bid to upend traditional power hierarchies was inconsistent. The internal inequalities, most prominently of class and gender, both at Catia TVe and within the broader Bolivarian revolutionary movement, went unaddressed. This failure eroded the possibility of confronting the crises that arose. The prominent notion advanced by Catia TVe's leadership that the redistribution of material resources would undermine other forms of oppression based on gender, race, or sexuality did not account for the ways social systems of domination are intertwined. Overlooking the relationships between class and gender and the social inequalities perpetuated and produced within the Bolivarian political process contributed to the ability of a newly ascendant power elite to assert control.

In granting singular emphasis to Chávez, many scholars and journalists make history the story of an individual personality. This narrow focus not only overlooks contingencies of global power relations, it also obfuscates the efforts of ordinary people to construct popular identities, collectivities, and mass movements in dialogic relation with the symbol and actions of a leader. Although Chávez undoubtedly centralized control over formal procedures and officially recognized mechanisms of accountability, his supporters used the symbol of his leadership and the concrete reforms advanced by his government in unanticipated ways. Chávez's supporters used the symbol of the president to bolster their challenge to class hierarchies and to encourage the leadership of poor people. Observers who see the first decade of the Bolivarian Revolution as laying the groundwork for the inevitable march toward centralized control underestimate the tension that Chávez's contradictory leadership and efforts to define "the people" created. This contradictory dynamic opened official institutions up to far greater debate and struggle than my interlocutors had ever experienced. We cannot overlook the dialectical relationship between social movements and leaders, between constitutive and constituted power. Nor can we, in appraising the Bolivarian Revolution, ignore the changing terrain of the world economy following the 2008 global economic crisis or the ongoing U.S. hostility to Venezuela's challenge to Washington's economic and political hegemony in Latin America.

Confronting Crisis: Revisiting Catia TVe in 2015

Returning to Caracas in 2015, twelve years after I first visited Catia TVe and seven years after I concluded my long-term fieldwork, I found that much had changed. I concluded my research just before a major crisis in capitalism unfolded in the United States and Europe. Governments in the world's richest countries imposed harsh austerity measures, further reducing public services and creating unprecedented levels of inequality. The immediate impacts of this world recession in Venezuela were unclear. The government's flawed exchange rate policy, combined with a precipitous and sustained decline in the global price of oil in 2014, created major inflation and contributed to scarcity (Weisbrot 2015, 214–17). In the midst of these considerable challenges, Chávez died of cancer in March 2013. His vice president, Nicolás Maduro, was narrowly elected president. In 2014, an emboldened opposition instigated a cycle of street protests against what it characterized as an authoritarian government with failed economic policies. These protests resulted in more than forty dead, most of whom were official state employees or chavistas.

In June 2015, I found my primary interlocutors engaged in a daily struggle to make ends meet. Imported goods such as food and medicine had become shockingly expensive and often impossible to find. Minimum wage salaries covered only a tiny fraction of people's basic needs. The poorest have been the hardest hit. The damage to social solidarity in the wake of the deep economic crisis has been far-reaching as people face desperate situations. Catia TVe producers I reconnected with were deeply critical of the Maduro government. They were frustrated, outraged, and saddened by the collapse of many of the institutions of the Bolivarian movement that they had worked to develop. A small number of my Catia TVe informants had begun to identify with the opposition around the time of Chávez's death in 2013. They were angry about inflation and scarcity and exhausted by the corruption they encountered in their dealings with people who claimed allegiance to revolutionary politics but who seemed dedicated only to personal profit.

Conversations with Catia TVe producers with whom I worked most closely during my research in 2006 and 2007—Ana, Margarita, Nestor, Carlos, Hector, Gregorio, Jesica, Rosemery, Edilson, Darnelis, Cristina, and Luis—made clear that they continued to align themselves politically with the government of Chávez's successor, Maduro, even in the face of a deepening political and economic crisis. Although they were wary and critical of the Maduro government, they had not given up on their efforts to remake the state in the interest of the poor. Ana, who served as Catia TVe's assistant director during the time of my research, noted, "Why should we give up our claim on state resources? The right wing never will!" She insisted that the Venezuelan state was theirs to build and fight for. Despite all the shortcomings, the Maduro government continued to represent to Ana, and to others who were long-term activists, the possibility of advancing the struggle to build socialism. They are adamant that efforts to bring down Maduro would ultimately resolve the crisis in the interest of capital, all while claiming to defend freedom and democracy. They viewed the opposition to Maduro as offering only a return to neoliberal rule. "We will not go back," Cristina, the former head of the production department, told me, reciting a refrain I heard repeated over the years of my fieldwork in Caracas.

By the time of my 2015 visit, Catia TVe had been off the air for almost a year. The station's transmitter was damaged and there were no funds to fix it. Catia TVe's contracts with state institutions to broadcast publicity had dried up. The paid staff had been cut back to five people, down from thirty during the time of my research. Brand new video equipment sat mostly dormant in locked cabinets. I learned that many of Catia TVe's staff had left to work for the Ministry of Communication and Information or had joined ViVe TV or other state-run media outlets. A handful were working at newer community media outlets that relied on Internet-based distribution. Many were unemployed.

Despite the losses in resources and staff, Catia TVe was bustling with activity. One afternoon I observed a crew of men, paid by the mayor's office, hard at work covering the interior walls of the station with a fresh coat of white paint. A group of preteen kids from the nearby barrio entered the station's basement classrooms for a dance class. A small group of young, mostly middle-class artists and documentary filmmakers had gathered in the station's small theater to host a screening as part of their weekly documentary film series. A core group of activists continued to devote time, energy, and their limited resources to advancing the goals of Catia TVe. The station was alive—at least for the moment—but very little of the activity involved producing media.

Spending time at Catia TVe in 2015, I wondered, by what metric and over what time frame should we judge the Bolivarian Revolution? What does the severe economic and political crisis that engulfed Venezuela a decade after I completed my fieldwork mean for how we evaluate community media projects aligned with the Bolivarian Revolution? How might the approach to the state and press freedom for which I have argued help us to understand the latest crisis?

While some conclude that the current political and economic crisis is the inevitable result of the top-down authoritarian nature of the Bolivarian movement from its beginning, my data and analysis reveal instead how the first decade of the twenty-first century was a period of profound uncertainty in Venezuela. It was a moment of tension, during which radical actors working inside, outside, and alongside official institutions were vying for power and were making some gains. While serious problems were already apparent during the time of my research, the relations and institutions being built were in flux. Assertions that the current crisis was unavoidable wrongly project the present into the past. The dispersed practice of statecraft that I have described in the previous chapters signals that the current crisis must be understood in terms of its particular conjuncture.

In the face of claims that the Bolivarian Revolution has faltered because of failed socialist policies, my informants at Catia TVe assert that the problem has been that the government has not been socialist enough. The Chávez government's contradictory approach to socialism combined efforts to collectivize property and production while at the same time leaving considerable portions of Venezuela's privately controlled banks and manufacturers untouched. Despite the vast gains that were made in social equality, dignity, and political participation, the structural continuities in the accumulation of capital meant that the material basis of social and political relations remained little changed (Purcell 2015, 165).

The plunge in the price of oil starting in 2014 has had deep and painful repercussions. Given that 95 percent of Venezuela's exports continued to come from its state-owned oil, when the international price dropped, the income flowing into state institutions declined precipitously. Despite much effort, the Chávez government was unsuccessful in diversifying the economy and expanding national production. Oil dependency typically creates conditions and incentives that make it enormously difficult to create an alternate economic future (Behrends, Reyna, and Schlee 2013; Karl 1997). The Bolivarian revolutionary government under Chávez expanded Venezuela's dependence on oil in its bid to end poverty, to extend financial support to its Latin American neighbors, and to underwrite nationalized businesses (Lander 2016).

My interlocutors at Catia TVe devoted little attention to analyzing the global oil industry beyond the demand that Venezuela's oil wealth be invested in improving living conditions for the majority. They saw investments in participatory programs in health care and education as having long-term positive consequences for radical democracy and capacity building. Yet, as I recounted at the outset of this book, when Hector lamented, "This revolution is too easy," he was in part remarking on the problems of challenging individual aspirations for upward class mobility in a context of easily accessible commodities and the apparent lack of need to develop forms of local food and commodity production. There was a sense among most of Catia TVe's producers that in the short term, they could continue to rely on the profits of the global oil economy to work toward an alternate system. At the same time, some Catia TVe producers were intensely preoccupied by the long-term ecological damage created by the burning of fossil fuels. But they were torn. It seemed entirely unfair to impose the cost of remaking the global energy system on the poorest sectors of the world's population.

Given these sentiments, some people I spoke with at Catia TVe in 2015 viewed the collapse of oil prices as a healthy development. They hoped it would provide the necessary push to try to analyze unsustainable extraction industries and remake Venezuela's mono-crop economy. Indeed, having the largest known oil reserves in the world has unclear long-term ramifications for Venezuela no matter the price of oil, given that these fossil fuels must remain in the ground in order to avoid catastrophic climate change (Lander 2016). My Catia TVe informants recognized the many contradictions of the Bolivarian Revolution, but most continued to see it as the only viable movement for change.

Looking Back, Looking Ahead

Looking back at the previous decade, my longtime interlocutors at Catia TVe debated what had gone wrong. In analyzing missteps, some Catia TVe leaders were critical of their own stagnant approach to organizing. Gregorio reflected, "We became very insular. We became an elite, in a way, isolated from the people. And if it's just about supporting our lives, sustaining ourselves and no one else, well, that wasn't the goal." Indeed, in the years following my 2007 research, the participation of Catia TVe's volunteer groups waned. After completing initial training workshops, new participants did not return, lacking material support and encouragement. Some seasoned volunteers grew frustrated with Catia TVe's leadership's lack of openness to change and internal criticism. A certain degree of tension had always been latent between the paid decision-making staff and the volunteers, who had gained skills and responsibilities but had neither salaries nor decision-making power. These issues were compounded by Catia TVe staff's reluctance to tackle inequality within their ranks. Insularity blossomed in the absence of internal criticism and reflection. The attrition that Catia TVe suffered was a result of internal power struggles, the collapse of state funding, and the challenge of maintaining a television station largely reliant on volunteer labor in the midst of an economy that was still fundamentally capitalist.

A further challenge that undermined Catia TVe's ability to sustain participation and media production was the constantly shifting political structure in which they operated. For example, the 2006 law that supported the development of local governance structures called communal councils presented a new possibility for how media might be produced by and for barrio communities. By 2007, Catia TVe leaders had begun to discuss how to adapt the existing organizational structure of their station to that of the communal council. For many revolutionaries, the communal councils and the nascent project of building a communal state represented the next step of the political process toward an equal and just socialist democratic society (Ciccariello-Maher 2016). Nevertheless, Catia TVe leaders struggled to figure out how to connect their project and the web of social relationships that made it possible with these newer experiments in direct democratic governance. To some degree, my interlocutors perceived newer experiments as threatening their hard-won gains, even as they agreed with the importance of taking steps to advance socialist production of food, goods, and media.

After decades of organizing, there was little consensus among the Catia TVe producers I reconnected with about how to approach the processes of media production, distribution, and consumption in ways that could advance struggles for social justice. Some questioned their long-standing emphasis on the process of production as the central organizing strategy and began to highlight the importance of the final products—compelling and persuasive programming—for advocacy and the dissemination of knowledge.

Hector, who during the time of my research shared the position of assistant director with Ana, insisted that both middle-class cultural producers working at state-run outlets and community media activists alike had been dishonest about the kind of television they wanted to see. Catia TVe producers were unsuccessful in generating support for the nonrenewal of RCTV's license, in part because they neither respected nor addressed the question of pleasure or the complexity of audience reception practices. The dismissal of people's passion for commercial media as simply false consciousness, a theme I explored in previous chapters, became a significant roadblock to engaging the complexity of people's lives.

Hector was adamant that many state media producers at ViVe TV responded to the constant barrage of commercial media attacks on state initiatives by focusing solely on the achievements and claiming the revolution as "already accomplished." Hector was deeply critical of ViVe TV for increasingly broadcasting official speeches, programming that featured traditional dances and celebrations, and dry discussions of politics largely devoid of the messiness of conflict, doubts, and confusion that people were experiencing. Hector noted that many producers at ViVe TV and other state outlets had little trust in the ability of poor people to make proposals and understand the revolution as a process in motion that inevitably faced gaps between revolutionary goals and everyday practice. The prevailing faction of ViVe TV continued to see poor audiences as dependent receivers of ideas and "beneficiaries" of the revolution rather than as producers. Hector argued that the conventional commercial media training and middle-class perspectives of most ViVe TV employees led them to approach the revolution as a finished product they needed to peddle to inert audiences. Yet, as Hector and Carlos were eager to acknowledge, for all of ViVe TV's many shortcomings, some of its programming, which featured the lives of the poor and historically disenfranchised populations of Venezuela and Latin America more broadly, was an improvement on the narrow, racist, and classist depictions that had made up the majority of commercial television programming for much of Venezuela's history.

Reimagining Press Freedom

The media world of Venezuela in June 2015 was remarkably different from what I encountered when I first started conducting research on media reception in the Venezuelan countryside in 1999. Activist and official efforts to make community media production legal and accessible, starting in the early 2000s, advanced a radical challenge to commonsense understandings about who could produce media. Even while many community outlets struggled to survive the economic crisis intact, people continued to experiment with new ways to shape the media world. The Chávez government's 2007 move to replace RCTV with an official state channel heralded the beginning of major transformations in Venezuelan mass media that have undermined the power of private media corporations. Since coming to power, the Maduro government has considerably narrowed the space for criticism of government policies on both private media outlets and official state-run media outlets.

While it is vital to question the possibilities for critical media to disseminate fact-based information, Catia TVe's practice of media making threw into sharp relief the inadequacy of liberal understandings of press freedom as private ownership, unfettered speech, and autonomy from the state. To advance a more rigorous understanding of communicative freedom and justice requires making central the importance of media production by, for, and about historically oppressed and exploited populations. To do so requires a holistic understanding of press freedom that includes not just the freedom to criticize those in official positions of power, but also access to education, health care, housing, physical mobility, self-determination, and the means of media production. Without broader recognition of the interconnection between political and economic rights, free expression is reduced in practice to a class-based privilege, accessible to those who have their stomachs full, as my informants explained.

Don't Just Watch, Make!

Over the past thirty years, there has been a remarkable continuity in the analyses that many scholars and pundits advance about problems in Venezuela. Observers on both the political right and left have claimed that at the root of the economic and political crisis in Venezuela today, as in the past, is a culture of dependency on the oil-rich state. Venezuelans, according to this line of thought, believe that the state should fulfill obligations to provide for the population, but that they do not have a work ethic. That is, many propagate the notion that Venezuelans do not want to work hard or to assume responsibility for their own problems. This appraisal relies on numerous faulty assumptions, including those of the discriminatory culture of poverty thesis, which explains poverty as the result of bad values and lack of self-discipline. What is especially striking, in light of the arguments I have elaborated in this book, is how this explanation remains mired in the perspective that all Venezuelans see the state as a magical, coherent, or separate force.

Catia TVe and other activists did confront people in their neighborhoods who hoped that Chávez or "the state" would solve their problems. But Catia TVe producers fought hard to upend this inclination, as did many activists who built and supported the Bolivarian Revolution. Although barrio-based activists and their allies faced intransigence, corruption, and confusion in many of their dealings with state institutions, Catia TVe producers argued that the only way to resolve problems and advance popular leadership was to encourage broader participation in barrio-based programs aligned with the Chávez-led state. They urged their neighbors to engage in statecraft rather than leaving it to a managerial middle class and elite.

Catia TVe and other activists did not wait for an outside force of unseen bureaucrats to do the work. People who engaged in the everyday statecraft of building the Bolivarian Revolution attended long meetings, worked in soup kitchens, volunteered in local healthcare clinics, engaged in oversight programs, cared for the homeless, and attended and facilitated educational workshops. Sometimes they were paid to do this work by state institutions; often they weren't. To grant the complex and uneven project of the Bolivarian Revolution any chance of success required constant social mobilization, community organization, and the continuous performance and display of signs of popular empowerment to deflect criticism and encourage widespread participation. This was challenging labor, but also meaningful. This work created social ties, granted activists status in their neighborhoods, and reaped rewards of better health outcomes, nutrition, and education. It gave them dignity and hope. My interlocutors carried out this collective labor in the face of fierce reaction from right-wing forces at home and abroad.

When Catia TVe producers urged their neighbors to make television, rather than watch it, they pointed to how people can remake the world they share. This task of transformation involved channeling the institutions and resources of the state. For Catia TVe producers and their allies, freedom meant the ability to engage in this process of statecraft, not declare autonomy from the process and its constellation of relations. Catia TVe producers worked hard to make revolution with the material available to them. The lessons will not be lost.

Notes

INTRODUCTION

1. In all but a few cases, I use pseudonyms to protect identities.

2. Scholars debate whether or not the Bolivarian Revolution was, in fact, a revolution. The central question is, as Benjamin Arditi asserts, "How radical must radical restructuring of the cosmos be in order to call it revolutionary?" I see "revolutionizing" as "a transgression that questions the existing consensus" (Arditi 2007, 117) and "an attempt rationally to design a *new* political order" (Donham 1999, 1). It was clear to me from the first extended period of fieldwork I conducted with Catia TVe in 2003 that community media activists and many of their allies aimed to radically restructure their social order. My participants sought broad, sweeping societal change and were part of a massive movement in popular political participation.

3. I have been strongly influenced by the work of Ferguson and Gupta (2002); Glick Schiller and Fouron (2001); Joseph and Nugent (1994); and Nugent and Alonso (1994).

4. Timothy Mitchell (1991) calls this the "state effect."

5. For further discussion of the state and the possibility of "taking power," see Wilpert (2007), debates over Holloway's *Change the World without Taking Power* (2002), and Ciccariello-Maher (2013).

6. In Venezuela, the affluent population is largely light-skinned, while people from poorer neighborhoods generally have darker complexions. Race is not understood in Caracas according to a black/white binary as it has been historically constructed in the United States. Racism works through a sometimes subtle demarcation of color hierarchy that, as elsewhere in Latin America, ultimately "enforces and promotes the idea that 'white' is 'better'" (Stam 1997, 45). Under the Chávez administrations, Afro-Venezuelan activist organizations had limited success in drawing attention to structural racism and advancing civil rights. The 1999 constitution and many government officials under Chávez continued to refuse to recognize Afro-descendant Venezuelans as a distinct group (García 2007). Nevertheless, Afro-Venezuelan groups made

strides. They worked to gain support for the 2011 Law against Racial Discrimination. Activist organizations also succeeded in their effort to include a question about ethnic descent in the 2011 national census. In this first effort to gather national data, 0.8 percent of those queried identified as Afro-descendants, 52.1 percent as *morenos* (dark and mixed race), 3 percent as black, 43 percent as white, and 2.7 percent as indigenous.

7. Founders of Venezuela's democracy combined liberal democratic commitments to private property, individual freedoms, universal suffrage, and the constitutional rule of law with Simón Bolívar's communitarian vision of the republic, which included communal rights to resources. Coronil calls this hybrid philosophy "rentier liberalism"; it combines core liberal tenets, such as the right to private property, with the landowner's commitment to distribute the profit from the oil trade, often called rent (1997, 88–89). The rentier liberal state, in other words, collects rents (or fees) for oil through contracts with oil companies and redistributes these rents to the population, while at the same time defending the rights of individuals to amass private capital (a basic commitment of liberalism). For an in-depth discussion of the relationship between land, capital, and labor, and the importance of the capture of foreign exchange, see Coronil (1997, 45–66) and Purcell (2015, 168–73).

8. I join a group of researchers who have analyzed how grassroots groups in Venezuela that were aligned with the Chávez-led state and supported financially by state institutions negotiated their autonomy, "outsider" militancy, and local control (Antillano 2005; Azzellini 2010; Ciccariello-Maher 2013; Fernandes 2010b; Valencia 2015; Velasco 2011). This scholarship challenges the mainstream political science approach that has long dominated research on Venezuela, as elsewhere in Latin America.

9. Liberal thought tends to mark dependency as negative and constraining, and sees autonomy and dependency as contradictory. Liberal approaches can make it difficult to recognize "other kinds of political and social projects and moral-ethical aspirations" (Mahmood 2007, 149). My understanding of dependence, independence, and interdependence draws on feminist and disability studies literature, as well as recent anthropological analyses of sovereignty. See Cattelino (2008), Fine and Glendinning (2005), and Fraser and Gordon (1994).

10. If the Chávez government's commitment to liberal norms was unclear, so were the liberal norms themselves. Internal debates among committed liberals rage about the limits of press freedom. What those who dismissed Chávez as censor-in-chief obscured was how, even within in the liberal Western tradition of freedom of expression, there is considerable disagreement about whether this freedom should be "absolute," i.e., whether people should be able to say whatever they want regardless of the consequences, or if governments should play a role in regulating speech, including by deeming certain expressions unacceptable "hate speech." While during Chávez's presidency a narrow understanding of press freedom dominated how prominent observers evaluated Venezuela's media world, the tradition of press freedom, like liberalism itself, is in fact "heteroglossic," meaning that it is "under constant negotiation, reformation and critique" (Coleman and Golub 2008, 258).

CHAPTER 1. STATE–MEDIA RELATIONS
AND THE RISE OF CATIA TVE

1. Crespo was president from 1884 to 1886 and again from 1892 to 1898.

2. Consejo Nacional de la Cultura, 1976, *Proyecto Ratelve: Diseño para una nueva política de radiodifusión del Estado venezolano*, http://saber.ucab.edu.ve/handle /123456789/31804.

3. Widespread disdain for the corruption and the lack of channels for democratic participation in the two-party puntofijista system pressured the government of Jaime Lusinchi (1984–89) to create the Presidential Commission for State Reform (COPRE). COPRE formulated proposals for major decentralization and electoral reform. Demands for decentralization dovetailed with an emerging neoliberal ideology (Hein 1980, 241).

4. The official figure is 277. Families of victims of the Caracazo claim 399 dead (Coronil 2011b, 65). Ellner notes that other estimates placed the death count above 2,000 (Ellner 2008, 95).

5. The Cisneros Group's partnership with DirecTV ended in 2005.

6. There are a variety of terms that practitioners, scholars, and activists use to categorize media produced by nontraditional nonprofessionals in the interest of social change. Categories include alternative media, which is identified principally by its methods of circulation and distribution (Anderson and Goldson 1993), and radical or guerrilla media, which refers to media made with the purpose of creating progressive social change informed by a political economy approach to media industries (Boyle 1997; Downing 2001). Building on Chantal Mouffe's approach to citizenship, Clemencia Rodríguez (2001) argues for the category of "citizen's media" as a practice that can facilitate a radically reconceptualized citizenship, based not on state-controlled legal status but on disrupting established power relationships. The category of indigenous media is often defined by the particular identification of its producers and their long-term struggles against the legacies of colonialism (Ginsburg 1995). These distinctions are not simply tedious taxonomies. They reveal a great deal about the interests and intentions of producers and scholars. I follow my interlocutors in Venezuela in using the term *community media*. The concept of community has its own limitations and possibilities, which I explore throughout this book. As I make plain in this chapter and others, I don't find it useful or theoretically rigorous to advance sharp distinctions between state-funded and supposedly autonomous media organizations. Each case and the power dynamics that constitute it need to be examined in their specificity of time and place, as the meaning of state shifts and presents different possibilities at distinct conjunctures.

7. See Alejandro Velasco's (2015) rich analysis of the violence and possibility of modern urban planning for Caracas's popular sectors during this period.

8. Many believed that state forces actively supported the drug trade to undermine the possibility of leftist organizing in militant neighborhoods of Caracas (Ciccariello-Maher 2013, 77).

9. See Bessire and Fisher (2012) for anthropological approaches to the ongoing importance of radio.

10. For a discussion of the history of community media in Venezuela, see Castillo (2003) and González (2001).

11. For further examples, see Dowell (2013), Fisher (2016), Ginsburg (1997), Himpele (2007), Turner (1991), and Wortham (2013).

12. The hospital was the highest building in the area—which provided a necessary boost for the signal—and had the infrastructure of security and air-conditioning to maintain the equipment.

13. By law, the station's staff could contribute only 15 percent of the station's content. Volunteers had to produce 55 percent. The remaining content could be filled by other noncommercial sources. The regulation also stipulates that the directors of community media cannot be party officials, members of the military, or work for private mass media.

14. Some of the most popular channels were Cartoon Network, Discovery Kids, Fox Kids, Nickelodeon, MTV, Discovery Channel, and Fox Warner.

15. This quotation, which I have translated, appeared on a page of the Internet site noticierodigital.com, no longer in existence. It was reposted later on page 21 of http://www.redescualidos.net/forum.

16. For a discussion of the varied histories of state broadcast regulation and control in Latin America, see Sinclair (1999) and Waisbord (1995).

17. The 2005 Law of Social Responsibility exerts little regulation over satellite and cable television, limiting itself to the networks granted concessions to broadcast on the electromagnetic spectrum.

CHAPTER 2. COMMUNITY MEDIA AS
EVERYDAY STATE FORMATION

1. The government borrowed this term from Doreen Massey, a British geographer and social scientist.

2. The community stations represented at the meeting were Televisora Michelena, TV Rubio, and Televisora Cultural from Rubio; Galopando TV from Guárico; Catia TVe from the Federal District of Caracas; Camunare Rojo from Yaracuy; Canal Z and Quijote TV from Zulia; Montaña TV and Jaureguina from Táchira; Lara TV from Lara; Selva TV from Amazonas; Teletambores from Aragua; TV Puerto from Anzoátegui; Coro TV from Falcón; and TV Petare and Telecimarrón from Miranda.

CHAPTER 3. CLASS ACTS

1. Recent ethnographies of class include Bettie (2003), Goldstein (2003), Ortner (2003, 2013), Jackson (2001), and Walley (2013).

2. It is also vital to recognize that a cadre of business elites in the private sector collaborated with the Chávez government at various junctures over the course of Chávez's rule. As Steve Ellner has explored (2015), while these business owners were focused on the short-term financial rewards of collaboration and did not endorse the political project of revolutionary state formation, a group of domestic capitalists in

the private sector were nevertheless important contributors in crafting the emerging state in ways that had long-term negative consequences for the ability of radical actors inside and outside official state institutions to develop collective worker control of wealth.

3. For differing analyses of poverty in Venezuela during the period of my research, see Francisco Rodriguez (2008) and Mark Weisbrot (2008). Weisbrot makes a convincing case that Rodriguez and other journalists have incorrectly asserted the increase of poverty in Venezuela under Chávez based on calculations that include the devastating impacts of the 2002–3 oil strike and management lockout, which opposition forces intentionally unleashed to cripple the economy.

4. Deronne, of course, borrows the term *organic intellectual* from Gramsci. For Gramsci, all intellectuals play a key role in maintaining and producing a given social order (Gramsci 1971). Gramsci scholar Nicholas Forgacs (2000) explains that in Gramsci's formulation, for the working class to challenge elite hegemony and become itself hegemonic, it must create its own "organic" intellectuals.

5. *Gorda* can also be a term of affection.

6. There are various meanings of *popular culture*, only some of which Daniel and his students invoked during the workshop. For a group of orthodox Marxist scholars known as the "Frankfurt School," popular culture is a term that suggests a defiled form of commercial culture that is manipulative, bereft of creativity, and imposed from "above." In contrast, many British cultural studies scholars rejected this notion. Drawing on Gramsci's notion of hegemony, they sought to understand popular culture neither as an arena of ideological domination by the ruling class nor of pristine expression of the oppressed, but rather a terrain of struggle and appropriation.

7. It may well be that communication scholarship that seeks to highlight "resistance" has overstated the ability of audiences to form their own transgressive readings. Nevertheless, the producer never completely determines what people learn from television (Abu-Lughod 2005; Mankekar 1999). For scholarship on the complexity of audience practices, see Ang (1985, 1991), Hall (1980), Martín-Barbero (1993), and Radway (1988). For an assessment of how the thesis of audience agency has been overextended, see Curran and Park (2000) and Miller (2004).

8. See Donna Goldstein's discussion of handwriting as one example of bodily movement that serves to distinguish an individual's cultural capital and class membership (2003, 91).

CHAPTER 4. CHANNELING CHÁVEZ

1. A denuncia may take the form of an official report of a crime filed with the police, a letter that expresses a grievance submitted to a relevant state institution, or a spoken complaint or demand. Denuncias are related to testimonial discourse, a genre of expression that usually denounces a situation of oppression or exploitation (Gugelberger 1996, 9; Himpele 2007).

2. Scholars have argued that media producers in Venezuela are well aware of the boundaries of acceptable speech established by their own speech communities (i.e.,

their set of political allies), as well as by the Chávez government and its legal regime, and thus exercise considerable levels of "self-censorship," making official acts of repression less necessary (Acosta-Alzuru 2013). My perspective, following Boyer (2003) and others, is that all knowledge production is a process of selection shaped by dominant hegemonies. From this perspective, the deployment of the concept of self-censorship to describe particular contexts and not others signals a struggle for power over and through the idea of free speech, rather than a move that helps us capture something unique about the process of knowledge production in a particular place and time.

3. My analysis here draws from a discussion that unfolded at a panel I participated in at the 2014 meeting of the American Anthropological Association on populist politics and mass mediation, organized by Amahl Bishara and Frank Cody. I am indebted to William Mazzarella's illuminating discussant remarks for advancing my understanding of the connections between liberalism and populism.

4. For six months in 2007, instead of the marathon Sunday program, Chávez appeared for an hour-and-a-half program on Thursday nights, with additional radio appearances on Monday, Tuesday, and Wednesday evenings.

5. *Aló Presidente*, no. 265, Thursday, February 15, 2007.

6. The program takes its name from Simón Bolívar's nurse, Hipólita Bolívar, an enslaved woman.

7. The health, education, and food distribution missions were created outside the traditional institutional structures of public health and education administered by state ministries. This alternative structure of services allowed for more local involvement in the administration of programs, but also left the programs vulnerable to strategic manipulation and inconsistent operation.

8. Barrio Adentro was designed to meet the 1999 constitution's mandate to create a health system that was "decentralized and participatory . . . guided by the principles of free cost, universal availability, intersectoriality, equity, social integration, and solidarity" (cited in Briggs and Mantini-Briggs 2009, 550).

9. Launched in 2006, the Madres del Barrio program aimed to provide poor women who have children a stipend of $176 a month, about 60 to 80 percent of the minimum wage, to work at home caring for their families. The program is based on Article 88 of the constitution, which recognizes women's work at home as economic activity. In 2006 about 200,000 women, or 8 percent of poor women, were enrolled in the program (Wilpert 2007, 143).

10. Corrales and Penfold argue that the Chávez government's programs were not unlike previous populist programs in Venezuela, some even claiming that Barrio Adentro and other programs were designed to "buy votes" (2007, 106). Kirk Hawkins, however, challenges this notion, finding that aid through the Chávez government programs was not dependent on overt or coercive demands for political support, even though programs were concentrated in areas that supported Chávez (2010, 213).

11. The language of "popular empowerment" and "participation," which formed a key aspect of Ana's approach, is a central component not only of progressive political projects, but also of neoliberal policies that have unloaded public services and labor to "responsibilized" citizens (Paley 2002, 2004). Unlike neoliberal discourses of

participation, the Chávez government's programs included heavy involvement of state institutions in redistributing resources, along with calls for local action. Despite these differences, Chávez's nascent socialist programs, like neoliberal programs, have placed the burden of community services on women, suggesting that gender oppression was extended rather than upended by the revolution's participatory programs in local governance and resource distribution. See my discussion in chapter 5. For an exploration of the Chávez government's reliance on neoliberal logics, see Fernandes (2010b).

CHAPTER 5. MEDIATING WOMEN

1. See Rakowski and Espina (2011) for a detailed analysis of the gains and shortcomings of the institutions, policies, and laws concerning women's rights advanced during the Chávez presidency.

2. The 2007 effort to alter the constitution also excluded the right to choose to terminate a pregnancy. As of 2015, abortion remains illegal even in cases of rape, incest, and fetal impairment (Buxton 2015).

3. Although there are four provisions in the constitution that prohibit employers, landlords, and financial institutions from discriminating against citizens based on sexuality, enforcement has been slow. As Buxton (2015) notes, as of 2015 there is no legal recognition of gender change, same-sex civil unions or marriage, or same-sex adoption. In the 2015 National Assembly elections, Tamara Adrian, a transgender woman and member of the opposition party Voluntad Popular, was elected, marking a major milestone for transgender visibility in Venezuela.

4. *Intersectionality* is a contested term. I approach the concept as a framework for understanding how race, class, gender, sexuality, and other factors are coconstitutive and interrelated. Rather than referring to points of intersection of different stable vectors of identity, as some theorists have suggested, I follow Yuval-Davis (2006) in highlighting how the term might capture how dimensions of social relations can never be disentangled. This framework, ideally, challenges the fragmentation and essentializing of social identities. Class, for example, always has gendered meanings in specific places and times, and these meanings and material consequences shift over time.

5. This broad categorization, as Guttman (1986) notes, negates important differences among classes, regions, ages, and ethnic groups throughout Latin America and Spain.

6. Lynn Stephen's book, *We Are the Face of Oaxaca* (2013) documents how the right to speak and be heard is equated with access to political citizenship.

7. See Jeff Himpele's exploration of similar dynamics on a Bolivian talk show (2007).

8. There is an extensive scholarly literature on the paradoxes and possibilities of state welfare assistance programs created to alleviate women's poverty. See Gordon (1990) and Orloff (1999).

9. Madres del Barrio, in its incarnation during the period of my research, depended on essentialized notions of gender difference. Later, Madres del Barrio began to challenge gendered labor ideologies. In December 2008, together with the Metro of Caracas, the Madres del Barrio launched a program to train women to be metro conductors in the Caracas subway system.

10. Many feminist scholars have argued that the distinction, first advanced by Maxine Molyneux (1985), between "practical" interests in improving access to nutrition, education, and local infrastructure and "strategic" efforts to challenge gender inequality is a false binary (Fernandes 2007; Lind 1992, 2005).

11. Elsewhere, Espina (2007) acknowledges and examines the complexity of the "fractured" and "multiple" subject whose experience of gender cannot be separated, for example, from that of race or class.

12. See bell hooks's foundational analysis of feminism (1984).

CHAPTER 6. RECKONING WITH PRESS FREEDOM

1. Liberalism is made up of numerous different traditions. Some traditions of liberalism are dedicated to maximizing individual liberty, while others more concerned with maximizing social equality (Brown 2003). Liberal ideals were first formulated over the course of the sixteenth, seventeenth, and eighteenth centuries in Western Europe, with the aim of redefining the limits of political authority. Early proponents opposed the arbitrary power of kings and the privileges granted by birth to the nobility. The development of liberal thought involved the formulation of a new notion of the individual. The sovereign, according to early liberal thinkers, needed to be subordinate to the liberty and rights of the individual. According to early and more recent proponents, the liberal state must be powerful enough to secure individual liberty but limited enough that it cannot impose restraints on individuals. The philosophical basis of the liberal state is a doctrine of natural rights that all "men" possess fundamental rights (life, liberty, security, and happiness) on which the state must not tread. In dominant contemporary versions of liberalism, "individual freedom" and "social constraint" are usually posed as binary concepts (Povinelli 2006, 2011). Yet liberal freedoms, as Isaiah Berlin famously pointed out, have included not only freedom from constraint, which he called "negative freedom," but also organized state coercion in the name of a greater social good and liberty, such as public education, which he called "positive freedom" (1969). For a review of recent anthropological approaches to liberalism, see Schiller (2015).

2. I draw on Jessica Winegar's use of the concept of "reckoning," which nicely captures "people's sense of having to deal with (or discover) things that appear to have already been set" (2006, 6).

3. For excellent work on press freedom in anthropology, see Bishara (2013), Boyer and Yurchak (2010), and Roudakova (2017).

4. A small body of anthropological scholarship builds on ethnographic studies of the state to explore the role of media producers in working with and contesting liberal premises (Bishara 2006; Boyer 2005; Hasty 2005; Roudakova 2009).

5. Scholars in communications and law have been at the forefront of exploring how media producers' autonomy from states might in fact undermine the very conditions needed to guarantee plural communications (Glasser and Gunther 2005; McChesney and Nichols 2011).

6. Governments around the world regulate the use of the electromagnetic spectrum—the finite spectrum of radio waves used to transmit radio, television, and

other data—through temporary frequency allocations. Governments distribute short-term licenses to broadcasters, who then have the exclusive right to transmit via that frequency for a specified geographic area (Peha 1998).

7. Agencia Bolivariana de Noticias, "Programación de TVes no será impuesta por el Ejecutivo," http://www.abn.info.ve/imprimir2.php?articulo=92441, accessed May 22, 2007.

References

Abercrombie, Thomas. 1998. *Pathways of Memory and Power: Ethnography and History among Andean People.* Madison: University of Wisconsin Press.

Abrams, Philip. 1988. "Notes on the Difficulty of Studying the State." *Journal of Historical Sociology* 1 (1): 58–89.

Abu-Lughod, Lila. 1990. "The Romance of Resistance: Tracing Transformations of Power through Bedouin Women." *American Ethnologist* 17 (1): 41–55.

Abu-Lughod, Lila. 1995. "The Objects of Soap Opera: Egyptian Television and the Cultural Politics of Modernity." In *Worlds Apart: Modernity through the Prism of the Local,* edited by Daniel Miller, 190–210. London: Routledge.

Abu-Lughod, Lila. 2005. *Dramas of Nationhood.* Chicago: University of Chicago Press.

Acosta-Alzuru, Carolina. 2003. "'I'm Not a Feminist . . . I Only Defend Women as Human Beings': The Production, Reproduction, and Consumption of Feminism in a Telenovela." *Critical Studies in Mass Communication* 20 (3): 269–94.

Acosta-Alzuru, Carolina. 2013. "Propaganda and Survival in Venezualan Television." *Venezuelan Politics and Human Rights.* Accessed March 17, 2013. http://venezuelablog.tumblr.com/post/45583925217/propaganda-and-survival-in -venezuelan-television.

Aguirre, Jesús María. 2005. "Democratizar la comunicación: El caso Venezuela." *Anuario Ininco* 17 (1): 17–38.

Alvarez, Sonia E., Evelina Dagnino, and Arturo Escobar. 1998. "Introduction." In *Cultures of Politics, Politics of Cultures: Re-Visioning Latin American Social Movements,* edited by Sonia E. Alvarez, Evelina Dagnino, and Arturo Escobar, 1–29. Boulder, CO: Westview.

Alvarez, Sonia E., Elisabeth Jay Friedman, Ericka Beckman, Maylei Blackwell, Norma Stoltz Chinchilla, Nathalie Lebon, Marysa Navarro, and Marcela Ríos Tobar. 2003. "Encontrando os feminismos latino-americanos e caribenhos." *Revista Estudos Feministas* 11 (2): 541–75.

Anderson, Kelly, and Annie Goldson. 1993. "Alternating Currents: Alternative Television inside and outside of the Academy." *Social Text* 35:56–71.

Ang, Ien. 1985. *Watching Dallas.* London: Methuen.

Ang, Ien. 1991. *Desperately Seeking the Audience.* London: Routledge.

Antillano, Andrés. 2005. "La lucha por el reconocimiento y la inclusión en los barrios populares: La experiencea de los comités de tierras urbanas." *Revista Venezolana de Economía y Ciencias Sociales* 11 (3): 205–18.

Antillano, Andrés. 2013. "Repolitizar la inseguridad." *Espacio Abierto Cuaderno Venezolano de Sociología* 22 (3): 581–91.

Arditi, Benjamin. 2005. "Populism and the Internal Periphery of Democratic Politics." In *Populism and the Mirror of Democracy,* edited by Francisco Panizza, 72–98. London: Verso.

Arditi, Benjamin. 2007. *Politics on the Edges of Liberalism: Difference, Populism, Revolution, Agitation.* Edinburgh: Edinburgh University Press.

Aufderheide, Patricia. 1993. "Latin American Grassroots Video." *Public Culture* 5:579–92.

Aufderheide, Patricia. 2000. "Grassroots Video in Latin America." In *Visible Nations: Latin American Cinema and Video,* edited by Chon A. Noriega, 219–38. Minneapolis: University of Minnesota Press.

Auyero, Javier. 2012. *Patients of the State: The Politics of Waiting in Argentina.* Durham, NC: Duke University Press.

Azzellini, Dario. 2010. "Constituent Power in Motion: Ten Years of Transformation in Venezuela." *Socialism and Democracy* 24 (2): 8–31.

Azzellini, Dario. 2015. "Venezuela's Social Transformation and Growing Class Struggle." In *Crisis and Contradiction: Marxist Perspectives on Latin America in the Global Political Economy,* edited by Susan J. Spronk and Jeffery R. Webber, 138–62. Chicago: Haymarket Books.

Barrios, Leoncio. 1988. "Television, Telenovelas, and Family Life in Venezuela." In *World Families Watch Television,* edited by James Lull, 49–79. Newbury Park, CA: SAGE.

Baxter, Judith. 2006. "'Do We Have to Agree with Her?' How High School Girls Negotiate Leadership in Public Contexts." In *Speaking Out: The Female Voice in Public Contexts,* edited by Judith Baxter, 159–78. Houndmills, UK: Palgrave Macmillan.

Becerra, Martín. 2014. "Medios de comunicación: América Latina a contramano." *Nueva Sociedad* 249:61–74.

Behrends, Andrea, Stephen Reyna, and Gunther Schlee, eds. 2013. *Crude Domination: An Anthropology of Oil.* New York: Berghahn Books.

Beltrán Salmón, Luis Ramiro. 2008. "Comunicación para la democracia en Iberoamérica: Memoria y retos de futuro." *Perspectivas de la Comunicación* 1 (1): 145–58.

Berlin, Isaiah. 1969. *Four Essays on Liberty.* Oxford: Oxford University Press.

Bessire, Lucas, and Daniel Fisher, eds. 2012. *Radio Fields: Anthropology and Wireless Sound in the 21st Century.* New York: New York University Press.

Bettie, Julie. 2003. *Women without Class: Girls, Race, and Identity.* Berkeley: University of California Press.

Bisbal, Marcelino. 2005. "En el aire nuestra pantalla televisiva." In *Televisión, pan nuestro de dada día,* edited by Marcelino Bisbal, 29–88. Caracas: Alfadil Ediciones.

Bisbal, Marcelino. 2007. "Los medios en Venezuela." *Espacio Abierto Cuaderno Venezolano de Sociología* 16 (4): 643–68.

Bishara, Amahl. 2006. "Local Hands, International News: Palestinian Journalists and the International Media." *Ethnography* 7 (1): 19–46.

Bishara, Amahl. 2013. *Back Stories: U.S. News Production and Palestinian Politics.* Stanford, CA: Stanford University Press.

Blanco, Jessie. 2007. "Feminismo revolucionario y socialismo." In *Ideas para debatir: El socialismo del siglo XXI*, edited by Margarita López Maya, 151–58. Caracas: Editorial Alfa.

Born, Georgina. 2005. *Uncertain Vision: Birt, Dyke and the Reinvention of the BBC.* London: Vintage.

Botía, Alejandro. 2007. *Auge y crisis del cuato poder: La prensa en democracia.* Caracas: Random House Mondadori, S.A.

Bourdieu, Pierre. 1984. *Distinction: A Social Critique of the Judgement of Taste.* Cambridge, MA: Harvard University Press.

Boyer, Dominic C. 2003. "Censorship as a Vocation: The Institutions, Practices, and Cultural Logic of Media Control in the German Democratic Republic." *Comparative Studies in Society and History* 45 (3): 511–45.

Boyer, Dominic C. 2005. *Spirit and System: Mass Media, Journalism, and the Dialectics of Modern German Intellectual Culture.* Chicago: University of Chicago Press.

Boyer, Dominic C., and Alexei Yurchak. 2010. "American Stiob: Or, What Late-Socialist Aesthetics of Parody Reveal about Contemporary Political Culture in the West." *Cultural Anthropology* 25 (2): 179–221.

Boyle, Deirdre. 1997. *Subject to Change: Guerrilla Television Revisted.* New York: Oxford University Press.

Briggs, Charles, and Clara Mantini-Briggs. 2009. "Confronting Health Disparities: Latin American Social Medicine in Venezuela." *American Journal of Public Health* 3:549–55.

Britto García, Luis. 2006. *Venezuela: Investigación de unos medios por encima de toda sospecha.* Caracas: Ministerio de Comunicación e Información.

Brown, Wendy. 2003. "Neo-Liberalism and the End of Liberal Democracy." *Theory and Event* 7 (1): 1–43.

Burton, Julianne. 1986. *Cinema and Social Change in Latin America.* Austin: University of Texas Press.

Butler, Judith. 1990. *Gender Trouble: Feminism and the Subversion of Identity.* New York: Routledge.

Buxton, Julia. 2003. "Economic Policy and the Rise of Hugo Chávez." In *Venezuelan Politics in the Chávez Era*, edited by Steve Ellner and Daniel Hellinger, 113–30. Boulder, CO: Lynne Rienner.

Buxton, Julia. 2011. "Foreword: Venezuela's Bolivarian Democracy." In *Venezuela's Bolivarian Democracy*, edited by David Smilde and Daniel Hellinger, ix–xxii. Durham, NC: Duke University Press.

Buxton, Julia. 2015. "Venezuela Lags Behind on Women's and LGBT Rights." Accessed July 10, 2015. http://lab.org.uk/venezuela-lags-behind-on-womens-and-lgbt-rights.

Cameron, Deborah. 1997. "Performing Gender Identity." In *Language and Masculinity*, edited by Sally Johnson and Ulrike Hanna Meinhof, 47–64. Oxford: Blackwell.

Cañizáles, Andrés. 2007. "Después de RCTV." *Revista Latinoamericana de Comunicación* 99:14–19.

Capriles, Oswaldo. 1996. *Poder y político y comunicación*. Caracas: Universidad Central de Venezuela, Consejo de Desarrollo Científico y Humanistico.

Carelli, Vincent. 1988. "Video in the Villages." *Commission on Visual Anthropology Bulletin* 4 (2) (May): 10–15.

Castillo, Juan Manuel Hernández. 2003. *Construcción del proceso histórico de los medios comunitarios en Venezuela: Aportes vivénciales*. Caracas: Comisión de Telecomunicaciones República Bolivariana de Venezuela.

Cattelino, Jessica. 2008. *High Stakes: Florida Seminole Gaming and Soveriegnty*. Durham, NC: Duke University Press.

Chase, Michelle. 2015. *Revolution within the Revolution: Women and Gender Politics in Cuba, 1952–1962*. Chapel Hill: University of North Carolina Press.

Chávez, Hugo. 2007. *Los cinco motores a máxima revolución*. Caracas: Gobierno Bolivariana de Venezuela.

Ciccariello-Maher, George. 2007. "Dual Power in the Venezuelan Revolution." *Monthly Review* 59 (4): 42–56.

Ciccariello-Maher, George. 2013. *We Created Chávez: A People's History of the Venezuelan Revolution*. Durham, NC: Duke University Press.

Ciccariello-Maher, George. 2016. *Building the Commune: Radical Democracy in Venezuela*. New York: Verso.

Coleman, Gabriella, and Alex Golub. 2008. "Hacker Practice: Moral Genres and the Cultural Articulation of Liberalism." *Anthropological Theory* 8 (3): 255–77.

Conklin, Beth. 1997. "Body Paint, Feathers, and VCRs: Aesthetics and Authenticity in Amazonian Activism." *American Ethnologist* 24 (4): 711–37.

Cooper, Amy. 2015. "What Does Health Activism Mean in Venezuela's Barrio Adentro Program? Understanding Community Health Work in Political and Cultural Context." *Annals of Anthropological Practice* 39 (1): 58–72.

Coronil, Fernando. 1997. *The Magical State: Nature, Money, and Modernity in Venezuela*. Chicago: University of Chicago Press.

Coronil, Fernando. 2008. "Chávez's Venezuela: A New Magical State?" *Revista: Harvard Review of Latin America* 8 (1): 36–39.

Coronil, Fernando. 2011a. "The Future in Question: History and Utopia in Latin America (1989–2010)." In *Business as Usual: The Roots of the Global Financial Meltdown*, edited by Craig Calhoun and Georgi Derluguian, 231–64. New York: New York University Press.

Coronil, Fernando. 2011b. "State Reflections: The 2002 Coup against Hugo Chávez." In *The Revolution in Venezuela*, edited by Thomas Ponniah and Jonathan Eastwood, 37–66. Cambridge, MA: Harvard University Press.

Coronil, Fernando, and Julie Skurski. 1991. "Dismembering and Remembering the Nation: The Semantics of Political Violence in Venezuela." *Comparative Studies in Society and History* 33 (2): 288–337.

Corrales, Javier, and Michael Penfold. 2007. "Venezuela: Crowding Out the Opposition." *Journal of Democracy* 18 (2): 99–113.

Corrigan, Philip, and Derek Sayer. 1985. *The Great Arch: English State Formation as Cultural Revolution.* Oxford: Basil Blackwell.

Creed, Gerald W. 2006. "Reconsidering Community." In *The Seductions of Community: Emancipations, Oppressions, Quandaries,* edited by G. W. Creed, 2–22. Santa Fe, NM: School for Advanced Research Press.

Curran, James, and Myung-Jin Park, eds. 2000. *De-Westernizing Media Studies.* New York: Routledge.

Dagnino, Evelina. 1998. "Culture, Citizenship, and Democracy: Changing Discourses and Practices of the Latin American Left." In *Cultures of Politics, Politics of Cultures: Re-Visioning Latin American Social Movements,* edited by Sonia E. Alvarez, Evelina Dagnino, and Arturo Escobar, 33–63. Boulder, CO: Westview Press.

Dávila, Arlene. 2015. *El Mall: The Spatial and Class Politics of Shopping Malls in Latin America.* Berkeley: University of California Press.

Dávila, Luis Ricardo. 2005. "Petróleo, cultura y sociedad en Venezuela." Accessed October 16, 2006. http://www.saber.ula.ve/db/ssaber/Edocs/papers/derecho/luis -davila/petroleo-cultura.pdf.

Delgado-Flores, Carlos. 2007. "Dos intentos para una radio televisión de servicio público en Venezuela." *Comunicación* 139:12–17.

Deronne, Thierry. 2009. *Venezuela en revolución: Diez propuestas para crear la televisión socialista.* Caracas: Vadell Hermanos Editores.

Deronne, Thierry. 2012. "Cómo nació la Escuela Popular y Latinoamericana de Cine, TV y Teatro." Accessed September 1, 2012. https://escuelapopularcineytv.wordpress .com/2012/07/01/como-nacio-la-escuela-popular-y-latinoamericana-de-cine/.

Díaz, Arlene. 2004. *Female Citizens, Patriarchs, and the Law in Venezuela, 1786–1904.* Lincoln: University of Nebraska Press.

Donham, Donald A. 1999. *Marxist Modern: An Ethnographic History of the Ethiopian Revolution.* Berkeley: University of California Press.

Dorfman, Ariel, and Armand Mattelart. 1975. *How to Read Donald Duck: Imperialist Ideology in the Disney Comic.* New York: International General.

Dowell, Kristen. 2013. *Sovereign Screens: Aboriginal Media on the Canadian West Coast.* Lincoln: University of Nebraska Press.

Downing, John. 2001. *Radical Media: Rebellious Communication and Social Movements.* Thousand Oaks, CA: SAGE.

Duno Gottberg, Luis. 2004. "Mob Outrages: Reflections on the Media Construction of the Masses in Venezuela." *Journal of Latin American Cultural Studies* 13 (1): 115–35.

Duque, José Roberto. 2000. "Catia en su pantalla." *Tal Cual* 1 (119) (September 26).

Edelsky, Carole. 1981. "Who's Got the Floor?" *Language in Society* 10:383–421.

Eekhout, Blanca. 2004. "La revolución en femenino." In *Bolivarianas: El protagonismo de las mujeres en la Revolución Venezolana,* edited by Monica Saiz, 37–43. Caracas: Ediciones Emancipación.

Eekhout, Blanca, and Gabriela Fuentes. 2001. "Cine de barrio: El discurso audiovisual producido por el Cineclub de la Comunidad de el Manicomio entre 1992–99." Communications, Universidad Central de Venezuela.

Ellner, Steve. 2008. *Rethinking Venezuelan Politics: Class, Conflict, and the Chávez Phenomenon*. Boulder, CO: Lynne Rienner.

Ellner, Steve. 2013. "Social and Political Diversity and the Democratic Road to Change in Venezuela." *Latin American Perspectives* 40 (3): 63–82.

Ellner, Steve. 2015. "Setting the Record Straight on Venezuela." *Jacobin*. Accessed December 4. https://www.jacobinmag.com/2015/12/venezuela-elections-hugo-chavez-maduro/.

Ellner, Steve, and Daniel Hellinger. 2003. "Conclusion: The Democratic and Authoritarian Directions of the Chavista Movement." In *Venezuelan Politics in the Chávez Era: Class, Polarization and Conflict*, edited by Steve Ellner and Daniel Hellinger, 215–26. Boulder, CO: Lynne Riener.

Espina, Gioconda. 2007. "El socialism del siglo XX no ocurrió, son cosas suyas. . . ." *Revista Venezolana de Estudios de La Mujer* 12 (28): 251–62.

Espina, Gioconda, and Cathy A. Rakowski. 2010. "Waking Women Up? Hugo Chávez, Populism and Venezuela's 'Popular' Women." In *Gender and Populism in Latin America*, edited by Karen Kampwirth, 180–201. University Park: Pennsylvania State University Press.

Espinosa, Julio García. 1979. "For an Imperfect Cinema." *Jump Cut* 20:22–26.

Ewell, Judith. 1984. *Venezuela: A Century of Change*. Stanford, CA: Stanford University Press.

Ferguson, James. 2004. "Power Topographies." In *A Companion to the Anthropology of Politics*, edited by Daniel Nugent and Joan Vincent, 383–99. Malden, MA: Blackwell.

Ferguson, James. 2006. *Global Shadows: Africa in the Neoliberal World Order*. Durham, NC: Duke University Press.

Ferguson, James, and Akhil Gupta. 2002. "Spatializing States: Toward an Ethnography of Neoliberal Governmentality." *American Ethnologist* 29 (4): 981–1002.

Fernandes, Sujatha. 2006. *Cuba Represent!: Cuban Arts, State Power, and the Making of New Revolutionary Cultures*. Durham, NC: Duke University Press.

Fernandes, Sujatha. 2007. "Barrio Women and Popular Politics in Chávez's Venezuela." *Latin American Politics and Society* 49 (3): 97–127.

Fernandes, Sujatha. 2010a. "Gender, Popular Participation, and the State in Chávez's Venezuela." In *Gender and Populism in Latin America*, edited by Karen Kampwirth, 202–21. University Park: Pennsylvania State University Press.

Fernandes, Sujatha. 2010b. *Who Can Stop the Drums? Urban Social Movements in Chávez's Venezuela*. Durham, NC: Duke University Press.

Fernandes, Sujatha. 2011. "Radio Bemba in an Age of Electronic Media: The Dynamics of Popular Communication in Chávez's Venezuela." In *Participation and Public Sphere in Venezuela's Bolivarian Democracy*, edited by David Smilde and Daniel Hellinger, 131–56. Durham, NC: Duke University Press.

Ferrandiz, Francisco. 2004. "The Body as Wound: Possession, Malandros and Everyday Violence in Venezuela." *Critique of Anthropology* 24 (2): 107–33.

Fine, Michael, and Caroline Glendinning. 2005. "Dependence, Independence, or Inter-Dependence: Revisiting the Concepts of 'Care' and 'Dependency.'" *Ageing and Society* 25:601–21.

Fisher, Daniel. 2016. *The Voice and Its Doubles*. Durham, NC: Duke University Press.

Forgacs, David, ed. 2000. *The Gramsci Reader*. New York: New York University Press.

Foucault, Michel. 1991. "Governmentality." In *The Foucault Effect: Studies in Governmentality*, edited by Burchell Graham, Colin Gordon, and Peter Miller, 87–104. Chicago: University of Chicago Press.

Fox, Elizabeth, and Silvio Waisbord. 2002. "Introduction." In *Latin Politics, Global Media*, edited by Elizabeth Fox and Silvio Waisbord, ix–xxii. Austin: University of Texas Press.

Fraser, Nancy, and Linda Gordon. 1994. "A Genealogy of Dependency: Tracing a Keyword of the US Welfare State." *Signs* 19 (2): 309–34.

Freire, Paulo. 1970. *Pedagogy of the Oppressed*. New York: Bloomsbury.

Friedman, Elisabeth J. 2000. *Unfinished Transitions: Women and the Gendered Development of Democracy in Venezuela, 1936–1996*. University Park: Pennsylvania State University Press.

Gal, Susan. 1991. "Between Speech and Silence: The Problematics of Research on Language and Gender." In *Gender at the Crossroads of Knowledge*, edited by Micaela di Leonardo, 175–203. Berkeley: University of California Press.

Gal, Susan. 1995. "Review Essay Language and the 'Arts of Resistance': Review of 'Domination and the Arts of Resistance: Hidden Transcripts' by James Scott." *Cultural Anthropology* 10 (3): 407–24.

Gal, Susan. 2001. "Language, Gender and Power." In *Linguistic Anthropology*, edited by Alessandro Duranti, 420–30. Malden, MA: Blackwell.

García, Jesús. 2007. "La deuda del estado venezolano y los Afrodescendientes." *Journal of Latin American and Caribbean Anthropology* 12 (1): 223–32.

García Canclini, Néstor. [1990] 1995. *Hybrid Cultures: Strategies for Entering and Leaving Modernity*. Minneapolis: University of Minnesota Press.

García Canclini, Néstor. [1995] 2001. *Consumers and Citizens: Globalization and Multicultural Conflicts*. Minneapolis: University of Minnesota Press.

García-Guadilla, María Pilar. 2011. "Urban Land Committees: Co-optation, Autonomy, and Protagonism." In *Venezuela's Bolivarian Democracy*, edited by David Smilde and Daniel Hellinger, 80–103. Durham, NC: Duke University Press.

Gates, Leslie. 2010. *Electing Chávez: The Business of Anti-Neoliberal Politics in Venezuela*. Pittsburgh: University of Pittsburgh Press.

Gershon, Ilana. 2008. "Email My Heart: Remediation and Romantic Break-Ups." *Anthropology Today* 24 (6): 13–15.

Ginsburg, Faye. 1995. "Aboriginal Media and the Australian Imaginary." *Public Culture* 5: 557–78.

Ginsburg, Faye. 1997. "'From Little Things, Big Things Grow': Indigenous Media and Cultural Activism." In *Between Resistance and Revolution*, edited by Richard Fox and Orin Starn, 118–44. London: Routledge.

Ginsburg, Faye, Lila Abu-Lughod, and Brian Larkin. 2002. "Introduction." In *Media Worlds: Anthropology on New Terrain*, edited by Faye Ginsburg, Lila Abu-Lughod, and Brian Larkin, 1–36. Berkeley: University of California Press.

Glasser, Theodore L., and Marc Gunther. 2005. "The Legacy of Autonomy in American Journalism." In *The Press*, edited by Geneva Overholser and Kathleen Hall Jamieson, 384–99. New York: Oxford University Press.

Glick Schiller, Nina, and Georges Fouron. 2001. *George Woke Up Laughing: Long-Distance Nationalism and the Search for Home*. Durham, NC: Duke University Press.

Goldfarb, Brian. 2000. "Local Television and Community Politics in Brazil." In *Visible Nations: Latin American Cinema and Video*, edited by Chon A. Noriega, 263–84. Minneapolis: University of Minnesota Press.

Goldstein, Donna. 2003. *Laughter out of Place: Race, Class, Violence, and Sexuality in a Rio Shantytown*. Berkeley: University of California Press.

González, Enrique. 2001. "Los medios communitarios en Venezuela." *Revista* sic 637 (August): 220–23.

Gordon, Linda. 1990. "The New Feminist Scholarship on the Welfare State." In *Women, the State, and Welfare*, edited by Linda Gordon, 9–35. Madison: University of Wisconsin Press.

Gramsci, Antonio. 1971. *Selections from the Prison Notebooks*. Translated by Quintin Hoare and Geoffrey Nowell Smith. New York: International Publishers.

Grandin, Greg. 2006. *Empire's Workshop: Latin America, the United States, and the Rise of the New Imperialism*. New York: Owl Books.

Gugelberger, Georg. 1996. *The Real Thing: Testimonial Discourse and Latin America*. Durham, NC: Duke University Press.

Gupta, Akhil. 1995. "Blurred Boundaries: The Discourse of Corruption, the Culture of Politics, and the Imagined State." *American Ethnologist* 22 (2): 375–402.

Guss, David. 2001. *The Festive State: Race, Ethnicity, and Nationalism as Cultural Performance*. Berkeley: University of California Press.

Gutmann, Matthew. 1986. *The Meanings of Macho: Being a Man in Mexico City*. Berkeley: University of California Press.

Gutmann, Matthew. 1993. "A Critique of the Theory of Everyday Forms of Resistance." *Latin American Perspectives* 20 (2): 74–92.

Hall, Stuart. 1980. "Encoding/Decoding." In *Culture, Media, Language*, edited by Stuart Hall, Dorothy Hobson, Andrew Lowe, and Paul Willis, 128–38. London: Hutchinson.

Hall, Stuart. 1998. "Notes on Deconstructing 'the Popular.'" In *Cultural Theory and Popular Culture: A Reader*, edited by John Storey, 442–53. Athens: University of Georgia Press.

Hansen, Thomas Blom. 1999. *The Saffron Wave: Democracy and Hindu Nationalism in Modern India*. Princeton, NJ: Princeton University Press.

Hartsock, Nancy. 2006. "Globalization and Primitive Accumulation: The Contribution of David Harvey's Dialectical Marxism." In *David Harvey: A Critical Reader*, edited by Noel Castree and Derek Gregory, 167–90. Malden, MA: Blackwell.

Harvey, David. 2003. *The New Imperialism*. Oxford: Oxford University Press.

Harvey, David. 2014. *Seventeen Contradictions and the End of Capitalism*. London: Profile.

Hasty, Jennifer. 2005. *The Press and Political Culture in Ghana*. Bloomington: Indiana University Press.

Hawkins, Kirk. 2010. *Venezuela's Chavismo and Populism in Comparative Perspective*. Cambridge: Cambridge University Press.

Hébrard, Véronique. 1998. "Opinión público y representación en el Congreso Constituyente de Venezuela (1811–1812)." In *Los espacios públicos en Iberoamérica*, edited by Francois-Xavier Guerra and Annick Lemperiere, 196–224. Mexico City: Centro Frances de Estudios Mexicanos y Centroamericanos.

Hein, Wolfgang. 1980. "Oil and the Venezuelan State." In *Oil and Class Struggle*, edited by Petter Nore and Terisa Turner, 224–51. London: Zed Press.

Hellinger, Daniel. 2007. "When 'No' Means 'Yes to Revolution': Electoral Politics in Bolivarian Venezuela." In *Venezuela: Hugo Chávez and the Decline of an "Exceptional Democracy,"* edited by Steve Ellner and Miguel Tinker Salas, 157–84. Lanham, MD: Rowman and Littlefield.

Hernández Díaz, Gustavo. 2008. *Las tres "T" de la comunicación en Venezuela: Televisión, teoría, y televidentes*. Caracas: Universidad Católica Andrés Bello.

Hetland, Gabriel. 2015. "Emergent Socialist Hegemony in Bolivarian Venezuela: The Role of the Party." In *Crisis and Contradiction: Marxist Perspectives on Latin America in the Global Political Economy*, edited by Susan J. Spronk and Jeffery R. Webber, 120–37. Chicago: Haymarket.

Himpele, Jeff. 2007. *Circuits of Culture: Media, Politics, and Indigenous Identity in the Andes*. Minneapolis: University of Minnesota Press.

Holloway, John. 2002. *Change the World without Taking Power: The Meaning of Revolution Today*. London: Pluto.

hooks, bell. 1984. *Feminist Theory: From Margin to Center*. Boston: South End.

Huggins, Magally. 2005. "Venezuela: Veinte años de ciudadanía en femenino." In *Venezuela, visión plural: Una mirada desde el CENDES*, 415–45. Caracas: BPR Publishers.

Hymes, Dell. 1972. "On Communicative Competence." In *Sociolinguistics*, edited by J. B. Pride and Janet Holmes, 269–85. Middlesex: Penguin.

Jackson, John L. 2001. *Harlemworld: Doing Race and Class in Contemporary Black America*. Chicago: University of Chicago Press.

James, Daniel. 1988. *Resistance and Integration: Peronism and the Argentine Working Class, 1946–1976*. Cambridge: Cambridge University Press.

Joseph, Gilbert, and David Nugent. 1994. "Popular Culture and State Formation in Revolutionary Mexico." In *Everyday Forms of State Formation*, edited by Gilbert Joseph and David Nugent, 3–23. Durham, NC: Duke University Press.

Karl, Terry. 1997. *The Paradox of Plenty: Oil Booms and Petro-States*. Berkeley: University of California Press.

Kulick, Don. 1993. "Speaking as a Woman: Structure and Gender in Domestic Arguments in a New Guinea Village." *Cultural Anthropology* 18 (4): 510–41.

Laclau, Ernesto. 1977. "Towards a Theory of Populism." In *Politics and ideology in Marxist theory*, edited by Ernesto Laclau, 143–98. London: New Left Books.

Laclau, Ernesto. 2005. *On Populist Reason*. London: Verso.

Lander, Edgardo. 2007. "Venezuelan Social Conflict in a Global Context." In *Venezuela: Hugo Chávez and the Decline of an "Exceptional Democracy,"* edited by Steve Ellner and Miguel Tinker Salas, 16–32. Lanham, MD: Rowman and Littlefield.

Lander, Edgardo. 2016. "La implosión de la Venezuela rentista." *Cuadernos de la Nueva Política* 1 (1): 3–23.

LaSpada, Salvatore. 1992. "Grassroots Video and the Democratization of Communication: The Case of Brazil." Ph.D. dissertation, Columbia University Teachers College, Columbia University.

Levine, Daniel H. 1973. *Conflict and Political Change in Venezuela.* Princeton, NJ: Princeton University Press.

Li, Tania Murray. 2005. "Beyond 'the State' and Failed Schemes." *American Anthropologist* 107 (3): 383–94.

Lind, Amy. 1992. "Power, Gender, and Development: Popular Women's Organizations and the Politics of Need in Ecuador." In *The Making of Social Movements in Latin America*, edited by Arturo Escobar and Sonia Alvarez, 134–49. Boulder, CO: Westview Press.

Lind, Amy. 2005. *Gendered Paradoxes: Women's Movements, State Restructuring, and Global Development in Ecuador.* University Park: Pennsylvania State University Press.

López Maya, Margarita. 2005a. *Del viernes negro al referendo revocatorio.* Caracas: Alfadil Ediciones.

López Maya, Margarita 2005b. "Venezuela 2002–2003: Polarization, Confrontation, and Violence." In *The Venezuela Reader*, edited by Olivia Burlingame Goumbri, 9–25. Washington, DC: Epica.

López Maya, Margarita, and Luis E. Lander. 2011a. "Participatory Democracy in Venezuela: Origins, Ideas, and Implementation." In *Venezuela's Bolivarian Democracy*, edited by David Smilde and Daniel Hellinger, 58–79. Durham, NC: Duke University Press.

López Maya, Margarita, and Luis Lander. 2011b. "Venezuela's Presidential Elections of 2006: Toward 21st Century Socialism?" In *The Revolution in Venezuela*, edited by Thomas Ponniah and Jonathan Eastwood, 131–54. Cambridge, MA: Harvard University Press.

López Maya, Margarita, and Alexandra Panzarelli. 2013. "Populism, Rentierism, and Socialism in the Twenty-First Century: The Case of Venezuela." In *Latin American Populism in the Twenty-First Century*, edited by Carlos de la Torre and Cynthia J. Arnson, 239–68. Baltimore: Johns Hopkins University Press.

Mahmood, Saba. 2004. *Politics of Piety: The Islamic Revival and the Feminist Subject.* Princeton, NJ: Princeton University Press.

Mahmood, Saba. 2007. "Ten." In *The Present as History: Critical Perspectives on Contemporary Global Power*, edited by Nermeen Shaikh, 148–71. New York: Columbia University Press.

Mankekar, Purnima. 1999. *Screening Culture, Viewing Politics: An Ethnography of Television, Womanhood, and Nation in Postcolonial India.* Durham, NC: Duke University Press.

Martín-Barbero, Jesus. [1987] 1993. *Communication, Culture and Hegemony: From Media to Mediations*. London: SAGE.

Martz, John D. 1988. "The Malaise of Venezuelan Political Parties: Is Democracy Endangered?" In *Democracy in Latin America: Colombia and Venezuela*, edited by Donald L. Herman, 155–74. New York: Praeger.

Mayobre, José Antonio. 1996. "Politics, Media and Modern Democracy: The Case of Venezuela." In *Politics, Media, and Democracy: International Innovations in Electoral Campaigning and Their Consequences*, edited by David L. Swanson and Paolo Mancini, 227–46. Westport, CT: Praeger.

Mayobre, José Antonio. 2002. "Venezuela and the Media: A New Paradigm." In *Latin Politics, Global Media*, edited by Elizabeth Fox and Silvio Waisbord, 176–86. Austin: University of Texas Press.

McCarthy, Michael. 2012. "The Possibilities and Limits of Politicized Participation: Community Councils, Coproduction, and *Poder Popular* in Chávez's Venezuela." In *New Institutions for Participatory Democracy in Latin America*, edited by Maxwell Cameron, Eric Hershberg, and Kenneth Sharpe, 123–48. New York: Palgrave Macmillan.

McChesney, Robert, and John Nichols. 2011. *The Death and Life of American Journalism: The Media Revolution That Will Begin the World Again*. Philadelphia: Nation Books.

Meza, Alfredo. 2002. "Cuatro horas frente a la pantalla de Catia TV." *El Nacional*, September 22.

Miller, Toby. 2004. "A View from a Fossil: The New Economy, Creativity, and Consumption—Two or Three Things I Don't Believe In." *International Journal of Cultural Studies* 7 (1): 55–65.

Mitchell, Timothy. 1991. "The Limits of the State: Beyond Statist Approaches and Their Critics." *American Political Science Review* 85 (1): 77–96.

Mitchell, Timothy. 1999. "Society, Economy, and the State Effect." In *State/Culture: State-Formation after the Cultural Turn*, edited by George Steinmetz, 76–97. Ithaca, NY: Cornell University Press.

Molyneux, Maxine. 1985. "Mobilization without Emancipation? Women's Interests, the State, and Revolution in Nicaragua." *Feminist Studies* 11 (2): 227–54.

Moraga, Cherrie, and Gloria Anzaldúa. 1983. *This Bridge Called My Back: Writings by Radical Women of Color*. Albany: State University of New York Press.

Mukerji, Chandra, and Michael Schudson. 1991. "Introduction: Rethinking Popular Culture." In *Rethinking Popular Culture*, edited by Chandra Mukerji and Michael Schudson, 1–61. Berkeley: University of California Press.

Muñoz, Carlos. 2003. "Identidades translocales y orientación sexual de Caracas." In *Políticas de identidades y diferencias sociales en tiempos de globalización*, edited by Daniel Mato, 219–55. Caracas: FACES.

Nugent, Daniel, and Ana María Alonso. 1994. "Multiple Selective Traditions in Agrarian Reform and Agrarian Struggle." In *Everyday Forms of State Formation*, edited by Gilbert Joseph and Daniel Nugent, 209–46. Durham, NC: Duke University Press.

Ochoa, Marcia. 2008. "Perverse Citizenship: Divas, Marginality, and Participation in 'Loca-Lization.'" *Women's Studies Quarterly* 36 (3–4): 146–69.

Orloff, Ann Shola. 1999. "Motherhood, Work, and Welfare in the United States, Britain, Canada, and Austrailia." In *State/Culture: State Formation after the Cultural Turn*, edited by George Steinmetz, 321–54. Ithaca, NY: Cornell University Press.

Ortner, Sherry B. 1973. "On Key Symbols." *American Anthropologist* 75 (5): 1338–46.

Ortner, Sherry B. 2003. *New Jersey Dreaming: Capital, Culture, and the Class of '58.* Durham, NC: Duke University Press.

Ortner, Sherry B. 2013. *Not Hollywood: Independent Film at the Twilight of the American Dream.* Durham, NC: Duke University Press.

Paley, Julia. 2002. "Toward an Anthropology of Democracy." *Annual Review in Anthropology* 31:469–96.

Paley, Julia. 2004. "Accountable Democracy: Citizens' Impact on Public Decision Making in Postdictatorship Chile." *American Ethnologist* 31 (4): 497–513.

Panizza, Francisco. 2005. "Introduction: Populism and the Mirror of Democracy." In *Populism and the Mirror of Democracy*, edited by Francisco Panizza, 1–31. London: Verso.

Panizza, Francisco. 2013. "What Do We Mean When We Talk about Populism?" In *Latin American Populism in the Twenty -First Century*, edited by Carlos de la Torre and Cynthia J. Arnson, 85–115. Baltimore: Johns Hopkins University Press.

Paramio, Ludolfo. 2006. "Giro a la izquierda y regreso del populismo." *Nueva Sociedad* 205:62–74.

Pasquali, Antonio. 2004. "La norma omite la radiotelevisión del sector publico." *El Universal*, November 15. Accessed July 25, 2013. http://www.eluniversal.com/2004/11/15/imp_apo_art_14158B.shtml.

Pedelty, Mark. 1995. *War Stories: The Culture of Foreign Correspondents.* New York: Routledge.

Peha, Jon M. 1998. "Spectrum Management Policy Options." IEEE *Communications Surveys* 1 (1): 2–7.

Portes, Alejandro. 1985. "Latin American Class Structures: Their Composition and Change during the Last Decades." *Latin American Research Review* 20 (3): 7–39.

Povinelli, Elizabeth A. 2006. *The Empire of Love: Toward a Theory of Intimacy, Genealogy, and Carnality.* Durham, NC: Duke University Press.

Povinelli, Elizabeth A. 2011. *Economies of Abandonment: Social Belonging and Endurance in Late Liberalism.* Durham, NC: Duke University Press.

Purcell, Thomas F. 2015. "Socialist Management and Natural Resource Based Industrial Production: A Critique of *Cogestión* in Venezuela." In *Crisis and Contradiction: Marxist Perspectives on Latin America in the Global Political Economy*, edited by Susan J. Spronk and Jeffery R. Webber, 163–92. Chicago: Haymarket Books.

Radway, Janice. 1988. "Reception Study: Ethnography and the Problems of Dispersed Audiences and Nomadic Subjects." *Cultural Studies* 2 (3): 359–76.

Rakowski, Cathy A. 2003. "Women's Coalitions as a Strategy at the Intersection of Economic and Political Change in Venezuela." *International Journal of Politics, Culture and Society* 16 (3): 387–405.

Rakowski, Cathy A., and Gioconda Espina. 2006. "Institucionalización de la lucha feminista/femenina en Venezuela." In *De lo privado a lo público*, edited by Elizabeth Meier and Natalie Lebon, 310–30. Buenos Aires: UNIFEM, United Nations, and Siglo XXI.

Rakowski, Cathy A., and Gioconda Espina. 2011. "Advancing Women's Rights from inside and outside the Bolivarian Revolution, 1998–2010." In *The Revolution in Venezuela: Social and Political Change under Chávez*, edited by Thomas Ponniah and Jonathan Eastwood, 155–92. Cambridge, MA: Harvard University Press.

Rangel, Eleazar Diaz. 2007. *La prensa venezolana en el siglo XX*. Caracas: Fundación Neumann.

Ranucci, Karen. 1990. "On the Trail of Independent Video." In *The Social Documentary in Latin America*, edited by Julianne Burton, 193–208. Pittsburgh: University of Pittsburgh.

Riaño, Pilar, ed. 1994. *Women in Grassroots Communication: Furthering Social Change*. Thousand Oaks, CA: SAGE.

Rivera, Raquel Z., Wayne Marshall, and Deborah Pacini Hernandez. 2009. *Reggaeton*. Durham, NC: Duke University Press.

Roberts, Kenneth. 2003. "Social Polarization and the Populist Resurgance." In *Venezuelan Politics in the Chávez Era: Class, Polarization and Conflict*, edited by Steve Ellner and Daniel Hellinger, 55–72. Boulder, CO: Reiner.

Rodríguez, Clemencia. 1994. "A Process of Identity Deconstruction: Latin American Women Producing Video Stories." In *Women in Grassroots Communication: Furthering Social Change*, edited by Pilar Riaño, 149–60. Thousand Oaks, CA: SAGE.

Rodríguez, Clemencia. 2001. *Fissures in the Mediascape: An International Study of Citizens' Media*. Ann Arbor, MI: Hampton.

Rodriguez, Francisco. 2008. "An Empty Revolution: The Unfulfilled Promises of Hugo Chávez." *Foreign Affairs* 87 (2): 49–62.

Rofel, Lisa. 1999. *Other Modernities: Gendered Yearnings in China after Socialism*. Berkeley: University of California Press.

Roncagliolo, Rafael. 1991. "The Growth of the Audio-Visual Imagescape in Latin America." In *Video the Changing World*, edited by Nancy Thede and Alain Ambrosi, 22–30. Montreal: Black Rose.

Rose, Nikolas. 1996. "Governing 'Advanced' Liberal Democracies." In *Foucault and Political Reason: Liberalism, Neo-Liberalism and Rationalities of Government*, edited by Andrew Barry, Thomas Osborne, and Nikolas Rose, 37–64. Chicago: University of Chicago Press.

Roseberry, William. 1994. *Anthropologies and Histories: Essays in Culture, History, and Political Economy*. New Brunswick, NJ: Rutgers University Press.

Roudakova, Natalia. 2009. "Journalism as 'Prostitution': Understanding Russia's Reactions to Anna Politkovskaya's Murder." *Political Communication* 26:412–29.

Roudakova, Natalia. 2010. "Press Freedom as Ethical Practice." Paper presented at the American Anthropological Association Annual Conference, Philadelphia.

Roudakova, Natalia. 2017. *Losing Pravda: Ethics and The Press in Post-Truth Russia*. Cambridge: Cambridge University Press.

Samet, Robert. 2012. "Deadline: Crime, Journalism, and Fearful Citizenship in Caracas, Venezuela." Ph.D. dissertation, Dept. of Anthropology, Stanford University.

Samet, Robert. 2017. "The Denouncers: Populism and the Press in Venezuela." *Journal of Latin American Studies* 49 (1): 1–27.

Samet, Robert, and Naomi Schiller. 2015. "Battles over Press Freedom in Venezuela." *Cultural Anthropology.* Accessed February 5, 2015. https://culanth.org/fieldsights /645-battles-over-press-freedom-in-venezuela.

Sánchez, Rafael. 2016. *Dancing Jacobins: A Venezuelan Genealogy of Latin American Populism.* New York: Fordham University Press.

Schiller, Naomi. 2009. "Framing the Revolution: Circulation and Meaning of *The Revolution Will Not Be Televised.*" *Mass Communication and Society* 12 (4): 478–502.

Schiller, Naomi. 2011. "Catia Sees You: Community Television, Clientelism, and Participatory Statemaking in the Chávez Era." In *Venezuela's Bolivarian Democracy*, edited by David Smilde and Daniel Hellinger, 104–30. Durham, NC: Duke University Press.

Schiller, Naomi. 2013. "Reckoning with Press Freedom: Community Media, Liberalism, and the Processual State in Caracas, Venezuela." *American Ethnologist* 40 (3): 540–54.

Schiller, Naomi. 2015. "Anthropology of Liberalism." In *The International Encyclopedia of the Social and Behavioral Sciences*, edited by James Wright. Oxford: Elsevier.

Scott, James C. 1985. *Weapons of the Weak: Everyday Forms of Peasant Resistance.* New Haven, CT: Yale University Press.

Scott, James C. 1990. *Domination and the Arts of Resistance: Hidden Transcripts.* New Haven, CT: Yale University Press.

Scott, James C. 1998. *Seeing Like a State: How Certain Schemes to Improve the Human Condition Have Failed.* New Haven, CT: Yale University Press.

Segura, María Soledad, and Silvio Waisbord. 2016. *Media Movements: Civil Society and Media Policy Reform in Latin America.* London: Zed.

Sennett, Richard, and Jonathan Cobb. [1972] 1993. *The Hidden Injuries of Class.* New York: W. W. Norton.

Sharma, Aradhana, and Akhil Gupta. 2006. "Introduction: Rethinking the State in the Age of Globalization." In *The Anthropology of the State: A Reader*, edited by Aradhana Sharma and Akhil Gupta, 1–41. Malden, MA: Blackwell.

Sinclair, John. 1999. *Latin American Television: A Global View.* Oxford: Oxford University Press.

Skurski, Julie. 1993. "The Leader and the 'People': Representing the Nation in Postcolonial Venezuela." Ph.D. dissertation, Department of Anthropology, University of Chicago.

Skurski, Julie. 2015. "Battles to Claim the 'Pueblo.'" *Cultural Anthropology.* Accessed February 5, 2015. http://www.culanth.org/fieldsights/634-battles-to-claim-the -pueblo.

Smilde, David. 2007. *Reason to Believe: Cultural Agency in Latin American Evangelicalism.* Berkeley: University of California.

Smilde, David. 2011. "Participation, Politics, and Culture: Emerging Fragments of Venezuela's Bolivarian Democracy." In *Participation and Public Sphere in Venezuela's*

Bolivarian Democracy, edited by David Smilde and Daniel Hellinger, 1–27. Durham, NC: Duke University Press.

Smilde, David, and Daniel Hellinger, eds. 2011. *Venezuela's Bolivarian Democracy: Participation, Politics, and Culture under Chávez*. Durham, NC: Duke University Press.

Stam, Robert. 1997. *Tropical Multiculturalism: A Comparative History of Race in Brazilian Cinema and Culture*. Durham, NC: Duke University Press.

Steinmetz, George. 1999. "Introduction." In *State/Culture: State Formation after the Cultural Turn*, edited by George Steinmetz, 1–49. Ithaca, NY: Cornell University Press.

Stephen, Lynn. 2011. "The Rights to Speak and to Be Heard: Women's Interpretations of Rights Discourses in the Oaxaca Social Movement." In *Gender at the Limits of Rights*, edited by Dorothy Hodgson, 161–79. Philadelphia: University of Pennsylvania Press.

Stephen, Lynn. 2013. *We Are the Face of Oaxaca*. Durham, NC: Duke University Press.

Sternbach, Nancy Saporta, Marysa Navarro-Aranguren, Patricia Chuchryk, and Sonia E. Alvarez. 1992. "Feminisms in Latin America: From Bogotá to San Bernardo." In *The Making of Social Movements in Latin America*, edited by Arturo Escobar and Sonia E. Alvarez, 207–39. Boulder, CO: Westview Press.

Straubhaar, Joseph D. 1989. "Television and Video in the Transition from Military to Civilian Rule in Brazil." *Latin American Research Review* 24 (1): 140–54.

Tanner Hawkins, Eliza. 2006. "Community Media in Venezuela." Paper presented at the 2006 meeting of the Latin American Studies Association, San Juan, Puerto Rico.

Taussig, Michael. 1993. "*Maleficium*: State Fetishism." In *Fetishism as Cultural Discourse*, edited by Emily Apter and William Pietz, 217–50. Ithaca, NY: Cornell University Press.

Taussig, Michael. 1997. *The Magic of the State*. New York: Routledge.

Thomas, Deborah. 2004. *Modern Blackness: Nationalism, Globalization, and the Politics of Culture in Jamaica*. Durham, NC: Duke University Press.

Tinker Salas, Miguel. 2009. *The Enduring Legacy: Oil, Culture, and Society in Venezuela*. Durham, NC: Duke University Press.

Tomaselli, Keyan G., and Jeanne Prinsloo. 1990. "Video, Realism and Class Struggle: Theoretical Lacunae and the Problem of Power." *Continuum: Journal of Media and Cultural Studies* 3 (2): 140–59.

Tomlinson, John. 1991. *Cultural Imperialism*. Baltimore: Johns Hopkins University Press.

Trouillot, Michel-Rolph. 2001. "The Anthropology of the State in the Age of Globalization." *Current Anthropology* 42 (1): 125–38.

Turner, Terence. 1990. "The Kayapo Video Project: A Progress Report." *Commission on Visual Anthropology Newsletter* (fall): 7–10.

Turner, Terence. 1991. "The Social Dynamics of Video Media in an Indigenous Society: The Cultural Meaning and the Personal Politics of Video-Making in Kayapo Communities." *Visual Anthropology Review* 7 (2): 68–76.

Valdeavellano, Paloma. 1989. "América latina está construyendo su propria imagen." In *El video en la educación popular*, edited by Paloma Valdeavellano, 73–130. Lima: IPAL.

Valdivieso Ide, Magdalena. 2004. "Confrontación, machismo, y democracia: Representaciones del heroísmo en la polarización política en Venezuela." *Revista Venezolana de Economia y Ciencias Sociales* 10 (2): 137–53.

Valencia, Cristobal Ramirez. 2015. *We Are the State! Barrio Activism in Venezuela's Bolivarian Revolution*. Tucson: University of Arizona Press.

Velasco, Alejandro. 2011. "'We Are Still Rebels': The Challenge of Popular History in Bolivarian Venezuela." In *Venezuela's Bolivarian Democracy: Participation, Politics, and Culture under Chávez*, edited by David Smilde and Daniel Hellinger, 157–87. Durham, NC: Duke University Press.

Velasco, Alejandro. 2015. *Barrio Rising: Urban Popular Politics and the Making of Modern Venezuela*. Oakland: University of California Press.

Waisbord, Silvio. 1995. "Leviathan Dreams: States and Broadcasting in South America." *Communication Review* 1 (3): 201–26.

Waisbord, Silvio. 2000. *Watchdog Journalism in South America: News, Accountability, and Democracy*. New York: Columbia University Press.

Waisbord, Silvio. 2013. "Democracy, Journalism, and Latin American Populism." *Journalism* 14 (4): 504–21.

Walley, Christine. 2013. *Exit Zero: Family and Class in Postindustrial Chicago*. Chicago: University of Chicago Press.

Weisbrot, Mark. 2008. "Poverty Reduction in Venezuela: A Reality-Based View." *ReVista: Harvard Review of Latin America* 8 (1): 36–39.

Weisbrot, Mark. 2015. *Failed: What the "Experts" Got Wrong about the Global Economy*. New York: Oxford University Press.

Weyland, Kurt. 2001. "Clarifying a Contested Concept: Populism in the Study of Latin American Politics." *Comparative Politics* 34 (1): 1–22.

Wilpert, Gregory. 2003. "Collision in Venezuela." *New Left Review* 21 (May–June): 101–16.

Wilpert, Gregory. 2007. *Changing Venezuela by Taking Power: The History and Policies of the Chávez Government*. London: Verso.

Winegar, Jessica. 2006. *Creative Reckonings: The Politics of Art and Culture in Contemporary Egypt*. Stanford, CA: Stanford University Press.

Wolfe, Thomas C. 2005. *Governing Soviet Journalism*. Bloomington: Indiana University Press.

Wortham, Erica. 2013. *Indigenous Media in Mexico: Culture, Community, and the State*. Durham, NC: Duke University Press.

Wright, Winthrop R. 1990. *Café con Leche: Race, Class and National Image in Venezuela*. Austin: University of Texas Press.

Yi Ng, Beliana. 1993. "Las dos caras de las comunidades: entre la denuncia y la autogestión." *Comunicación: Estudios Venezolanos de Comunicación* 19 (82): 22–26.

Yúdice, George. 2003. *The Expediency of Culture: Uses of Culture in the Global Age*. Durham, NC: Duke University Press.

Yurchak, Alexei. 2006. *Everything Was Forever, Until It Was No More: The Last Soviet Generation*. Princeton, NJ: Princeton University Press.

Yuval-Davis, Nira. 2006. "Intersectionality and Feminist Politics." *European Journal of Women's Studies* 13 (3): 193–209.

Zubillaga, Verónica, and Roberto Briceño-León. 2001. "Exclúsion, masculinidad y respeto." *Nueva Sociedad* 173 (May–June): 34–48.

Index

Caracazo, 21, 37, 41, 82, 97, 243n4. *See also* Chávez, Hugo; media

Catia TVe: Caracas milieu and, 54–57; Chávez's relationship with, 47–48, 50–51, 53–54, 65, 128–31, 133–34, 227; class and, 98–107, 139–44, 196–200, 205, 209–22, 232–38; communal councils and, 24–29, 64, 71–73, 75–76; cultural essentialism and, 110–15; denuncias and, 128–32, 144–63, 220, 245n1; ECPAI and, 51–52; election coverage of, 62–65, 84–88; everyday state formation and, 4, 22, 66, 71–78, 152, 230, 240; founders of, x, 23, 25, 39–46, 59, 168–69; gender and, 22, 27, 60, 154, 166–89, 192–95, 232, 236–38; images of, *9, 26, 57, 63, 75, 105*; Maduro government and, 234–36; poor people's leadership and, xi, xii, 4, 6–14, 16, 22–24, 39, 44–45, 50–51, 61, 71–72, 108–10, 139–44; press freedom and, 17–18, 22, 54–57, 68–69, 128–29, 196–204, 207–10, 213–22, 224–26, 238–39; social mobility and, 119–27; statecraft of, 4–5, 64–78, 239–40; state's relationship to, 3–6, 13, 15–17, 19–20, 23–29, 43–45, 49–52, 60–61, 64–84, 87–88, 161–62, 174–75, 179–80, 198–200, 207–13, 215–26, 229, 231–33, 236–38; ViVe TV and, 3, 23, 79–84, 98–104, 107–11, 115–19, 174–90, 204–6, 209–10, 234–35, 238. *See also* media; people; state, the

censorship, 30–31, 59, 128–29, 205, 245n2

Centro Internazionale Crocevia, 40

Chalbaud, Román, 43

Chávez, Hugo: 1999 constitution and, 47–48; Catia TVe and, 47–54, 65, 128–31, 139–44, 227–28; censorship and, 128–29; class heterogeneity and, 93–95, 126–27, 208–9; coup against, 12, 53–55, 72, 78, 82–83, 145, 174–80, 199–200, 221; death of, 13, 233; denuncias and, 148–51, 154–63; elections of, ix, 2, 11, 47–48, 78; gender and, 166–67, 171–72, 174–95; media presence of, 1–3, 4–5, 10, 17–18, 19–21, 23–24, 26, 36, 38–39, 47–49, 53–57, 65–67, 89, 94, 134–39, 145, 150–52, 154–63, 196–200; oil wealth and, 2, 11–12, 25, 55–57, 94–95, 149–50, 245n3; persona of, 129–30, 133, 134–39, 150–52, 227, 230, 232; poor people's cause and, xi, xii; populism and, 131–39, 148–53; rise to power of, 37–38,

43; social welfare programs of, 72–74, 97–98, 119–27, 135, 146–47, 190, 206; twenty-first-century socialism and, 3, 10–14

chavismo, 93–95, 131–39, 156, 232–33

Chile, 7, 70, 103

Cineclub Manicomio, 42–44, 46–47

Cine Mujer, 39

Cisneros, Gustavo, 37, 53

Cisneros Group, 38

class: authenticity discourses and, 108–19, 157–59; chavismo and, 93–95, 131–39, 156, 232–33; cultural capital and, 102–4, 115–19; denuncias and, 129–32, 144–63, 220, 245n1; gender and, 96–97, 166–68, 191–95; injuries of, 102–4, 119, 126–27; media control and, 98–104, 140–44, 196–200, 205, 209–18, 220–22, 232–33, 236–38; oil wealth and, 2, 7–13, 25, 29–41, 55–57, 90–98, 145, 149–50, 233–36, 245n3; the people and, 91–92, 105–7, 130–31, 142–54, 158; performativity and, 102–4; race and, 94, 118, 140–41, 241n6; social mobility and, 119–27, 140–41; ViVe TV and, 102–7, 115–19

clientelism, 66, 149–50, 191

Cobb, Jonathan, 102

Cody, Frank, 246n3

Cold War, 35

Colombia, 143

communal councils, 24–29, 64, 71–73, 75–76

Communist Party of Venezuela, 30–32

community media (definitions), 2–12, 19–21, 243n6. *See also* Catia TVe; media

Community Outreach Department (Catia TVe), 146

CONATEL. *See* National Commission of Telecommunications

Conklin, Beth, 114

contradictions (of Chávez), 131–32, 134–39, 162, 232–33

COPEI (Independent Political Electoral Organizing Committee), 7, 33, 42, 96

COPRE (Presidential Commission for State Reform), 243n3

Coronil, Fernando, 242n7

Corrales, Javier, 245n10

corruption, 36, 38, 144–45, 155–58, 234, 243n3

Crespo, Joaquín, 25, 243n1

Cuba, 60, 70, 125–26

New Latin American Film movement, 39, 42, 91–92

New World Information and Communications Order (NWICO), 34–36, 57–58

NGOs, 46

Nicaragua, 58

1999 constitution (of Venezuela), 47–48, 154, 165, 241n6, 246n8

NWICO. *See* New World Information and Communications Order

Ochoa, Francisco, 157–59

oil (Venezuelan), 2, 7–13, 25, 29–30, 34–41, 55–57, 90–98, 145, 149–50, 233–36, 245n3

One World, Many Voices (MacBride Report), 34–35

oversight committees, 155–58

Pacifica Radio, 217–18

Panizza, Francisco, 131–32

Pasquali, Antonio, 34, 56

paternalism, 111–15

PDVSA, 56

Pedagogy of the Oppressed (Freire), 33

Peña, Alfredo, 56–57

Penfold, Michael, 245n10

the people: ambiguity of, 91, 135–44; authenticity discourses and, 100–101, 108–15; class heterogeneity and, 93–98, 100, 105–7, 135, 142–54; democracy and, 2–8, 11, 16–22, 28–40, 48–60, 66, 73, 108, 131–37, 150–57, 227–34, 242n7; denuncias and, 129–32, 144–63, 220, 245n1; gender and, 183–89, 194–95; leadership by, 138–39; media's invocation of, 29, 200–204, 213–16; representations of, 130–31; state resources and, 216–18, 225–26. *See also* authenticity discourses; Catia TVe; Chávez, Hugo; class; poor people

Pérez, Carlos Andrés, 37–38

Perón, Juan, 200–201

Pinochet, Augusto, 103

poor people: as audience, 91–92, 135; authenticity discourses and, 108–15; Catia TVe's recruitment of, 1–2, 4, 6–10, 12–13, 22–24, 40–47, 50–51, 61, 64–65, 71–72, 236–38; chavismo and, 93–95, 131–39, 156, 232–33; class consciousness and, 105–7; commercial media portrayals of, 53; communal councils

and, 24–29; leadership of, xi–xii, 138–39, 153–54, 162–63; living conditions of, 121–27; media as weapon of, 50–51, 59–61, 64–71, 84, 86–87, 98–102, 108–10, 115–19, 128–29, 139–44, 229–30, 239–40; middle class and, 6–11, 22–24, 42–53, 89–90, 104, 111–19, 200, 208–10, 223–24, 230–31, 239–40; oil collapse and, 13, 233–36; "the people" idea and, 91–100, 105–7, 130–31, 135, 138–39, 142–54, 216–26; race and, 94, 118, 140–41, 241n6; social mobility and, 119–27; statecraft and, 15–17, 96, 230–33, 239–40; Venezuela's liberal democracy and, 7–8, 32–40, 57, 60–61, 136–37, 191–209, 213–18, 222–29, 238–39, 242n7, 242nn9–10. *See also* Bolivarian Revolution; class; populism; state, the

popular culture, 108–10, 148–51, 210–13, 245n6

populism, 22, 130–39, 148–51, 245n2, 245n11

Primera, Alí, 98

Psycho (Hitchcock), 103–4

Puma, 58

race: class and, 94, 118, 140–41, 241n6; gender and, 7, 192–94; the people idea and, 135–36; popular culture and, 111–15

racism, 53, 110–15, 127, 132, 171, 192–93, 220, 238, 241n6

radical interdependency, 17, 40, 67, 79, 152, 164, 200, 217, 225, 230

RATELVE (Project of Radio and Television in Venezuela), 34, 36, 56, 59

RCTV (Radio Caracas Television), 31, 37, 53, 56, 104, 199–216, 218–24, 226, 230, 239

reggaeton, 111–15

Regulation of Community Media, 52

Reporters without Borders, 48

Resolution 3178, 33

revolution, 241n2. *See also* Bolivarian Revolution

Rodriguez, Francisco, 245n3

Rodriguez, Lil, 223

Rodríguez, Simón, 41

Rope (Hitchcock), 104

Rouch, Jean, 103

Salas, Miguel Tinker, 93

Scott, James, 15–16

Sennet, Richard, 102

tourism and, 196–97; U.S. hegemony and, 11, 13, 31–39, 58, 95–96, 100–101, 110–15, 197, 210–11, 220, 227–29, 233. *See also* Bolivarian Revolution; media; people; state, the; *specific laws and ministries*

Video nas Aldeias, 39

virtual immediacy, 136–37

ViVe TV, xi, 21, 44, 58–59, 79–88, 91–92, 95, 98–104, 107–11, 115–19, 140, 171–72, 174–90, 203–6, 209–10, 225–26, 238

Voluntad Popular, 247n3

VTV (Venezolana de Televisión), 30, 54, 58, 89, 134–35, 179, 206

We Are the Face of Oaxaca (Stephens), 247n6

Weisbrot, Mark, 245n3

WIDF (Women's International Democratic Federation), 171

Winegar, Jessica, 248n2

women: class divisions and, 191–93; of color, 7; family labor and, 164–66, 168–74, 189–90, 247n2; feminism and, 39, 96, 189–95; machismo and, 176–77; pay scales and, 27, 190–91; political activism of, 165, 169, 171–72; social welfare programs and, 147–50, 152, 247n8; speaking roles and public space and, 180–89; structural inequality and, 7, 101–2, 184–95. *See also* Catia TVe; feminism; gender; maternalist discourses; media

World Council of Churches, 40

Yuval-Davis, Nira, 247n4